LIGHTS AND SHADOWS

OF

ARMY LIFE

FROM BULL RUN TO BENTONVILLE

William B. Westervelt

LIGHTS AND SHADOWS
OF
ARMY LIFE

FROM BULL RUN
TO BENTONVILLE

BY

WM. B. WESTERVELT

OF

THE 27TH NEW YORK INFANTRY AND

THE 17TH NEW YORK VETERAN ZOUAVES

EDITED BY
GEORGE S. MAHARAY

 BURD STREET PRESS

This Burd Street Press publication was printed by

Beidel Printing House, Inc.
63 West Burd Street
Shippensburg, PA 17257 USA

In respect for the scholarship contained herein, the acid-free paper used in this book meets the guidelines for permanence and durability of the Committee on Production Guidelines for Book Longevity of the Council on Library Resources.

First edition, 1886 by
C. H. Cochrane, Book and Pamphlet Printer, Marlboro, N.Y.

Second edition by
Burd Street Press, Division of White Mane Publishing Co., Inc., Shippensburg, PA USA

For a complete list of available publications please write

Burd Street Press, a division of
White Mane Publishing Company, Inc.
P.O. Box 152
Shippensburg, PA 17257 USA

Library of Congress Cataloging-in-Publication Data
Westervelt, Wm. B. (William B.), 1838–1927.
    Lights and shadows of army life : from Bull Run to Bentonville /
by Wm. B. Westervelt ; edited by George S. Maharay.
        p.   cm.
    Originally published: Marlboro, NY : C.H. Cochran, Book & Pamphlet Printer, 1886.
    Includes bibliographical references and index.
    ISBN 1-57249-115-9 (alk. paper)
    1. Westervelt, Wm. B. (William B.), 1838–1927.   2. United States-
-History--Civil War, 1861–1865--Personal narratives.   3. United
States.   Army.   New York Infantry Regiment, 27th (1861–1863)
4. United States.   Army.   New York Veteran Infantry Regiment, 17th
(1863–1865) 5. New York (State)--History--Civil War, 1861–1865-
-Personal narratives.   6. Soldiers--New York (State)--Biography.
I. Maharay, George S. II. Title.
E601.W53 1998
973.7'81'092--dc21
[B]   97-50174
                                                                 CIP

PRINTED IN THE UNITED STATES OF AMERICA

This book is affectionately dedicated

TO MY BRAVE FALLEN COMRADES

Who shared in my haversack, tent or canteen,
And now rest 'neath the sod of Virginia's broad acres,
Or sleep their last sleep 'neath the grass ever green.

'Neath Georgia's tall pines, in the morass or thicket,
No white, sculptured tablet may speak of our dead
Who fell, clad in blue, in the charge or on picket,
Where the feet of the stranger now ruthlessly tread.

TABLE OF CONTENTS

TABLE OF CONTENTS

ILLUSTRATIONS AND MAPS

ILLUSTRATIONS AND MAPS

ILLUSTRATIONS AND MAPS

PREFACE

In offering this little work to the public it is not in the expectation of any fame as an historian, but to place in the hands of my comrades, in readable form, an account of some of the events as they occurred during the war, and as they appeared from the standpoint of a private soldier. Trusting these unvarnished facts will stand the criticism as to correctness of those whom the writer felt the "touch of elbow" when we marched forth to breathe the hot breath of the enemy's cannon, on the fields of Bull Run, Gaines' Mill, Fredricksburg Heights, Jonesboro, Bentonsville and other well known battle fields,

WM. B. WESTERVELT.

Middle Hope, N.Y., Sept. 30, 1886.

William B. Westervelt

INTRODUCTION

About This Edition

William B. Westervelt fought in the 27th New York Infantry Regiment from Bull Run to Chancellorsville and in the 17th New York Veteran Zouaves in the West, with Sherman in the Atlanta Campaign, from Atlanta to the Sea, and in the Carolinas' Campaign to the end of the war. This is his account of the Civil War as he saw it—a Union Soldier who served nearly four years in two theaters of war.

Westervelt describes how he took part in 22 engagements (see Appendix 1), including Bull Run, The Seven Days', Antietam, Fredericksburg, Chancellorsville, Jonesboro, Averasboro, and Bentonville. But his book is about far more than battles. It is about Army life in the Civil War—little fights and skirmishes not recorded in most histories of the War, long periods of inactivity as seen by the common soldier. He records the importance of food, the campfire, shelter, and weather to the enlisted man; memories of home; judgements of officers and other soldiers; and the stoic acceptance of wounds, disease, and death.

In his nearly four years of service, Westervelt rose in the ranks from private to first lieutenant. But his perspective remained that of an enlisted man. This is reflected in the title of his book, first published in 1886, *Lights and Shadows of Army Life, as Seen by a Private Soldier*.

William B. Westervelt, whose daughter married one of my favorite uncles, C. Scott Satterly, kept a diary throughout his entire wartime service. My brother, Arthur Maharay, recalls that as a child he watched and listened as the old veteran poured through his voluminous diary and talked about the war. This was around 1919. Time passed, Westervelt died, and the diary disappeared. No one we know was aware that he had written a book.

Over fifty years later, 1976, a client of Arthur's—who was then a retired attorney—found a copy of Westervelt's book, knew the family relationships involved and gave it to Arthur. Upon inspection, it was clear that the book, published in 1886, was based upon the diary Arthur had seen earlier. It was also clear that Westervelt had privately published the book—probably in limited numbers—for his comrades-in-arms. I believe it is worthy of republication as do others who have read it.

Westervelt as a Reporter of the Civil War

In the research for this edition, I found that Westervelt was a major contributor to the Regimental History of the 27th New York. That book, entitled *History of the 27th New York Vols.*, was published in 1888.[1] Westervelt's role in contributing to that history is an indication of how well he was accepted by his comrades and superiors as a soldier and as a reporter of the Civil War.

The entire group of contributors to the Regimental History of the 27th New York was as follows:

INTRODUCTION

Henry W. Slocum - First colonel of the 27th New York, later major general in charge of the XII Corps at Chancellorsville and Gettysburg; in charge of the XX Corps from Atlanta to the Sea; and in charge of the XIV and XX Corps (The Army of Georgia) in the Carolinas' Campaign.

Joseph J. Bartlett - Second colonel of the 27th New York; later brevet major general; appointed to receive the overall surrender of Lee's army at Appomattox.

Curtiss C. Gardiner - Major in the 27th New York; later brevet lieutenant colonel.

Charles A Wells - Captain, Company C of the 27th New York; later major by brevet.

Charles Bryant Fairchild - Second lieutenant, Company D of the 27th New York   (Note— he is listed as the author of the Regimental History).

Eri S. Watson - Second lieutenant, Company C of the 27th New York.

Joseph L. Ross - First sergeant, Company F of the 27th New York.

William B. Westervelt - Corporal, Company F of the 27th New York; later first lieutenant.

It is significant to note that Westervelt was a key participant in preparing the Regimental History and that extensive passages from his book are contained intact in it. Specifically, pages 11-14 relating to the Bull Run Campaign are from his book, as are pages 33-34, relating to West Point, Va.; pages 95-96 relating to Antietam; pages 116, 122 and 123, relating to Fredericksburg; page 136 regarding the Mud March; and page 171 regarding Chancellorsville.[2] It is also significant that I was able to verify his reports by comparison with information in the *Official Records*.

The Format of This Edition

Westervelt's book was written for his comrades and presumes detailed knowledge of the events, the participants and the environment of the Civil War. Further, his book contains many items which are of historic significance and others which were important to the common soldier. These are not highlighted in his book and deserve to be.

Therefore, this edition of William Westervelt's book, *Lights and Shadows of Army Life*, is designed to provide today's reader with some perspective of the events of the war in which Westervelt was involved. I have reorganized his work around battles and campaigns, and highlighted significant items in his reports. This is done without changing any of Westervelt's original text.

Westervelt's book consists of two parts (one for each enlistment) and fifty-three numbered but untitled chapters. I have eliminated his numbers for chapters, and titled the chapters in this edition using, for the most part, names of the engagements or campaigns as they appear in historical records.[3]

INTRODUCTION

His manuscript has been retained intact but his chapters have been grouped or split based upon how they pertain to an engagement or campaign. Where errors have been found in his work or where further brief comment seems appropriate, these have been annotated through footnotes, thus preserving the basic manuscript.

Each chapter in this edition starts with background information on the campaign: what the Federal army was trying to do and why it was trying to do it; where Westervelt's regiment—the 27th New York or the 17th Veteran Zouaves—fit into the picture; and where the regiment was located (through the use of maps). This is followed by highlights of significant or interesting aspects of army life that Westervelt saw or experienced. William B. Westervelt's manuscript then follows, copied exactly as originally published.

Background information for each chapter has been developed from Official Records, the Regimental History of the 27th New York, books published during or right after the Civil War and standard references. Maps used are, to the extent possible, those published in the period 1861-1900. The same is true of the pictures and sketches used in this edition.

The new material is in full page format. The original manuscript is in italics and in two columns; the same format as the original publication—printed in 1886. Thus, added material is carefully delineated from the original, permitting the reader to read all or part of the added material and the original or just the original.

The references to individuals are by the rank the person held when first mentioned in this book.

It is my hope that this edition will highlight William B. Westervelt's original work and will provide it the recognition it so richly deserves.

George Satterly Maharay

1997

William B. Westervelt and his Civil War Tent Mate

BIOGRAPHICAL SKETCH — WILLIAM B. WESTERVELT

William B. Westervelt was born in Poughkeepsie, New York on November 5, 1838. He was educated in that city, his first day in school being the first day on which free schools were opened in Poughkeepsie. He moved to New York City in 1858 and remained there until 1860. In that year, he returned up the Hudson River to Newburgh in Orange County where he resided until he enlisted in 1861.

Westervelt's first enlistment was in the 27th New York Volunteer Infantry Regiment. He entered service at Binghamton, New York on May 6, 1861, as a private in Company F. Promoted to corporal on September 1, 1861, he carried that rank for the remainder of his two-year term of service. He was mustered out with the regiment at Elmira on May 31, 1863.

Westervelt's second enlistment on September 8, 1863, was as a private in the 38th Infantry in New York City. This organization was then transferred to the 17th Veterans Zouaves on September 14, 1863. Westervelt was assigned to Company K and became its first sergeant on or before November 1, 1863. He was promoted to first lieutenant on May 30, 1865, and was mustered out with the regiment at Alexandria, Virginia on July 13, 1865. His total military service was sixteen days short of four years.

A significant fact not mentioned by Westervelt in his book is that his commanding officer recommended him for the War Department's Medal of Honor. On March 24, 1865, Captain A.S. Marshall, Capt. Commanding, 17th Regiment, New York Veteran Volunteers cited seven enlisted men for gallantry during the period from January 20-March 24, 1865; Westervelt was one of the seven named (see Report No. 93, *Official Records*, Vol. XLVII, pp. 507-509).

Upon discharge from the service, Westervelt returned to Orange County, New York where he resided until his death.

In physical appearance, William B. Westervelt was a small man by today's standards, 5' 7 ½" tall and weighing about 150 lbs. He was of light complexion with blue eyes and brown hair.

William B. Westervelt married Annie E. Ehrnfeldt in Newburgh, New York on May 8, 1867. They had six children—John William, b. Sept. 26, 1868; Charles Ehrnfeldt, b. Jan. 4, 1871; Andrew Barnes, b. Aug. 28, 1874; Harry Irving, b. May 5, 1879; Jennie Stevens, b. Dec. 22, 1880; and Fred Thorton, b. Oct. 1, 1882.

Westervelt's oldest son went into the military service also and retired as master sergeant at the age of 77 in 1945; the oldest enlistee in the army at the time of his retirement. His obituary states:

> It was his boast that Westervelts had been fighting ever since 1671, when the Wampanoag Indians went on the warpath in what is now southern New England. His grandfather fought at Stony Point with "Mad Anthony" Wayne, his father was in the Civil War, and his brother in battle at San Juan Hill.[4]

Westervelt's occupation before the war was as a clerk and a silversmith. After the war, he worked in his brother's shop as a silversmith from 1865 until 1874 when he had to give up that occupation because of failing eyesight caused by a wartime bayonet injury.

A fact that he did not mention in his book is that he was injured in arresting a drunken soldier of his regiment at Alexandria, Virginia on September 2, 1861. While making the arrest, ordered by the officer of the day, the soldier hit Westervelt between the eyes with a bayonet. One witness said

BIOGRAPHICAL SKETCH — WILLIAM B. WESTERVELT

that the incident caused so much disturbance that Colonel Bartlett appeared and drew his pistol to subdue the man. This injury had a profound effect upon Westervelt's career after the war because of loss of sight. For this reason, Westervelt applied for a disability pension on June 30, 1880. Since his medical records were incomplete, he had to furnish affidavits from his comrades and from the regiment's surgeon, Barnes. In the process of examining the claim, an official in the Pension Bureau wrote to the deputy commissioner, "General Bartlett [who commanded the 27th New York at the time of the incident]—do you remember the facts stated by the claimant?" Bartlett responded, "June 8, 86—Yes, the time, place and circumstances were as nearly as possible as the claimant states them —one of the guard was wounded by a prisoner that night by a blow from a bayonet while taking him to the Guard House. J.J. Bartlett, Deputy Commissioner." The pension was granted and continued until Westervelt's death.

From 1874 to 1875, Westervelt worked as an insurance agent and as a newspaper correspondent for a local newspaper. From 1880 until his retirement around 1915, he served as superintendent of both Cedar Hill and Woodlawn Cemeteries in Middle Hope, New York and New Windsor, New York respectively. During this time, he also continued as a writer for the press.

After retirement, Westervelt lived at Woodlawn Cemetery with his daughter and son-in-law, Mr. & Mrs. C. Scott Satterly. Pictures of him at age 74 on page xiii and the one with his Civil War tent mate in 1912, page xvii, were taken by my Uncle C. Scott Satterly. My family would frequently visit Uncle Scott and Aunt Jen (Westervelt's daughter). I can just barely remember the old gentleman, sitting on the porch at Woodlawn Cemetery, visiting with us. Then, he would politely excuse himself and go up to his room to rest. He passed away when I was seven years old. He died on August 27, 1927, at the age of 88 years.

Westervelt's obituary in the *Newburgh News* of August 27, 1927, provides insights on his character and his standing in the community.[5] Excerpts follow:

> Mr. Westervelt was one of the founders of Ellis Post, Grand Army of the Republic and served as a member of the First Memorial Day Committee here. He was the last survivor of that committee.

> Mr. Westervelt was a picturesque figure in any company. Even when approaching his 90th year he never seemed to have lost his youth. His face preserved much of its freshness. His eyes twinkled merrily. In his long life there had been amusing and interesting incidents which he could relate most entertainingly. A deeply religious man he found real joy and happiness in his religion, which he did not obtrude, but which he made very manifest in his living and in his standards of living. Though he had at times served as a preacher and could deliver a very good sermon, he practiced religion, rather than preached it. He found life very good and enjoyed it and was an exponent of gladness. Although fortune was not always kind to him, he found the good so overshadowing that under all conditions he maintained unfailing good humor and optimism.

INTRODUCTION and BIOGRAPHICAL SKETCH

Notes

1. Charles Bryant Fairchild, *History of The 27th Regiment, New York Vols.* (Binghamton, New York, Carl and Matthews, 1888), p. vi.

2. Ibid.

3. Frederick H. Dyer, *A Compendium of the War of the Rebellion* (Cedar Rapids, Iowa, Torch Press, 1908; reprint, Dayton, Ohio, Morningside Bookshop, 1978), Vol. III, pp. 1411-12, 1414-15.

U.S. War Department, *War of the Rebellion. Official Records of the Union and Confederate Armies. 128 Volumes* (Washington, D.C., Government Printing Office, 1880-1901). (Hereafter referred to as *O.R.*)

4. *Newburgh News* (Newburgh, N.Y.), October 20, 1946.

5. *Newburgh News*, August 27, 1927.

LIGHTS AND SHADOWS

OF

ARMY LIFE

FROM BULL RUN TO BENTONVILLE

COL. HENRY W. SLOCUM.

Chapter 1

MUSTERING IN —- A NEW RECRUIT IN A NEW REGIMENT

Background

The year 1861 was one of turmoil. By January, South Carolina had seceded from the Union; other states were about to follow. On March 4, Lincoln was inaugurated as president and on April 15, he announced an insurrection in seven Southern states (South Carolina, Georgia, Alabama, Florida, Mississippi, Louisiana, and Texas). Further, he called upon the loyal states to supply 75,000 militia for a period of three months to put down the rebellion.[1]

New York was asked to furnish seventeen regiments, each with 780 officers and men.[2] Elmira was designated by the War Department as one of the points where the militia would be organized, quartered, and dispatched "to the seat of danger."[3] New York anticipated Lincoln's call, for the Legislature acted on April 15, 1861 to provide funds for arming and equipping troops for immediate service.[4] New York furnished more than Lincoln requested.

Henry W. Slocum, a West Point graduate, organized the 27th Regiment of Infantry at Elmira where it was accepted by the State of New York on May 21, 1861, and mustered into service for a period of two years.[5] Slocum's regiment consisted of ten companies (A through K, without J) and a total of 780 men, one of whom was William B. Westervelt, a private in Company F.

The regiment left Elmira, New York for Washington, D.C. on July 10, where it was attached to Porter's Brigade of Hunter's Division in Brigadier General Irvin McDowell's Army of Northeast Virginia (First Brigade, Second Division) until August 14, 1861. It became one of the first nine regiments of what was to become the famous "Army of the Potomac."[6] The regiment would spend its two years of service in the Army of the Potomac fighting and marching in Virginia and Maryland.

For a lad raised near Poughkeepsie, New York whose farthest travels had been along the Hudson River to New York City and back, the two years would be William B. Westervelt's greatest adventure. Most of his time would be spent in the District of Columbia, Virginia, and Maryland. Names of places such as Washington, Fredericksburg, Yorktown, West Point, Hanover Court House, Gaines Mill, Sharpsburg, and Chancellorsville would become part of his life, indelibly imprinted in his memory.

General McDowell had been assigned command of the army on May 28, five days after Virginia voted to secede.[7] On June 29, McDowell presented his plans to the Cabinet for attacking the Confederates.[8] By July 16, his army of 35,000 was on its way to Manassas and then, presumably, "on to Richmond." Richmond by then, was the new capital of the Confederacy.

The Southern commander at Manassas, Brigadier General P.T. Beauregard, had 22,000 troops at Manassas Junction guarding the railroad from Manassas to Richmond as well as the railroad that ran from Manassas to the Shenandoah Valley. In the Valley was another Confederate army under Brigadier Joseph E. Johnston. Near the Maryland line at Williamsport, Maryland, was a Federal army of 16,000 troops comanded by Major General Robert Patterson. His job was to keep Johnston's forces from joining Beauregard at Manassas.

MUSTERING IN — A NEW RECRUIT IN A NEW REGIMENT

Two factors forced General McDowell to hasten his green troops into battle: first, pressures from the public, the administration, and the Congress; and second, the fact that the 90-day term of enlistment for many of the militia was about to expire. (McDowell reported that if he had waited a few days, he would have lost 10,000 of his best troops because of expiration of their 90-day tour.)

Highlights

There are two points to note in Westervelt's reports on his first 73 days of service before the Battle of Bull Run:

1. The Flogging: Westervelt and his comrades were required to watch a flogging on July 19. This involved whipping a soldier with a lash; a form of disciplinary action that was a carry-over from the Revolutionary War where 100 strokes were authorized.[9] Westervelt is correct in that this practice was abolished in 1861; he probably witnessed the last flogging in the army.[10]

2. Washington - A Southern City: Colonel Slocum told Corporal Westervelt, who was on sentry duty, to be on guard for the citizens of Washington were not friendly. Slocum's admonition reflects the feelings of Northern officers about the capital city and its inhabitants. Harpers states, "Treason was rife in every department of the government at Washington...the Confederate government was fully informed of every movement made or contemplated at Washington."[11]

MUSTERING IN — A NEW RECRUIT IN A NEW REGIMENT

In the Spring of 1861, while rumors of war were the principal, and in fact about the whole topic of conversation, I caught the infection, and like other young men looking for adventure concluded to enlist, and was not long in putting this resolution into practice. A few days found me enrolled as member of Company F, 27th Regt. N. Y. Vols., to serve for two years unless sooner discharged. We were quartered in barracks in Elmira, N. Y., and were commanded by Colonel, since Major General Henry W. Slocum, now Congressman-at-Large from this state.

In looking over a diary I kept from day to day during the whole four years of my army life, I find that, while its leaves are turning yellow with the age of nearly a quarter of a century, there may be some facts of interest to the reading public; so I will send you a few extracts. Not to discuss any great stragetic movements of our armies; or how this campaign was a success, or that one a failure; rather leaving that to the historian, or the commanding officers to tell, while we devote our time to the "lights and shadows" of army life as they appeared to the private soldier, whose blood made the general's glory, and whose greatest strategy was often exhausted in the momentous question of securing a good dinner or refilling the empty haversacks.

Passing over the "backaches," etc., that every recruit knows accompany the drill of the awkward squad in getting the positions, facing, wheeling, and other movements taught in the "school of the soldier;" but by devoting about 8 hours each day to the tiresome work, we soon got so far advanced that we could fall into line, and march through the streets of Elmira creditably.

About the first of July we received our uniforms, and as we dressed ourselves in blue and took charge of our guns and equipments, and knapsacks, haversacks and canteens, we realized more fully than ever that we were no longer citizens, but soldiers in the service of the government.

On the eleventh of July[*] we received orders to start for Washington, and for the first time, we packed our haversacks preparatory to a move; and it is surprising and amusing to look back after three or four years' service and think of the useless things that found their way into that receptacle. But we were then inexperienced in the art of making our load as light as possible, in fact we found one of the hardest lessons for a soldier to learn was how many things one can do without.

The next evening we arrived in Washington and were quartered in barracks in Franklin sq. On the following morning we were put on guard, and as I walked up and down the sidewalks that surrounded our camp, Col. Slocum approached and said "Sentry, many of the citizens are not friendly toward a soldier, but if any of them attempt any liberties with you hit them over the head with your gun." How well I remember what my feelings were, as I braced up and waited impatiently for one of them to give me a slight excuse for carrying out this order.

For the next four days our time was spent in drilling, in loading and firing, and at target practice. About noon on the 16th orders came to move. We packed up hastily and soon crossed the Long bridge into Virginia.

---

[*] Official Records show that the regiment left Elmira on July 10, 1861.

MUSTERING IN — A NEW RECRUIT IN A NEW REGIMENT

After passing the fortifications at Arlington we passed the fertile plantations of the Lees, the Balls, Bailys* and Arlingtons†, that had not yet felt the devastating hand of war, but were destined to be left a barren waste, from which they have not yet recovered. We marched about twelve miles and at ten P.M. reached the main army which was encamped on the Annandale hills, and for the first time slept on the ground with no covering but our blankets.

July 17th, Wednesday. — At sunrise the bugle called us, and soon after we were on the march, taking the road towards Fairfax Court House. After a few hours marching at "route step" we were called to quick time and moved by platoons closed to half distance. Soon our mounted rifles and cavalry were ordered to the front, and as they moved forward at a gallop we almost held our breath in the excitement and expectation of hearing them open fire and commence an engagement. But the enemy retreated on their approach, with but a few scattering shots from our men to accelerate their progress. We then marched leisurely on, and entered the village of Fairfax Court House, with our colors flying, bands playing, and men singing the "Star Spangled Banner," more confident than ever that nothing could stop our victorious march, right through the Southern Confederacy. After passing two or three lines of works we went into camp. The men being under but little discipline, were allowed to do as they pleased, and many acts were committed that a veteran would be ashamed of.

---

* Bailey's

† Arlington—not the name of a family, but Lee's wife's home overlooking Washington.

Houses were pillaged and burned, women and children were insulted, barns were fired, and immense amounts of property unnecessarily destroyed.

July 18th, Thursday. — At 9 A.M., we were called in line and moved out to the road, where we waited until three P.M., when we started, taking the road towards Centreville. The day was hot, and the men but little used to marching, so it came very hard to us. But our Colonel then, as ever after, looked out for the comfort of his men and favored us all he could, so we got along much better than a regiment of regulars, and a battalion of marines that were just ahead of us. After a march of about five miles we went into camp, where we soon built bough houses to protect us from the dew and sun.

July 19th, Friday. — Remained in camp; in the morning the regiment of regulars, who were encamped next to us, were called in line and formed a square, when two of their number were whipped, receiving thirty cuts each on their bare backs. It was a sickening, disgusting sight, the blood flowing from every blow of the whip. The first one, after receiving his punishment, was so weak that he had to be helped into his clothes; but the second pushed the man aside who attempted to help him put on his shirt, and very coolly dressed himself, buttoning every button as carefully as though preparing for dress parade. When he had finished he took out his pipe and tobacco pouch, and after filling the pipe seated himself for a comfortable smoke. This was the last case of this kind of punishment in our army, as it was abolished soon after.

In the afternoon there was some sharp skirmishing a few miles in front of us, and soon after some prisoners were brought in, who were the first rebels we had seen.

6

They attracted a good deal of attention, and we, in the innocence of our maiden soldiering, discussed the question among ourselves whether we should shoot or hang them. Fortunately the question was not left to the private soldiers to decide. At dark we went on picket, and our men thinking every leaf that stirred was an enemy approaching kept up a continual firing all night, and deprived those of us who were on the reserve of what sleep we might otherwise have had.

July 20th, Saturday. — Relieved from picket about 9 o'clock and returned to camp, where we remained quiet all day. Some skirmishing in front of us in the afternoon in the direction of Bull Run. Were ordered to move the next morning.

MUSTERING IN — A NEW RECRUIT IN A NEW REGIMENT

Notes — Chapter 1

1. Orville J. Victor, *History of The Southern Rebellion* (New York, James D. Torrey, Publishers, 1863), Vol. II, pp. 81-83.

2. Alfred H. Guernsey and Henry M. Alden, *Harper's Pictorial History of the Civil War* (Harper & Bros, 1866), p. 65 f. Reprint (date not shown).

3. Victor, *History of the Southern Rebellion*, p. 140.

4. Ibid., p. 140.

5. Frederick Phisterer, *New York in the War of the Rebellion 1861-1865* (Albany, J. B. Lyon Company, Publishers, 1912), Volume III, p. 2039.

6. William C. Davis, *Battle at Bull Run* (New York, Doubleday & Co., Inc., 1977), p. 14.

7. E.B. Long, *The Civil War Day by Day* (Garden City, New York, Doubleday and Company, 1971), pp. 77, 79.

8. Ibid., p. 88.

9. Russel F. Weigley, *History of the United States Army* (New York, The Macmillan Company, 1967), p. 63.

10. Ibid., p. 231.

11. Guernsey and Alden, *Harper's Pictorial History of the Civil War*, p. 148.

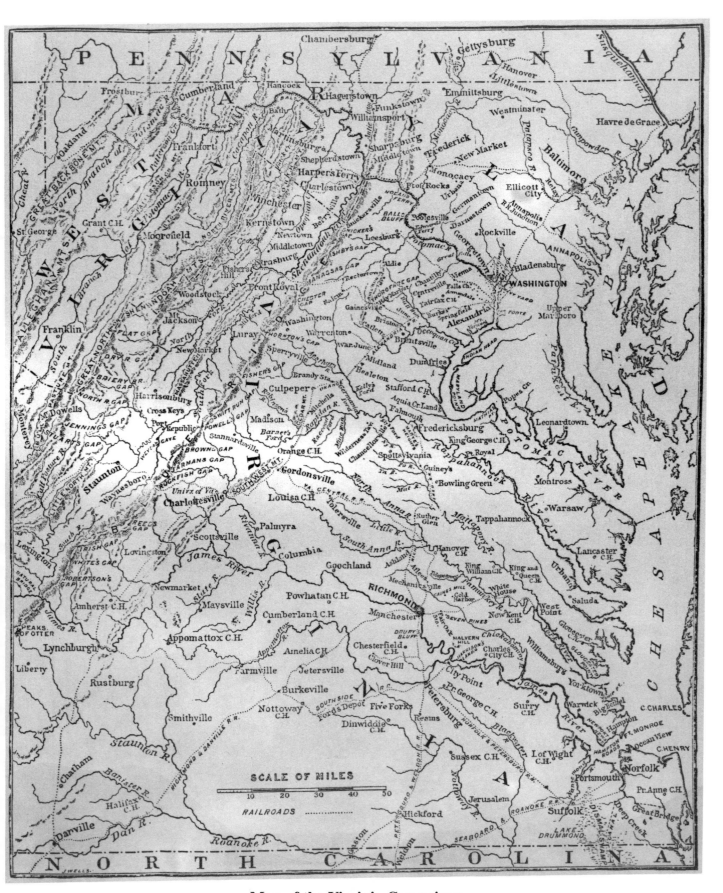

Map of the Virginia Campaigns

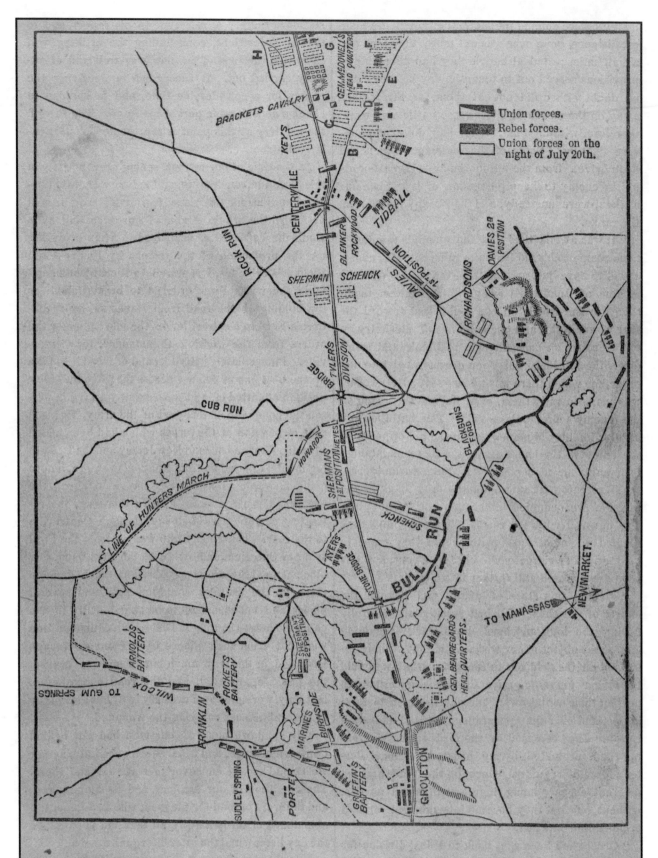

Giving the disposition of the forces [: :: :: : :: ::] the night before the battle, and the position assumed on the field by the several divisions and batteries. The line of retreat of the Union forces was by the direct routes to the Potomac by which the divisions marched on to Centreville.

General McDowell's Official Map of the Battle of Bull Run

Chapter 2

THE BULL RUN CAMPAIGN

Background

McDowell's plan of attack against the Rebels at Bull Run or Manassas was to throw his right at the Confederate left in a surprise flanking movement. Colonel David Hunter's Division, which included the 27th New York, played a major role in this thrust on July 21, 1861. (Note: The North typically named battles after geographic features—hence, they called the battle Bull Run; the South typically named battles after towns—thus they called the same battle Manassas.)

What happened to the 27th New York at Bull Run is described in Colonel Porter's Report as commanding officer of both the brigade and the Second Division:[1]

"...The brigade was silently paraded in light marching order at 2 o'clock in the morning of that day composed as follows, viz: Griffin's battery; marines, Major Reynolds; Twenty-seventh New York Volunteers, Colonel Slocum; Fourteenth New York State Militia, Colonel Wood; Eighth New York State Militia, Colonel Lyons; battalion regulars, Major Sykes; one company Second Dragoons, two companies First Cavalry, four companies Second Cavalry, Major Palmer. Total strength, 3,700....

"Owing to frequent delays in the march of troops in front, the brigade did not reach Centreville until 4.30 a.m., and it was an hour after sunrise when the head of the column turned to the right to commence the flanking movement.

"...the rattle of musketry and the occasional crash of round shot through the leaves and branches of the trees in our vicinity betokened the opening of battle.

"...Griffin's battery found its way through the timber to the fields beyond, promptly followed by the marines, while the Twenty-seventh took direction more to the left, and the Fourteenth followed upon the trail of the battery, all moving at a double-quick step. The enemy appeared drawn up in a long line, extending along the Warrenton turnpike from a house and haystacks on our extreme right to a house beyond the left of the division. Behind that house there was a heavy masked battery, which with three others along his line on the heights beyond, covered the ground upon which we were advancing with all sorts of projectiles. A grove in front of his right wing afforded it shelter and protection, while the shrubbery along the road, with fences, screened somewhat his left wing. Griffin advanced to within a thousand yards, and opened a deadly and unerring fire upon his batteries, which were soon silenced or driven away. Our right was rapidly developed by the marines, Twenty-seventh, Fourteenth, and Eighth, with the cavalry in the rear of the right, the enemy retreating with more precipitation than order as our line advanced."

....

"The rebels soon came flying from the woods towards the right, and the Twenty-seventh completed their rout by charging directly upon their center in the face of a scorching fire, while the Fourteenth and Eighth moved down the turnpike to cut off the retiring foe, and to support the Twenty-seventh which had lost its gallant colonel, but was standing the brunt of the action, with its ranks thinning in the dreadful fire. Now the resistance of the enemy's left was so obstinate that the beaten right retired in safety.

"Griffin's and Ricketts' batteries were ordered by the commanding general to the top of the hill on our right, supporting them with Fire Zouaves and marines, while the Fourteenth entered the skirt of woods on their right, to protect the flank, and a column composed of the Twenty-seventh New York, Eleventh and Fifth Massachusetts, First Minnesota, and Sixty-ninth New York, moved up towards the left flank of the batteries; but so soon as they were in position, and before the flanking supports had reached theirs, a murderous fire of musketry and rifles, opened at pistol range, cut down every cannoneer and a large number of horses. The fire came from some infantry of the enemy, which had been mistaken for our own forces, an officer on the field having stated that it was a regiment sent by Colonel Heintzelman to support the batteries.

"The evanescent courage of the zouaves prompted them to fire perhaps a hundred shots, when they broke and fled, leaving the batteries open to a charge of the enemy's cavalry, which took place immediately....Soon the slopes behind us were swarming with our retreating and disorganized forces, whilst riderless horses and artillery teams ran furiously through the flying crowd. All further efforts were futile....

"Upon our first position the Twenty-seventh was the first to rally, under the command of Major Bartlett, and around it the other regiments soon collected their scattered fragments."

Thus ended the Battle of Bull Run.

For the 27th New York, the early part of July 21 and 22 went like this:

July 21, 1861

1:00 A.M.	Called for duty
2:00 A.M.	Started marching
4:30 A.M.	Reached Centreville
9:00 A.M.	Passed Sudley Church
10:30 A.M. - 5:00 P.M.	In battle, constantly under fire
5:00 P.M. -12:00 P.M.	Retreated, reaching Fairfax at midnight

July 22, 1861

8:00 A.M.	Reached Franklin Square in Washington, D.C.

THE BULL RUN CAMPAIGN

This was the 27th's first battle, on a very hot day, and the men were dressed in regulation blue wool uniforms. The regiment suffered 130 casualties (26 killed, 44 wounded, and 60 missing). This represented 17% of its strength. It was next to the worst single day's loss in the history of the regiment. Westervelt survived unscathed.

Highlights

There are several points to note in Westervelt's reports on Bull Run and the periods before and after the battle.

1. Uniforms - Friend or Foe?: Bull Run was a battle in which there was confusion as to who was friend and who was foe. Some of the Northern troops wore gray and some of the Southern troops wore blue. Westervelt indicates that the 8th New York Militia was dressed in gray. The turning point in the battle occurred when the 33rd Virginia Regiment, dressed in blue, got close enough to Griffin's and Ricketts' batteries, due to mistaken identity, to shoot down the gunners and horses and drive off the Zouaves and marines who were supporting the guns.[2]

2. "Stonewall" Jackson: At an early point in the battle, the troops of the 27th New York mistook for friends the 8th Georgia and the 4th Alabama under Brigadier General Barnard E. Bee. This initial error, however, did not stop the 27th New York and other Federal troops from driving the Rebel troops back and shattering their organizations. It was in this retreat that General Bee called to his troops, "Look, there is Jackson standing like a stone wall! Rally behind the Virginians!"[3] Thus, Westervelt and the 27th New York played a part in nicknaming "Stonewall" Jackson, formally known as Brigadier General Thomas J. Jackson, Commanding Officer of the First Brigade of Joseph E. Johnson's Division of the Army of the Shenandoah.

3. U.S. Cavalry Panic: Westervelt states that the Federal rout after the battle was, in part, due to the fact that the Federal cavalry literally ran through the infantry in the retreat. This fact, not mentioned in official reports nor in standard references is verified in the Regimental History of the 27th New York as well as in a contemporary history.[4]

4. Medical Care 1861: After Bull Run, Westervelt talks about the devastating effects of diarrhea upon the Army. The medical director of the Army of the Potomac reported that, in August 1861, "thirty-three percent of some of the regiments were reported sick with diarrhea, intermittent, and typhoid fevers."[5] In the course of two years, the period of existence of the 27th New York, the regiment lost two officers and 70 enlisted men because of death due to disease. This is almost the same number it lost through death on the battlefield and from wounds received on the battlefield (2 and 72, respectively).[6]

First Battle of Bull Run

July 21st, Sunday. — At one A.M. we were called and ordered to get ready to move. Soon after we formed in line where we stood waiting two hours, while the private soldier exercised his prerogative of grumbling. I never knew the cause of this long delay until a few weeks ago, while in Elmira attending a re-union of the survivors of the 27th Regt. Gen. Slocum, in an after dinner speech, alluded to this delay, and said it was caused by a government wagon being broken and left across the road, and no one seemed to have the authority to move it out of the way. Things were quite different a year or so later, when we got down to a basis of more fighting, and less red tape.

On starting from here we moved very slowly, and at sunrise we reached Centerville. On passing through the village we turned to the right, into a heavy timber. Here we put out one company of our regiment as skirmishers and continued to advance. The day was hot, and this is a portion of Virginia noted for scarcity of water, so we suffered both from heat, and thirst. At nine A.M. we reached Sudley's church when the firing in front of us became quite lively. We soon left the woods, and as we came into the open field one of Gen. McDowell's aids met us, and ordered Col. Slocum to move forward, and with a wave of his hand exclaimed "You will find the enemy down there somewhere;" then turning to us said as we moved past: "Hurry up, boys, or your dinners will be cold before you get there." But as the sequel proved, it was hotter than we could digest when we got it. On we went, apparently on our own hook, with no lines on either flank, or to support our rear.

We were soon under fire, where the solid shot and shell began to pass our heads and made us do some involuntary dodging.

Still we continued to advance, every step the shot coming thicker and faster. As yet we had met with no casualties. We passed the 8th N. Y. Militia, who, dressed in the gray state uniform, were caring for some of their wounded comrades.

On we went, when our Colonel, seeing a battery on a hill, on the Warrenton turnpike, in advance of us, started to take it. This soon brought us under a heavy fire, of both artillery and musketry, and here I saw the first man killed. Private Wesley Randall, of Binghamton, who was marching just in front of me, was struck with a grape shot over the left eye. He gave an unearthly screech, and leaping into the air, came down on his hands and knees, and straightened out dead.

Finding we were overmatched, and no troops coming to support us, Slocum took us from the road to an adjoining field, where under shelter of the celebrated "Stone House", at the junction of the Warrenton turnpike and Newmarket road, our ranks, that had been thrown into some disorder, were reformed. From here we advanced a few rods, when we saw two regiments coming towards us from a direction we did not expect the enemy. They were dressed in gray and we could not tell whether they were some of our militia, or the enemy. Colonel Slocum rode forward between our lines and waving his white handkerchief (that is always recognized as a flag of truce) asked, "What regiment are you?" He was answered by them unfurling the Confederate colors and firing a volley, when he rode back, exclaiming, "Give it to them, boys! We can whip any two regiments that do as cowardly an act as that." They proved to be the 8th Georgia and 4th Alabama regiments. The fight now commenced in earnest. It was give and take. Soon Slocum fell, shot through the hip, and

An Incident in the Retreat at the Battle of Manassas

was sent to the rear to the surgeons. Then Major Bartlett took command. Our line was continually growing shorter as we closed up the gaps, but we had the grim satisfaction of seeing our opponents getting the same punishment as ourselves, and finally break in disorder and retreat. Just at this time the regulars and marines came up and relieved us.

As our ammunition was about expended, we withdrew to the woods in our rear, where we rested awhile and refilled our cartridge boxes. We then advanced again to the Stone House, where we took shelter under a bank by the roadside, and were moved from one point in the field to another, where it was thought our service would be the most needed, taking but little active part in the fight, yet continually under fire.

At five P.M., when we thought the fight was all in our hands, we saw a heavy column of troops arrive on the field at the left, that we supposed was Gen. Patterson coming to our help, and gave them three cheers. But as they advanced we soon saw our mistake, as they proved to be the rebel reserve of twelve thousand troops under General Johnson. This turned the table very effectually, and a retreat was ordered, with Major Bartlett riding at the head of our regiment, and our colors flying we marched off the field in good order. Although our numbers were few, and our line was short, yet our ranks were kept closed up until passing Sudley's Church, when some of our panic stricken cavalry rode through our ranks and ordered us to cover their retreat. This move broke our ranks and scattered our men among the fragments of other regiments, so that it was impossible to rally them again.

It then became a stampede, with every man for himself. A few miles from the field we came to the Stone Bridge across Cub Run. Here was a blockade of cannons and cassions*, while the troops were turning to the right and fording the stream just below the bridge. As I came up I saw a familiar face of one riding on a limber chest. The second glance showed me it was private, afterward Major James Taggart, of Newburgh, then a member of Capt. Ellis' company, attached to the 71st N.Y. Militia. His face was drawn with pain from the rough riding of this uncomfortable conveyance, and on enquiry I found he had been badly wounded during the day, but with that indomitable will that did not desert him to the day of his death, had determined not to be left behind, so with a little assistance had climbed upon this artillery attachment, and by this means escaped being taken prisoner, which was a fate worse than death. Just before midnight we reached the camp we left in the morning near Centerville, when we were ordered to move on to Fairfax. We started again and traveled all night.

July 22d, Monday. — From midnight until daylight we kept trudging along toward Washington. We passed through Fairfax Court House—this time without music—while the cry "On to Richmond!" seemed to have lost all its charm as a rallying cry. About sunrise we reached Arlington, and two hours after we were back to our old quarters at Franklin Square. Thus ended the first battle of Bull Run, where both armies were for the first time under fire, and for hard fighting and stubborn resistance they challenged the admiration of the world.

---

* caissons

After our return from the battle of Bull Run, we occupied our quarters at Franklin Square, in Washington, until near the middle of August. That terrible disease camp diarrhoea, more destructive than the enemy's bullets, broke out in our regiment, and for a few weeks made sad havoc with the men. Drilling was dispensed with and all other duties not absolutely necessary. Even then those who were well had extra duty to perform. I, being one of the well ones, was sent to take charge of the cook house of our company. Not having any great talent in the art "de cuisine" the duties were particularly irksome to me. Our cooking utensils, furnished by the government, were of the most primitive description. The kettles, mess pans and frying pans were all made of sheet iron, and were used out of doors, over a fire made between two rows of bricks. The fuel was Virginia pine, so burned bean soup seldom failed to appear on our bill of fare.

Some of the most ridiculous mistakes were made by me, that thinking of them even to this day excited my risibilities. One day the commissary issued about eight pounds of rice to our company. I inquired if I was to make an immense rice pudding of it, and was informed that the proper way to cook it was by boiling in water with a little salt. So dumping the whole eight pounds into a mess kettle, I filled it with water, and put it on the fire. Soon it began to climb out of the top of the pot, and I began to dip it out, and continued the bailing process until nearly every kettle in the cook house was filled. Then filling the one on the fire with water, made a good hot fire under it, and soon had the finest mess of burned-half-cooked rice one would wish to see. In disgust I left the cook house and reported to our captain that I had discovered my mission in the army was not to destroy any more government rations, but would hereafter try to earn my pay and allowances in the ranks.

On Aug. 14th we left Washington, and crossing the Long Bridge marched to Alexandria, where we received our first tents and commenced our life under canvas. We now spent most of our time drilling by battalion or brigade, and the men seemed to show the effects of it in their improved soldierly appearance, while some of the officers seemed dull and hard to understand their duties, and often made very ridiculous mistakes, that brought down on them some sharp reprimands from Gen. Slocum or Col. Bartlett; in fact many of them seemed to think their only duty was to keep well supplied with whiskey and shuffle through what duties they could not shirk.

Notes — Chapter 2

1. *O.R.*, Vol. II, Chapter IX, pp. 383-387.

2. Vincent J. Esposito, Col, *The West Point Atlas of the Civil War* (Frederick A. Prager, New York 1962), P. Explanation of Map 23.

3. E.B. Long, *The Civil War Day by Day*, p. 98.

4. J.T. Headley, *The Great Rebellion, A History of the Civil War in the United States* (Hurlbut, Williams and Co., Hartford, Conn. 1862), Vol. I, p. 118.

5. *O.R.*, Series I, Vol. V, p. 81.

6. Dyer, *A Compendium of the War of the Rebellion*, Vol. III, p. 1415.

COL. J. J. BARTLETT.

Chapter 3

POHICK CHURCH, VIRGINIA

Background

After Bull Run, things were rather uneventful for the 27th New York until October 1861. The regiment was assigned to Heintzelman's Brigade, Division of the Potomac on August 4, and then to Slocum's Brigade, Franklin's Division, Army of the Potomac on October 15, 1861. Slocum was promoted to command the brigade in September 1861, and Joseph J. Bartlett was moved up to command the regiment.

On October 3, 1861, Westervelt's Company, Company F, was detailed to go on an expedition to Pohick Church, Virginia. What the Federal unit was trying to do is described in General Slocum's report.[1] The expedition was an acknowledged failure, and Westervelt provides the unvarnished reasons for lack of success as he perceived them.

General Slocum's report follows:

"October 3, 1861 - Expedition to Pohick Church, Virginia.
Report of Brig. Gen. Henry W. Slocum, U.S. Army.

HEADQUARTERS SECOND BRIGADE,
Alexandria, VA., October 6, 1861.

SIR: I received information on the 3d instant that a body of the enemy's cavalry was at Pohick Church, about 12 miles from these headquarters, together with such other information as led me to suppose that the force could be captured without difficulty. The plan of an expedition for this purpose was fully matured and verbally communicated to Colonel Christian, Twenty-sixth New York Volunteers, who was detailed to command. An order was then issued of which I herewith inclose a copy.

The expedition proved an entire failure, and this result I am informed and believe is to be attributed to the fact that my orders relative to the manner of the execution were not obeyed; and what is still more annoying to me and disgraceful to my command is the fact that instead of being marched back to camp in good order, a large portion of the command was allowed to disband beyond our line of pickets, and, as might have been anticipated from such a proceeding, this force sent to operate against the troops of the enemy was converted into a band of marauders, who plundered alike friend and foe.

I deem it my duty to lay these facts before the commanding general, and to suggest that a court of inquiry be convened for the purpose of a thorough investigation of all the circumstances attending the expedition.

I am, sir, very respectfully, your obedient servant,

H.W. SLOCUM
Brigadier-General Volunteers, Commanding.

Major S. Williams, Assistant Adjutant-General.

POHICK CHURCH, VIRGINIA

(Inclosure.)

HEADQUARTERS SECOND BRIGADE,
October 3, 1861.

Col. William H. Christian:

SIR: You will take command of a detachment of 300 infantry from the regiments composing this brigade and one company of cavalry, and will endeavor to cut off and take prisoners a body of the enemy's cavalry, numbering probably 50 men, stationed at or near Pohick Church.

You will proceed with 225 infantry, according to verbal directions already given to you, to certain points in the rear of the enemy's position, and will make your attack at precisely 6 o'clock to-morrow morning.

You will send out 75 infantry and the company of cavalry on the Richmond road, with instructions for them to be at Potter's store, 4 miles from Pohick Church, and 6 miles from these headquarters, at 5.45 o'clock, driving in the enemy's pickets and advancing as rapidly as possible towards Pohick Church, in order to cut off the enemy or to render assistance to the other detachments of your command.

The object of the expedition being accomplished, you will return without delay.

By order of Brigadier-General Slocum:

JOSEPH HOWLAND,
Assistant Adjutant-General."

POHICK CHURCH, VIRGINIA

Highlights

In this chapter, two items are worthy of note: Westervelt's criticism of his officers, and the execution of a "deserter."

1. Criticism of Officers: In this part of his book, Westervelt is highly critical of Colonel Christian. This criticism of certain officers of the 27th New York is a theme that runs through his report of his service with that regiment. However, his criticism of officers other than Colonel Christian is confined to lower ranking persons, captains, and lieutenants or company grade officers, while he has high praise for field grade officers; majors, lieutenant colonels, colonels, and generals.

Research on the officers of the 27th New York shows that five field and staff officers were authorized for the regiment, exclusive of surgeons and chaplains. These were colonel, lieutenant colonel, major, adjutant, and quartermaster. Two—Slocum and Bartlett—were promoted out of the regiment and became general officers; six were discharged, and five were mustered out with the regiment at the end of two years of service. A total of thirteen served in the five positions over the two-year period.[2]

For the 30 officer positions authorized in the 10 companies (captain, 1st lieutenant and 2nd lieutenant in each company), 86 persons were appointed. Of these, five were promoted out of the companies, four were killed or died in service, 51 resigned or were discharged, and 30 mustered out with the regiment. On the basis of this data alone, it appears that leadership at the company level was a problem for the 27th New York and that Westervelt had cause to be critical.[3]

2. Executing a Deserter: The second item of significance in this chapter is the execution of a deserter. Westervelt believed that the execution he was required to watch was the first of its kind in the war.

Deserters were fairly common for both the North and the South during the war. The History of the 27th New York indicates that 104 (against an authorized strength of 780), or 13.3%, deserted. Not all were true desertions, for some men simply moved over and joined another outfit in their army. Few were executed, a total of 147 out of 2,778,304 who served in the Union armies.[4]

What makes this case unusual is that the soldier was both a deserter and a spy. The fact that the execution was so brutal apparently was intended as a lesson for others.

POHICK CHURCH, VIRGINIA

On Sept. 12th we moved our camp to the grounds afterwards occupied as Fort Lyons, and after removing a heavy growth of timber, commenced building that large earthwork, and for the next month we put aside our drilling and exchanged our guns for the pick and shovel. We looked and acted more like railroad laborers than soldiers. Discipline was rather loose, and our army life was quite different from what we expected to find it.

The only break that occurred in the monotonous labor was on the night of Oct. 3rd, when on our return to camp we were ordered to hurry through our suppers and "fall in", in light marching order. It did not take us long to get through, when after receiving a supply of cartridges we took our place at the head of the column. We were the only company from our regiment; the rest of the column was made up of companies from the 5th Maine and the 16th and 26th N.Y., and was commanded by Colonel Christian, of the 26th, a man who evidently mistook his calling when he entered the army, and who afterwards at the battle of Antietam, distinguished himself by advancing to the rear, when he was given his choice of being cashiered or sending in his resignation, to read — "I resign from inability to stand fire." He choose the latter, and that is the way his resignation is on file at the war department.

Soon after dark we started, taking the road towards Mt. Vernon. A few miles took us to Gum Spring, where we passed outside the picket line. Then a small squad of us were sent ahead and ordered to keep about one hundred yards in advance of the main column. This I think was one of the most interesting night marches I ever had. The road ran through the woods most of the way, and it was so dark we could not see 5 paces in advance

of us, and expected to come upon the enemy's pickets at every step. I can't say I enjoyed it much. About midnight orders came forward to halt our squad and picket the road, so we quietly sat down by the roadside and tried to penetrate the darkness of night until about three A.M., when we were ordered to advance. We soon emerged from the woods and passed through the village of Occoaquan, and just at daylight, when near Pohick church, we came upon the enemy's pickets, when instead of making a rush and capturing some or all of them, our doughty Colonel called us back and sent us around to the left, as he said, to cut off their retreat, but it looked as though it was to give them a chance to get away before they hurt some one. They were not slow to avail themselves of this opportunity, leaving behind them their commissary stores and a half cooked breakfast. This we soon disposed of and took what spoils from the stores we could carry, and after examining the church, and the pew that Gen. Washington and his family used to occupy, we started to return, reaching camp about four P.M., having marched some thirty miles on the round trip on about as useless an errand as a body of tired men were ever sent upon.

This with an occasional tour of picket duty was the only variation we had from our "pick and shovel" duty until October, when we moved our camp near Fairfax Seminary, where we built log foundations to our tents, and went into winter quarters, and once more resumed our drilling that was kept up almost uninterruptedly until the mud became so deep on our drill ground about midwinter that it had to be discontinued. On the 13th of December, soon after noon hour, we were ordered to fall in line, and amid many conjectures of what it was for we were marched out of our camp to a large plain near *by, to witness the execution of a deserter named Johnson. The story of his crime was as follows: He came north from New Orleans about the commencement of the war, and joined the 1st N.Y. Cavalry, for the purpose of better serving the Southern cause, than by remaining in their ranks. One day while a squad of his company were on picket he attempted to desert to the enemy. Meeting one of our scouts dressed in gray, Johnson mistook him for a Confederate, and confided to him his little scheme of having his company captured while on the picket post. The scout pretended to readily fall in with his plan, but in an unguarded moment covered private Johnson with his revolver, disarmed him, and marched him into our lines a prisoner. The result was a speedy court martial, and sentence to be shot, and this afternoon the sentence was to be executed. We marched out with the rest of our division and formed three sides of a square. Johnson was then placed in a conspicuous position, blindfolded and kneeling upon his coffin. Then ten members of his company marched to within ten paces of him, and at the word of command fired their carbines into his breast. He fell forward upon his face, when the Sergeant of the squad stepped to within a few feet of him, and with his large revolver fired six shots into his body. Then the troops were marched past his body, where they could all have a good view of it, and leaving the sickening sight we marched back to our quarters. This I believe was the first execution of the kind during the war.*

POHICK CHURCH, VIRGINIA

Notes — Chapter 3

1. *O.R.*, Series I, Vol. V, pp. 236-237.

2. Phisterer, *New York in the War of the Rebellion*, pp. 2039-2052.

3. Fairchild, *History of the 27th Regiment, N.Y. Vols.*, pp. 258-292.

4. Long, *The Civil War day by Day*, pp. 705, 714.

Chapter 4

THE PENINSULAR CAMPAIGN — AN OVERVIEW

A simple explanation of Westervelt's and the 27th New York's activities in the Peninsular Campaign would be that they joined McClellan at Yorktown on April 22, 1862; fought at West Point, Virginia on May 7; supported Porter in the Hanover Court House Expedition on May 22 and 27; and fought with Porter at Gaines' Mill on June 27. Westervelt was injured at Gaines' Mill and found his way back to Harrison's Landing on July 4 where the entire army had retreated and where the Peninsular Campaign ended.

But the events surrounding the regiment and Westervelt were far more complicated than that; they were related to the following:

-the geography of the Peninsula and its impact upon the Campaign,

-McClellan's relationship with Lincoln and with his corps commanders, and his perception of the size of the enemy facing him, and

-the amount of time, months gone by, without a significant Northern victory in Virginia and with the administration constantly calling for action.

Each of these three major factors had a direct impact upon the 27th New York and Westervelt, and are discussed below.

The Geography of the Peninsula

The Peninsula of Virginia lies between the York River and its tributaries on the north, and the James River on the south. Fortress Monroe is on the eastern end of the Peninsula, and Richmond on the James River is near the western end of the Peninsula. The Chickahominy River runs from a point north of Richmond (northwest of Mechanicsville) and splits the upper Peninsula. The Chickahominy is normally a small river, but it can flood as it did in May, June, and July of 1862.

McClellan landed at the eastern end of the Peninsula at Fortress Monroe, moved westward after battles at Yorktown, Williamsburg, and West Point and established his supply base at White House on the Pamunkey. His forces continued moving toward Richmond and found the Confederates drawn up about six miles east of that city; their lines running from the James north to the Chickahominy and thence west on the south side of that river. North of the Chickahominy were scattered Confederate troops and about forty miles northeast of Mechanicsville was Fredericksburg and McDowell's Union Corps. East of Mechanicsville were important geographic features that could be used in defense—first, Beaver Dam Creek (used at the Battle of Mechanicsville); and second, Boatswain's Swamp (used at the Battle of Gaines' Mill, also known as First Cold Harbor).

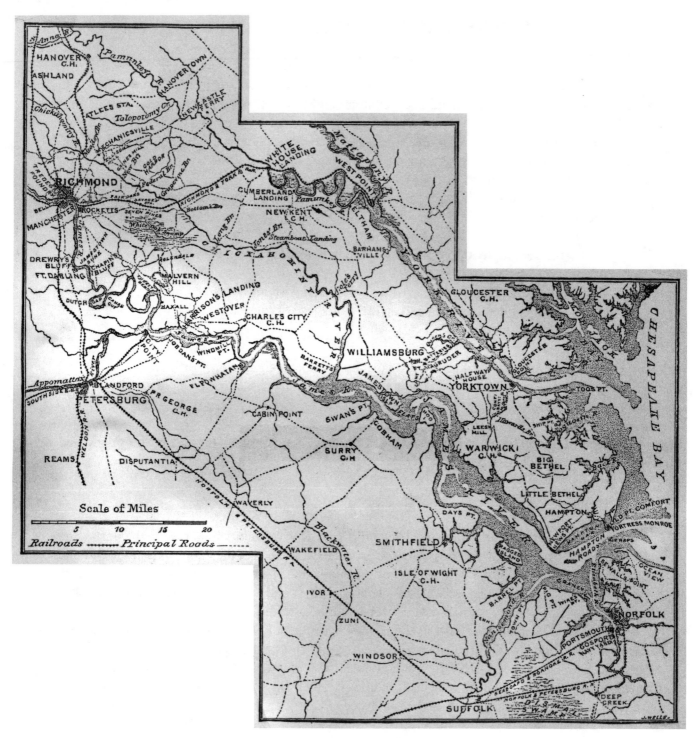

Map of the Peninsular Campaign

THE PENINSULAR CAMPAIGN — AN OVERVIEW

McClellan's alternate supply base, which was more accessible to the navy and its gunboats, was Harrison's Landing on the James. To transfer his base from White House to Harrison's Landing required a movement below White Oak Swamp, a swamp that McClellan had to control to protect such a move.

McClellan planned to attack Richmond by moving west between the Chickahominy and the James. But he also had to protect the area north of the Chickahominy to keep the way clear for McDowell to join him and to protect his supply line and rail line for his heavy guns (the line ran from White House Landing to Fair Oaks and west). McClellan tried to protect the area north of the Chickahominy with Major General Fitz John Porter's V Corps supported by Brigadier General George A. McCall and some of Franklin's VI Corps. The rest of the army was south of the Chickahominy which was at flood stage and was, therefore, a divisive barrier between the two wings of the army. Lee took advantage of the geography and the flood to attack Porter. Then Porter made use of the geography (Beaver Dam Creek and Boatswain's Swamp) in his withdrawal back to the main body of the army and Harrison's Landing. Westervelt and the 27th New York were involved in supporting Porter north of the river and were directly involved in the Battle of Gaines' Mill.

McClellan — his relationships with Lincoln and his corps commanders; his perception of the size of the enemy facing him.

McClellan assumed command of the Army of the Potomac on July 27, 1861.[1] He became commander in chief of all the Union armies on November 1, 1861.[2] Despite these heady advancements, he immediately ran into difficulties.

First, McClellan refused to reveal his plans for his campaign to the president, and to indicate when he would act. So, from July 1861 until January 1862, he organized, trained, and provisioned the Army of the Potomac but made no attempt to go after the Confederates or to indicate how or when he would do so. Then, McClellan became ill with typhoid and things appeared to be at a standstill.[3] Lincoln became so frustrated that he is quoted as saying, "if something were not done soon, the bottom would be out of the whole affair; and if General McClellan did not intend to use the Army of the Potomac, he would like to borrow it for a while."[4]

To get some action started, Lincoln met with Generals McDowell and Franklin on January 10, 1862.[5] Another meeting was held on January 13; this time McClellan was present. The president had his plan for a campaign (via Manassas to Richmond).[6] McClellan had his own plan which he revealed to the president a few days later (from the lower Chesapeake to Richmond).[7] McClellan and Lincoln argued about the plans and McClellan was forced to put the two proposals to a vote by the twelve senior generals in the Army of the Potomac. They voted for McClellan's plan —eight to four.[8] Now, McClellan was a captive of his generals. To complicate matters further, on March 8, 1862, over McClellan's objections, Lincoln organized the Army of the Potomac into four corps and named McDowell, Sumner, Heintzelman, and Keyes to command them. Three of these men had voted for Lincoln's plan, and one—Keyes—had voted for McClellan's plan with reservations.[9]

When Lincoln finally agreed to the Peninsular Campaign, he did so providing certain conditions were met—the most important of which was that a force be left in or about Washington

Col. A. D. Adams.

as "in the opinion of the General-in-Chief and the Commanders of the Army Corps shall leave said city entirely secure."[10]   This McClellan—in Lincoln's eyes—did not do, particularly in view of Jackson's success in the Shenandoah Valley and the potential threat he posed to the Federal capital. Therefore, on April 4, Lincoln detained McDowell's Corps to protect Washington. He did assure McClellan that the corps would join him later.[11] To compensate for this and other losses, McClellan specifically requested and got Franklin's Division which, of course, included Westervelt and the 27th New York.[12]

Second, according to a contemporary biographer of Lincoln, McClellan did not like organizing the army into corps and on May 9, 1862, asked President Lincoln's and Secretary of War Stanton's permission to return to the organization by divisions. Lincoln wrote a private letter in response in which he said that McClellan's struggle against the corps organization was seen as an effort "to pamper one or two pets," that McClellan was reported to have had no communication with Sumner, Heintzelman, and Keyes, and that he only consulted with Fitz John Porter and perhaps Franklin.[13]

After he received this letter on May 18, 1862, McClellan then created two new corps—The V under Fitz John Porter and the VI under William B. Franklin.[14] Now, McClellan had two of "his" generals as corps commanders. For Westervelt and the 27th New York, this meant that Slocum, the first colonel of the regiment was now their division commander; Bartlett, the second colonel of the 27th was now their brigade commander; and Lieutenant Colonel Adams, who had been second-in-command of the regiment, now became the third and last colonel of the organization.

Third, as McClellan moved toward Richmond with his main body south of the Chickahominy, he sent Porter supported by Slocum's Division and McCall's north of the river to link up with McDowell. While the army was thus divided, Stanton notified McClellan that McDowell would not be sent at all.[15] McClellan's plans had always been based on an attack with at least 140,000 men.[16] When he reached the outer defenses of Richmond, he was convinced that Lee had 180,000 soldiers defending the capital.[17] The news about McDowell changed McClellan's posture from one of offense to one of defense and retreat. One contemporary author whose writings were very sympathetic to McClellan flatly stated, "McClellan never proposed or promised, or expected to take Richmond with the forces given him."[18] In other words, without McDowell, the question, as McClellan saw it, became one of saving the army via the James in the face of the overwhelmingly superior forces of the enemy.

Therefore, Mechanicsville and Gaines' Mill were the beginnings of the withdrawal. When Porter needed help at Gaines' Mill, Slocum's Division moved in and virtually saved the day.[19] The four corps commanders appointed by Lincoln said they could not help Porter because the enemy forces in front of them were too strong and too active.[20]

Time—Months without a significant Northern victory

The chronology of events concerning Westervelt and the 27th New York illustrates how months went by without a significant Northern victory. Only Yorktown (May 4), Williamsburg (May 5), and Hanover Court House (May 27), could be claimed as victories. In contrast, Stonewall Jackson started his offensive in the Shenandoah Valley on May 19, fought the battles of Front Royal,

THE PENINSULAR CAMPAIGN — AN OVERVIEW

Winchester, Port Republic, and Cross Keys by June 9, totally disrupting Federal activities in that area, and was then in a position to threaten Washington or join Lee near Richmond.

Chronology of Events—The 27th New York in the Peninsular Campaign

Date	Event
April 11, 1862	- Franklin's Division ordered to join McClellan at Yorktown
April 22, 1862	- 27th New York arrives at Yorktown
May 3, 1862	- Yorktown evacuated by the Confederates*
May 5, 1862	- Battle of Williamsburg*
May 7, 1862	- Battle of West Point
May 27, 1862	- Battle of Hanover Court House
May 31-June 1, 1862	- Battle of Fair Oaks or Seven Pines*
June 25-July 1, 1862	- The Seven Days' Battles
July 4, 1862	- The Regiment moved to Harrison's Landing
August 14, 1862	- Regiment left Harrison's Landing for Alexandria, Virginia
August 24, 1862	- The 27th New York returned to Fort Ellsworth, Alexandria, Virginia

*27th New York Regiment not engaged in this battle

THE PENINSULAR CAMPAIGN — AN OVERVIEW

Notes — Chapter 4

1. J.T. Headley, *The Great Rebellion, A History of Civil War in the United States* (Hartford, Conn.: American Publishing Company, 1862), Vol. I, p. 124.

2. T. Harry Williams, *Lincoln and His Generals* (New York: Alfred A. Knopf, 1952), p. 43.

3. Ibid., p. 55.

4. Orville Victor, *History of the Southern Rebellion*, Vol. III, p. 480.

5. Ibid.

6. Ibid.

7. John Laird Wilson, *Pictorial History of the Great Civil War* (John Laird Wilson, 1878), p. 192.

8. Guernsey and Alden, *Harper's Pictorial History of the Civil War*, p. 330.

9. Victor, *History of the Southern Rebellion*, Vol. III, p. 51.

10. Ibid., Vol. III, p. 53.

11. Headley, *The Great Rebellion, A History of the Civil War in the United States*, Vol. I, p. 384.

12. J.G. Holland, *The Life of Abraham Lincoln* (Springfield, Mass: Gurdon Bill, 1866), p. 367.

13. Ibid., p. 369.

14. Robert U. Johnson and Clarence C. Buel, Editors, *Battles and Leaders of the Civil War* (New York, N.Y.: The Century Co., 1884-1887), Vol. 2, p. 173.

15. Headley, *The Great Rebellion, A History of the Civil War in the United States*, Vol. I, p. 501.

16. Alexander S. Webb, *Campaigns of the Civil War, The Peninsula* (New York: Scribner's Sons, 1881), p. 32.

17. Ibid., p. 182.

18. Headley, *The Great Rebellion, A History of the Civil War in the United States*, Vol. I, p. 421.

19. Johnson and Buel, *Battles and Leaders of the Civil War*, Vol. II, p. 339.

20. Ibid., p. 180.

Chapter 5

THE BATTLE OF WEST POINT, VIRGINIA

Background

On April 5, McClellan laid siege to Yorktown. At McClellan's specific request, Franklin's Division, including the 27th New York, left Alexandria and arrived at Yorktown on April 22. On May 4 and 5, Yorktown was evacuated by the Confederates.

Then, on May 5, Franklin's Division was sent on up the York River to West Point on transports. McClellan writes, "The moment the evacuation of Yorktown was known, the order was given for the advance of all disposable cavalry and horse batteries, supported by infantry divisions, and every possible effort was made to expedite the movement of a column by water upon West Point, to force the evacuation of the lines at Williamsburg, and if possible, cut off a portion of the enemy's forces and trains.

The heavy storms which had prevailed recommenced on the afternoon of the 4th, and not only impeded the advance of the troops by land, but delayed the movement by water so much that it was not until the morning of the 7th that the leading division—Franklin's—disembarked at West Point and took up a suitable position to hold its own and cover the landing of reinforcements. The division was attacked not long after it landed, but easily repulsed the enemy."[1]

Headley, a contemporary author, writes of West Point, "While this battle (Williamsburg) was raging, Franklin was approaching West Point with his troops to intercept the retreat of the rebel army. It effected a landing, and on Wednesday was attacked by the enemy. A battle followed, in which we lost two hundred killed and wounded and a large number of prisoners. Nothing of consequence seems to have been accomplished by this movement, save the rapid transportation of a large force far in advance, where it could cooperate with McClellan's army. Franklin's division was too weak to attack the whole retreating force of the enemy."[2]

Highlights

There are three items of significance in Westervelt's report on the Battle of West Point; they are as follows:

1. The Death of Lieutenant Bailey: While death was no stranger to the regiment, Westervelt and the men of the 27th New York really felt the loss of Lieutenant Bailey who was killed by a Confederate scout. This incident is mentioned in detail in the Regimental History of the 27th New York, and it is covered in a footnote and a picture of Bailey's roll-book in *Battles and Leaders*, Vol. 2, page 433. Also of interest is the fact that the roster in the Regimental History appears to indicate that Bailey did not receive his commission before he was killed for he is not included on the list of officers of the regiment.

2. Hood's Star Begins to Rise: Westervelt points out that the Confederate killed by his unit was from the First Texas; one of Brigadier General John B. Hood's regiments. Douglass Southall Freeman states that at Eltham (the Confederate name for the Battle of West Point) General Hood made his first bid for fame. In fact, one chapter in *Lee's Lieutenants* is titled "Eltham Introduces John B. Hood."[3]

Westervelt and the 27th New York seemed to have a knack for helping Southern generals gain fame. First, they were involved at the beginning of Stonewall Jackson's rise to fame at Bull Run, and then they opposed John Bell Hood at West Point, as his star began to rise.

3. Perceptions of the Battle: Senior Officers vs. Men on the Line: Official reports of the Battle of West Point submitted by Franklin and Slocum and Newton indicate that the Confederates attacked first in the battle.[4] Franklin, writing about West Point in 1881, said, "My instructions were to await orders and not to advance....We had not made any attempt to advance, as such an attempt would have been in conflict with my orders."[5]

Corporal Westervelt flatly states that his unit attacked first under orders from a drunken captain and that it was a useless, costly exercise. Interestingly, that officer, Captain Jay of Company F, Westervelt's commanding officer, was favorably mentioned in Franklin's report and in Newton's report. The section in the Regimental History of the 27th New York on the Battle of West Point is consistent with Westervelt's version of the affair.[6]

The perceptions of this battle from the top and the bottom were vastly different!

THE BATTLE OF WEST POINT, VIRGINIA

The close of the winter of '62 found us still in our winter quarters near Fairfax Seminary, Alexandria. About the first of March we began to hear rumors of a move, and on the 10th of that month we left our camp and marched to Fairfax Court House, and on the 15th returned to our quarters at Alexandria. Here we remained until the 4th of April, when we took the cars to Manassas Junction, that had been evacuated by the enemy some four weeks previous. The 7th found us at Catlett station, on the Orange & Alexandria R.R., in a wet, muddy camp, in the midst of a severe snow storm—something unusual for Virginia at this time of year.

On the 12th we were once more on the cars on our way to Alexandria, where we remained until the 17th, when we embarked on the steamship S.R. Spaulding, and sailed down the Potomac. We remained on the steamer several days, which was not very pleasant. We were quartered on the upper deck, without shelter from the rain, that fell in copious showers, and with no facilities for cooking our food. We ate our salt pork raw, and sometimes (by paying the cook) we could get enough hot water from the galley to make a cup of coffee; other times we drank water.

On the 24th we disembarked near the mouth of the York River, and put up our tents in a beautiful grove of pines on the shore. Here oysters and clams were plenty and while the main part of the army was besieging Yorktown, we quietly remained at this safe distance at the rear, and fairly reveled in the bivalves, fresh from the beds.

On May 3rd Yorktown was evacuated; the next day we bid a sorrowful good-by to our camp, and oyster beds, and loaded on the transport, and started up the York river. On

the 5th while anchored off Yorktown we listened to the fierce engagement at Williamsburg, and on the following day ran up the river as far as West Point, where the junction of the Pamunkey and Mattapony rivers forms the York. There was no landing for heavy craft vessels, so our steamer ran as near the shore as the water would allow and anchored.

On looking shoreward we saw a squad of the enemy's cavalry about a mile distant, watching our movements.

Soon six companies of our regiment were landed in row boats and ordered to advance far enough to establish a line of pickets, to protect the troops while landing, which could have been done without loss of life, but our captain, having imbibed a fresh supply of "Rum-an courage", from a canteen he carried under his arm, started to accomplish some wonderfully daring feat, that is, if it could be done without the risk of his precious skin being perforated—so, deploying our company as skirmishers, he ordered us to advance.

This brought some of us short ones on the left of the company, to a dark muddy stream, that we were ordered to ford. The water was about up to our shoulders, so taking off our cartridge belts, we held them aloft on our guns, and through we went. After advancing a few rods we were ordered to retrace our steps, when we had the cool pleasure of fording the stream again. This brought us about a mile in advance of the ground he was ordered to occupy when we landed, and here he established the picket line, with one flank on the river bank, and the other stretched way off into the woods without any protection. Darkness soon came on, the night was very cold, but we, with our wet clothes, were placed on post and shivered through the long dark hours until morning. During the night one of the enemy's scouts crawled around the unprotected flank of our line, and shot an officer in command of a company adjoining ours—Lieutenant Baily,[*] of Binghamton, a young officer of great promise and a favorite of the whole regiment. He had received his commission a few days before, and this was his first tour of duty as an officer. The triumph of the scout was but momentary, as he was shot almost instantly by Surgeant[†] Elliot, of the same post, and the scout and his victim fell dead within two rods of each other.

At daylight on the morning of the 7th we advanced our line of skirmishers, and soon had our picket line established, extending in a half circle, with the York river on the left, and the Mattapony on the right, without accident or fear of bringing on an engagement, that was considered unnecessary as the force in front of us, like our own, was small, and an engagement, even if successful, would cause an unnecessary loss of life, and then again the whole rebel army was not many miles distant, and could turn and crush us before our army, that was advancing from Williamsburg, could come to our assistance.

About nine A.M. our captain had got well filled with whiskey, and as usual felt very brave, when seeing two of the enemy's cavalry about a mile in advance of us, sent Sergeant Ronk, of company C, with a squad of men to cut them off, and then sent me with a squad of ten men to capture them, while he held a safe position behind a fence. We knew it was a fool's errand, but it was our place to obey. As we advanced the cavalrymen leisurely fell back over the brow of the hill, as if inviting us on, and on we went. When we reached the top of the hill we found ourselves within shot range of a heavy "line of battle." But as we had taken the trouble to come to the top of the hill, we did not propose to run back and stand chagrin and ridicule for not firing a shot, so I ordered my squad to fire, and then retreat to the cover of the woods in the direction in which we came. At the discharge of our pieces an officer seated on a gray horse fell to the ground, and as I afterwards learned it was the Major of the 1st Regiment of Texans who was killed by our volley. We then fell back towards our reserve, losing two of our men on our retreat.

The enemy followed us closely and a general engagement came on, and lasted with varying success until sunset and ended by the enemy retreating.

Our loss during the day was 176 killed and wounded, and what was accomplished? Nothing! A drunken officer attacked the rear guard of Gen. Lee's[‡] army, who held us in check until their supply train was out of the way, and then fell back, and this 176 men of our army, and whatever number the enemy lost, was a sacrifice upon the altar of rum and imbecility.

This captain, however, never lead our company into another fight. His course was steadily downward, and finally he left the army. For some years after the war I lost all trace of him, until about the year '78, while in

---

[*] Bailey

[†] Sergeant

[‡] It was Johnston's army—Lee did not assume command until Johnston was injured at Fair Oaks or Seven Pines, May 31, 1862.

THE BATTLE OF WEST POINT, VIRGINIA

Binghamton, I found him peddling popcorn and peanuts from a handle basket about the streets, willing to do anything to gather a few nickels to satisfy his appetite for rum, a standing reproach to many members of this old company who were obliged to acknowledge him as the captain they served under during the war, until finally he sunk to a drunkard's grave.

THE BATTLE OF WEST POINT, VIRGINIA

Notes — Chapter 5

1. Johnson and Buel, *Battles and Leaders of the Civil War*, Vol. 2, p. 172.

2. Headley, *The Great Rebellion A History of the Civil War in the United States*, Vol. I, p. 411.

3. Douglass Southall Freeman, *Lee's Lieutenants* (New York: Charles Scribner and Sons, 1942), Vol. I, pp. 193-200.

4. Fairchild, *History of the 27th Regiment, N.Y. Vols.*, pp. 37-40.

5. Johnson and Buel, *Battles and Leaders of the Civil War*, Vol. 2, p. 222 footnote.

6. Fairchild, *History of the 27th Regiment, N.Y. Vols.*, p. 35.

Chapter 6

THE HANOVER COURT HOUSE EXPEDITION

Background

After West Point, the 27th New York proceeded west past Cumberland, White House, and Tunstall's Station to Cold Harbor. The Federal command wanted to find out about the Rebel opposition north of the Chickahominy and on May 22, Colonel Bartlett took the 27th New York, the 16th New York, and some cavalry and artillery on a reconnaissance towards Mechanicsville.[1] Bartlett was highly commended for this action and, as Westervelt reports, lost only two cavalrymen in the process.[2]

After this reconnaissance, General Porter and the V Corps moved in and cleared the area around Mechanicsville on May 25, and around Hanover Court House on May 27. The purpose of Porter's action, according to McClellan, was to dislodge the enemy force near Hanover Court House which threatened the Federal communications and was in a position to reinforce Jackson or oppose McDowell, who was then moving south and was eight miles below Fredericksburg.[3]

As a part of Porter's activities, the 27th New York moved into Mechanicsville on May 27 and took possession of it.[4] The regiment was alerted to help in the Battle of Hanover Court House, but was not actually engaged in that battle.

Similarly, on May 31, the regiment was alerted for the Battle of Fair Oaks, but was not engaged in the battle.

Highlights

There are two highlights in this chapter; one has to do with food, and the other with returning the enemy's twelve-pound shell.

1. Craving for food: Near Ellerson's Mill, Westervelt's craving for food overcame his normal good judgement. He started for a house in "no-man's land" between the Federal and Confederate lines only to be halted by a shot fired by a Rebel who was 3,000 feet away. It was a near miss. Westervelt at once lost his appetite and at the same time paid his respects to the enemy marksman.

2. Returning the Enemy's Artillery Shell: On June 1, a Confederate twelve-pound shell landed in the middle of a group of Federals that included Westervelt. When the shell failed to explode, the men took it to one of their gunners who put a new fuse in the thing and returned it to the Confederates "with the compliments of the 27th New York." The incident reinforces the point that both sides in the Civil War used the same weapons and ammunition. Westervelt's report of the incident is picked up in the Regimental History.[5] This incident and the way it is reported is a fine illustration of Civil War humor.

THE HANOVER COURT HOUSE EXPEDITION

After the battle of West Point, on May 7th, we moved leisurely up the peninsula in the rear of the Rebel Army, who were gradually drawing closer to Richmond. At Cumberland we joined our main army, who had come from Williamsburg. Our next stop was at White House, where Washington first met the widow Custis. We camped here a few days, while our Q.M. established this point as the base of supplies for the army of the Potomac.

From here we marched to Tunsall's[*] Station, and then to Cold Harbor, on the Chickahominy river.

On the morning of the 22nd we were sent on a reconnoissance[†] towards Mechanicsville. On reaching Ellistin's[‡] Mills, a small squad of the First N.Y. Cavalry rode past us, and took the advance. Not two minutes after, as they passed a turn in the road, they were fired upon by the enemy's pickets. The cavalry came riding back, and on reaching us stopped, and on counting their number found a sergeant and corporal missing. We then turned to the right, and ascended a small hill, where we found ourselves in plain sight of the enemy's pickets.

Here we remained for some time, when seeing a house some distance in advance I thought it a good plan to see what it contained —perhaps a good dinner—that is one of the objects in life of a soldier, when campaigning in an enemy's country. Before reaching the house I saw one of the enemy's pickets watching me very attentively and suddenly his

piece came to an aim, followed by a puff of smoke, and "zip" went a bullet in the ground about ten feet in front of me. It was a splendid line shot, but the distance (about 1000 yards) was too great. As the smoke cleared away I raised my cap to him in acknowledgement of his compliment, I did not care anything about taking dinner at the house between our lines that day, and suddenly remembered I was not hungry, so turning around came back to our company, when Lieutenant Brainard, in command, met me with a bland smile, and said, "Corporal, as you seem so anxious to go to the front, just take a walk down the road and see what has become of the two missing cavalrymen." I replied, "Certainly, I will be delighted, but, as the road is rather lonely, won't you just walk along for company?" This drew the attention of our company to him, so he could not well back out.

We started down the road and were soon joined by our company joker, Jim Bogart, with the remark, "I guess I will go along too, for fear you go too far and get lost." Corporal Truesdell soon joined us, and we walked on down the road, and as we approached the turn where the enemy's pickets were but two hours before, we expected we would be fired upon, so I raised the hammer of my piece to try and get one shot anyway, but we found their pickets had been withdrawn. We soon came to the remains of the cavalry sergeant, who had been shot through the heart, the ball entering the left side, going clear through, and was found in the pocket of his shirt, where a five dollar piece in his pocket-book had stopped it. His horse was gone, and beside him stood the corporal's horse with a leg broken. The corporal had been taken prisoner. The enemy

---

[*] Spelling—Tunstall's

[†] reconnaissance

[‡] Ellerson's

UNION ARTILLERY AT MECHANICSVILLE SHELLING THE CONFEDERATE WORKS SOUTH OF THE CHICKAHOMINY.

This sketch was made several days before the beginning of the Seven Days' Battles. The road to Richmond
crosses the stream by the Mechanicsville Bridge, the
half-dozen houses composing the town being to the left

of the ground occupied by the battery. It was by this
road that the troops of D. H. Hill's and Longstreet's
division crossed to join Jackson and A. P. Hill in the
attack upon the right of McClellan's army.

had evidently fallen back immediately after firing on the cavalry, as they left behind the corporal's saddle and bridle; even the sergeant's watch and pocket-book were not disturbed. We carefully took up the remains and carried them to the rear where some of his company took charge and gave them a decent burial.

On the 24th Gen. Porter advanced with his artillery, and taking the position held by us on our reconnoissance [sic], shelled the enemy out of Mechanicsville, and on the 27th of May our brigade with a battery moved up and took possession of the village. It consisted of about a half dozen houses; one was a hotel, with a fine grove attached, and from information gained from the negroes, it had been, in the ante bellum days, a fashionable drive for the young bloods of Richmond, that was about five miles distant.

Every house showed unmistakable marks of the handiwork of Porter's artillerymen. One house had been struck on one side, cutting off both corner posts, and the studding the whole length of the side. Another shot had struck a tree, fifteen inches in diameter, and had gone clear through and out of the other side, while the splintered wood had closed up the hole so a ramrod could not be pushed through. But the most curious (if there is anything curious about the murderous things) was where one had passed through a wheat field, fired at point blank range, and striking few inches below the heads. It had cut as clean as could be done with a sickle. Just the size and shape of the under side of the shot could be seen across the field. We put up our tents in the hotel grove, and in looking about the gardens of the deserted houses, I found a patch of green peas just fit to pick. I mention this as it was the only time I indulged in that toothsome luxury the whole four years

I wore the army blue. We were on the extreme right of the army, with our pickets joining McCall's division on the left, while on the right, in the words of facetious Jim Bogart, it extended to "nowheres."

In front of our camp the ground gradually descended about a mile to the Chickahominy, a small and almost insignificant stream at this point, where the road crossed, running straight to the rebel capital. On crossing the bridge the ground rose rather more abruptly, and at half a mile distance was a line of breastworks, that we soon learned was armed with a battery of field guns with which the enemy seemed to enjoy shelling our camp, and picket lines.

On May the 31st we heard heavy cannonading, that proved to be the battle of Seven Pines, or Fair Oaks. We were called in line and marched down the road, across the bridge, and started to ascend the hill on the opposite side. When within about two hundred yards of the enemy's works, we about faced and returned to our camp. Not a gun was fired from the enemy's works. They had evidently withdrawn all their force to help at Fair Oaks, and I believe had Slocum, our commander, had permission to advance, we could have entered Richmond with but little opposition.

On our return to camp one of our batteries was run out, and shelled the enemy's works for an hour, but received no response. The next day our company went on picket near the bridge. Soon the enemy trained a battery on them, that made it very uncomfortable although there were no casualties. A party of us were about a half mile back from the bridge acting as a reserve, and congratulating ourselves on being in a less exposed position than the outpost, when suddenly a twelve-pound conical shell came whistling through *the air, and buried itself in the ground directly in the center of our group. To say there was some lively tumbling backwards would not half express it; but finding the "critter" was not going to explode, we went back and dug it up, when we found it was a handsome made shell, of English manufacture, but with a defective fuse. One of us took it to a gunner of Upton's battery, who inserted a new fuse, and waiting for a favorable opportunity sent it back. As many of our company were watching him, he tried to make a good shot, and sustained his reputation of being one of the best gunners in the Army of the Potomac. It was fired at a supply train that was passing about two miles distant, and struck a wagon loaded with ammunition at about the center. Whether the shell exploded or not, it would be hard to say, but the contents of the wagon did, and the next few seconds the air in that vicinity was filled with dead and live mules, and parts of wagons, while the mules attached to the remainder of the wagons in the train started on a stampede, and were soon out of sight.*

Notes — Chapter 6

1. Fairchild, *History of the 27th Regiment, N.Y. Vols.*, p. 44.

2. Ibid., pp. 44-45.

3. Johnson and Buel, *Battles and Leaders of the Civil War*, Vol. II, p. 175.

4. Fairchild, *History of the 27th Regiment, N.Y. Vols.*, p. 46.

5. Ibid.

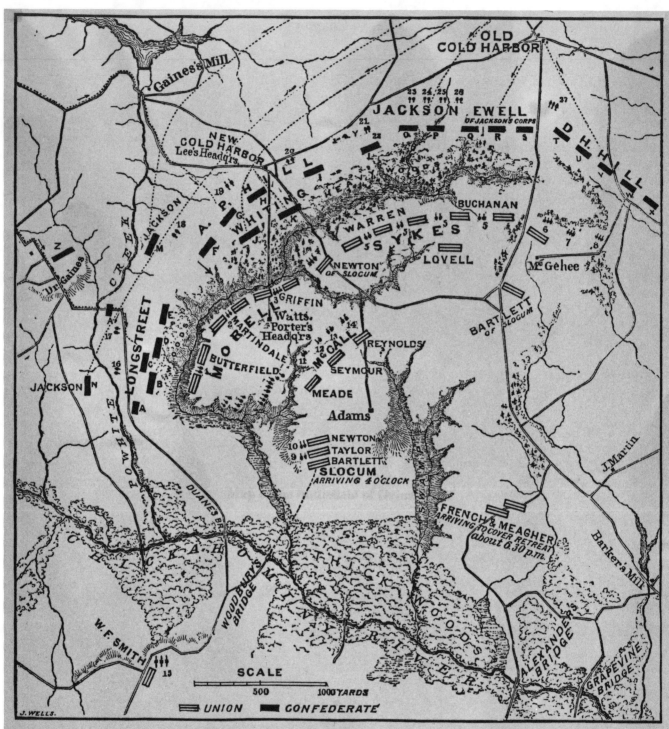

MAP OF THE BATTLE-FIELD OF GAINES'S MILL, SHOWING APPROXIMATELY THE POSITIONS OF INFANTRY
AND ARTILLERY ENGAGED. (THE TOPOGRAPHY FROM THE OFFICIAL MAP.)

Chapter 7

THE BATTLE OF GAINES' MILL

Background

    The period of May 31-June 26, 1862, was one of relative inactivity for Westervelt and the 27th New York. On May 31 and June 1, the Battle of Fair Oaks took place, and, as Westervelt indicated, the regiment was placed on alert, but was not engaged in the action.[1] Fair Oaks or Seven Pines, as the Confederates called it, was where General Joseph E. Johnston was wounded with the result that Robert E. Lee took command of the Confederate forces around Richmond.

    During this period, McClellan had been pleading for and waiting for additional troops. Despite promises, none arrived. Finally, on June 25, McClellan saw himself about to be overwhelmed by a superior enemy force. He believed that Lee had 200,000 men[2] while he had only 75,000 effectives.[3] He wired Washington for help and he also decided to change his base from White House Landing to Harrison's Landing.

    Porter had the chore of defending the area north of the Chickahominy. He selected, with McClellan's approval, the eastern bank of the Beaver Dam Creek and made his stand there on June 26.[4] The Confederates attacked and were severely beaten; Lee's losses were 1,350 compared to Porter's 361.[5] The men of the 27th New York heard the battle but were not in it.

    Porter retreated, under orders, to the eastern bank of Boatswain's Swamp where Lee found him entrenched and ready for battle on June 27. The respective strengths of the Union and Confederate armies was as follows:[6]

	North of the Chickahominy	South of the Chickahominy	Total
Federal	30,000	75,000	105,000
Confederate	55,000-60,000	25,000	80,000-85,000

    The figures vary depending upon the source. Regardless of the differences, it is obvious that, north of the Chickahominy, Lee had at least a 5 to 3 advantage over Porter and that he risked all by expecting Major General John B. Magruder to keep the Federals south of the river occupied and confused.

    It was clear that there would be a fight at Gaines' Mill on June 27. The 27th New York was called out at 8:00 A.M., marched down to the river and remained there south of Woodbury's Bridge until afternoon.[7] Porter had expected to have the regiment's help early in the day and didn't get it. (He had requested that McClellan send help but for some strange reason, the request never reached the Northern commander.[8]) Porter called for help again in the early afternoon, and Slocum's Division crossed the river at that bridge and went in to support him.[9]

THE BATTLE OF GAINES' MILL

Westervelt's account of the battle covers it well and parallels the reports of General Slocum, General Bartlett, and Lieutenant Colonel Adams (Division, Brigade and Regiment reports, respectively). The division was broken up and the 27th New York was assigned the job of reinforcing Sykes' regulars on the right side of the Federal line (see Map on page 46).

The 27th, upon call, charged the front and helped repulse a Rebel attack about 4:30 P.M.[10] At 6:30 P.M., the Confederates attacked again in great strength and broke the Federal line.[11]

Sykes' Regulars, with Slocum's support, are credited with holding fast and preventing a disaster. At dusk, French's and Meagher's Brigades arrived on the field. Their approach and darkness halted the battle and, at first, the two armies settled down in their respective positions.[12] Later in the night, the Federals retreated again and returned south of the Chickahominy.

Lee lost about 8,500 men at Gaines' Mill; Porter lost 6,837.[13] The 27th New York lost 162; 12 killed, 118 wounded, and 32 missing or captured. It was the regiment's worst day in its history.

Highlights

Gaines' Mill, as reported by Westervelt, is unusual in many respects and typical in others. (Note: The Battle of Gaines' Mill is also called First Cold Harbor and Boatswain's Swamp.) The six most significant aspects of Westervelt's report are highlighted below.

1. <u>Union Cheers vs. Rebel Yells</u>: Much has been written about the "Rebel Yell" and its impact upon the enemy in battle. At Gaines' Mill, the 27th New York employed its yell as it charged to support Sykes' Regulars in driving Hill's troops late in the afternoon. Fairchild writes in the Regiment's History, "No rebel troops, however brave, could stand the unearthly yell that we had learned to give."[14]

And at dusk, the shouts or yells of Meagher's and French's Brigades coming on the field of battle discouraged the Confederates from making a final attack that might have destroyed Porter's wing of the Army of the Potomac.[15]

2. <u>The Straw Hat Brigade</u>: Then there is the story of "The Straw Hat Brigade." Westervelt's story about them is picked up in the Regimental History.[16] The incident is also mentioned in a footnote on page 339, Vol. II, *Battles and Leaders*.[17]

3. <u>Hardee Tactics</u>: Westervelt refers to the final and successful advance of Hill's men with begrudging admiration for their use of Hardee Tactics. These men advanced across an open field at a double quick time of 165 steps per minute in the face of heavy rifle and artillery fire. Their guns were at a trail or right shoulder shift; no firing was permitted. No wonder Westervelt respected the courage of these enemy troops!

4. <u>Anticipation of McDowell's Joining McClellan</u>: Everyone in the Army of the Potomac, from McClellan to the lowest private, expected McDowell's Corps as reinforcements. Westervelt makes reference to McDowell's forces both in terms of reuniting with his friends and the added strength they would provide. Headley, a contemporary writer who was sympathetic to McClellan,

wrote, "...forever and anon came the rumor that McDowell had started. Four times was the army raised to the highest pitch of excitement by the news, only to sink back into disappointment and angry mutterings."[18]

5. <u>Medical Treatment, 1862</u>: Westervelt's attitude about medical treatment for his own injury reflects the soldiers' feelings about care available at   that time. Medical practice, in the early part of the war, was at an almost primitive state. Hence Westervelt wasn't going to the hospital with his injured ankle as his surgeon suggested. He'd rather take his chances in the field.

6. <u>Lee's Star Rises</u>: Westervelt and the 27th New York had been in on the beginning of both Jackson's and Hood's rise to fame. Gaines' Mill was the first battle where Lee had his famed Army of Northern Virginia.[19] Again, Westervelt and the 27th New York had a knack for being in battles that started Southern generals on the road to renown!

The Battle of Gaines' Mill, June 27, 1862

THE BATTLE OF GAINES' MILL

While camped at Mechanicsville in the early part of June, '62, some of the scouts of McDonal's* army reached our lines with the welcome intelligence that the army was then within a few days' march of us, and would soon join us. This was encouraging news, for we knew the greater our numbers the shorter would be our work in front of the rebel capital; besides many of us had friends with McDoual [sic] whom we were anxious to see. For my own part I looked forward to meeting with a company from Poughkeepsie commanded by Capt. Holiday, then in the 30th N.Y., among whom were many of my old friends and schoolmates.

On June 3rd the paymaster arrived, and put up his table in our camp, within easy shelling distance of the enemy, and then paid off our regiment. He soon finished his work of paying our division, and returned to Washington, as he found "the front" not a healthy or pleasant place to tarry.

On the 6th McCall's division, consisting of Pennsylvania troops, came to Mechanicsville, and we were ordered to return to Bottom Bridge. The Pennsylvanians were a rugged set, known as "The Bucktails," as each wore the tail of a buck in his cap, and were destined to make an enviable reputation for themselves before the close of the war. The burden of their complaint at this time was that they had never yet had an opportunity of meeting the enemy; but in this they were more than satisfied before many weeks.

We left Mechanicsville just before sunset, and made a detour of several miles to the right of the direct route, and instead of seven miles by direct road we went some thirteen before reaching our camp at midnight. The next morning we were called in line at 3 A.M., and stood under arms until daylight, evidently to guard against surprise. On the following morning as we stood under arms, just as day was dawning, the enemy got the range with a battery, of one of the adjoining camps, and gave them a lively shelling. We supposed a general engagement coming on, but soon all became quiet.

During the day our regiment was engaged building corduroy roads across the Chickahominy swamp. This kind of life was kept up with variations until the morning of the 18th, when we received orders to move. A twelve mile march took us across the Chickahominy river, and we went into camp, near the battlefield of Fair Oaks. We were now so close to the enemy's lines that when on picket, in the still morning hour, we could hear roll-call in their camp.

Our lines had gradually drawn closer around Richmond, and we were waiting for McDoual's [sic] army to form a junction on our right, when the combined armies could strike a decisive blow. McDoual's [sic] forces had been within two miles of our outposts on the right, when Banks was driven from the Shenandoah Valley, and the authorities at Washington, fearful of the safety of the city, called McDoual [sic] away from Richmond, and sent him on a foolish errand—pursuing Stonewall Jackson. This left our right exposed, and Jackson, quick to seize the advantage, eluded the pursuit of McDoual [sic] and formed a junction with Lee near Mechanicsville.

Wednesday, June 25th. — During the day we heard heavy cannonading in the direction of Mechanicsville, and expected a general engagement was coming. At dark, however, all became quiet. Twice during the

---

* References are to McDowell's Corps.

night we were called under arms. Of course we in the ranks knew nothing of what was going on, but from the manner in which the orderlies and aiddecamps [sic] were riding about, we could see the officers felt anxious as though things were not going as they should.

Thursday, June 26th. — During the forenoon all was quiet; but it proved to be the calm that preceeds* the storm. Suddenly, at 3 P.M., a perfect storm of cannonading burst on our right at Mechanicsville, and continued late into the night. From this direction it moved towards Gaines' Mill. It seemed as though our troops were falling back. Towards midnight all became quiet; and ended the battle known as Gaines' Mill, or the first of the "Seven Days Fight"† before Richmond, and the Pennsylvania reserves had no longer reason to complain that they "had never yet been able to meet the enemy."

Friday, June 27th, at 8 A.M., we were called in line, and after receiving a fresh supply of cartridges, moved in light marching order about two miles, and stopped near the Chickahominy river. Our brigade, I think, never looked better than it did that morning. General Slocum had been advanced to the command of our division, while General J. J. Bartlett, our former Colonel (a man whose vocabulary did not contain the word "fear"; or if it did, he never learned the definition of it), now commanded our brigade, that was made up of the 5th Maine, composed of hardy lumbermen from the northeastern part of that state, commanded by Colonel Jackson; the 96th Pennsylvania, from the coal regions of Luzerne county, and commanded by Colonel John Cake, a jolly fellow of about two hundred pounds weight, whom the boys dubbed "Johnnycake"; the 16th N.Y., from St. Lawrence county, commanded by Colonel Joseph Howland, of Fishkill, who the day before, at his own expense, furnished his regiment with neat, comfortable straw hats. As we, wearing our fatigue caps that hot morning, looked with envious eyes at his regiment, more than one of us violated the commandment that says: "Thou shalt not covet thy neighbor's" straw hats (or words to that effect).

As the colonel rode at the head of his regiment, his features, of a deligate‡ effeminate cast, adorned with a blonde mustache, no one would believe him to be the brave and dashing officer, that ere the sun went down he proved himself to be, even at the expense of a wound that I believe has ever since made life to him almost a burden. Then came our regiment, the 27th N.Y., commanded by Colonel D. Adams, of Lyons, N.Y., a man of education and refinement, but lacking the dash of our former colonel.

We remained quiet during the day, stretched under the shade of the trees, where we ate our dinner, and smoked our pipes. Some played cards, while others dozed away the time under the soothing influence of the sound of cannon on the opposite side of the river, little thinking, many of them, that it would be their last day on earth, but so it proved to scores of our brigade, and to hundreds of our army.

---

* precedes

† The battle on the twenty-sixth is known as the Battle of Beaver Dam or Mechanicsville; Gaines' Mill was on the twenty-seventh as Westervelt correctly notes later.

---

‡ delicate

THE BATTLE OF GAINES' MILL

Meantime Gen. Fitz John Porter with his corps was gradually falling back, but gallantly disputing the ground, inch by inch, under the incessant hammering of all of Stonewall Jackson's army, heavily reinforced from Lee's army from around Richmond. About 4 P.M., the Duc de Chartres, a young officer of the royal family of France, who was on Gen. McClellan's staff, arrived, and after a few hurried words with Gen. Slocum, galloped away. Soon our division were in line, and we supposed we were to return to camp. However, we turned to the left, and took the road toward Woodbury's bridge, across the Chickahominy River. Gen. Porter pays the following tribute to our division on page 316 of the Century for June, 1885:

"While withdrawing from Beaver Dam, I had seen, to my delight, Slocum's division of Franklin's corps crossing the river to my assistance. McClellan had promised to send it, and I needed it. It was one of the best divisions of the army. Its able, experienced and gallant commander, and his brave and gifted subordinates, had the confidence of their well-trained soldiers. They were all worthy comrades of my well-tried and fully-trusted officers, and of many others on that field, subsequently honored by their countrymen."

After crossing the Chickahominy river we ascended a hill, when there was plain evidence that our army was getting the worst of the fight. One evidence was, a company of pioneers were cutting the spokes out of some of our army wagons, to render them useless if they fell into the enemy's hands. This clearly proved that our army anticipated retreating, if they were not already moving in that direction.

We halted a few moments in a small ravine, when up rode a staff officer, and called out, "Bring up Bartlett's brigade, at double quick!" With an agility that would have done credit to an athlete, Gen. Bartlett sprang into his saddle, and calling "attention!" we were quickly moving to the front. One hundred yards brought us face to face with the enemy, where we relieved the 5th N.Y. (Duryea's Zouaves), whose uniforms were strewn thickly over the ground, showing some desperate fighting. We immediately got to work, and for a few minutes the fighting was fast and furious. We lost many but managed to hold our ground. Soon the firing slacked in our immediate front, as the enemy fell back, under cover of some woods, where they seemed to be massing on our right, in front of one of our batteries, which was supported by the 16th N.Y., who held the extreme right of our line.

We were not long kept in suspense, for looking to the right of our regiment we saw them forming just outside of the woods, and here we witnessed as complete a move by the enemy as could be made on drill or parade. They came out of the woods at double quick, with guns at "right shoulder shift" (Hardee tactics) and by a move known as "on the right by file into line," formed their line of battle complete. Every man on taking his place brought his piece to the shoulder and stood waiting until the battalion was formed (unless knocked over by a shot) when they moved forward, and made room for another battalion to form in the same way. We thought troops that could make that move, under a concentrated fire of artillery and musketry, were, to say the least "safe to bet on." We had not long to admire them; forward they came, intending to strike our line on the right. Not a gun did they fire, until within less than fifty yards, when, after a volley they gave a yell and charged, five lines deep. No single line

Woodbury and Alexander's Bridge

could stand the onslaught. The 16th N.Y. was crowded back, disputing the ground inch by inch, while the artillerymen stood by their guns, until the enemy closed in and actually struck them down, or knocked the cartridges out of their hands.

Meantime Col. Howland, chaffing under the fear of defeat, was riding from right to left of his regiment, urging his men to stand firm. Soon they rallied, and under the head of the colonel, drove the enemy back and recaptured the battery. Here Col. Howland was severely wounded, and carried from the field. Once more the enemy came forward, and the word passed down the line. "Come help the 16th." Without waiting for Col. Adams to give the order, but following the example set by Gen. Bartlett, and led by his brother, Lieut. L. C. Bartlett, of the General's Staff, we turned by the right flank, and were soon among the 16th, each man on his own hook. Here was some of the most desperate fighting we had ever done; the blue and the gray were mixed, and in the gathering darkness, we could scarce detect friend from foe. The ground was fairly covered with dead and wounded. The gray, the blue, and the red-trimmed artillerymen's uniforms lay side by side, while the blood from their wounds mingled together as it wet the ground. Every artillery horse was killed. Finally the enemy dragged off two of the cannon, while we held possession of the ground, and kept the other two, and as night closed upon the second of the "seven day's fight" in front of Richmond, known as the battle of Gaines' Mill, it found your correspondent limping to the rear with a dislocated ankle, using his Springfield rifle for a crutch.

Being unable to find our surgeon or hospital, I went into the woods by the roadside. Here, with the help of a soldier, I got my ankle in place, and, finding a pool of water, I placed my foot into it. The pain was intense, but toward morning, being tired and worn out, I fell asleep.

How long I slept I don't know, but on awakening found the sun well up, and hearing a noise in the road near me, I hobbled out, when I found some of our men running towards the river, pursued by the enemy's cavalry. I quickly took in the situation: that our forces had fallen back across the Chickahominy during the night, and these were some wounded and stragglers the enemy were picking up. I was suffering such pain that I thought it impossible to place my foot upon the ground, but in the excitement and by using my gun for a crutch, managed to get over the ground at a lively rate, and soon reached the bridge, only to find it blown up. Some of the wounded now gave up, but I determined to make one more effort to save myself from being taken; so climbing on a convenient log I paddled over. On reaching the opposite shore I found myself so much exhausted that I had to be helped up the bank, and was laid under a tree. I will pass hastily over the next week, as the sufferings endured are not pleasant to recall. Finding our army were retreating I determined not to be left behind, so I managed to keep up, and on July 4th joined our regiment at Harrison's Landing.

It seemed almost like getting home to be once more with our company. I found I had been reported killed at Gaines' Mill on June 27th, which report I most emphatically denied. One of the first men I met was the irrespressible Jim Bogart, with the side of his face badly swollen, that gave him a doubly ridiculous look and obliged him to talk with one corner of his mouth. On inquiry I found he had been struck in his face with a small bullet, but brimful of good nature, declared that the rebels saw him take a chew of tobacco and tried to knock it out of his mouth, and added, "I tell you, Corporal, that was a -- mean trick."

Our surgeon wished to send me to the hospital, but I preferred to remain with the company, and in a few weeks went on duty again; but it was years before my ankle entirely recovered.

On the river side of our camp we were guarded by our gunboats. While on the land side, we were soon well entrenched, and were continually on the alert for fear of an attack. Nothing occurred until July 31st, when the enemy placed a battery on the opposite side of the James river, and about midnight opened a perfect fusilade upon the camp nearest the river. We were far enough away to be out of range of their guns, so remained quiet spectators. Soon our gunboats and monitors that were anchored on the James, got into position and not only silenced their battery, but drove off the gunners and disabled some of the guns so they could not remove them, and the next morning the sailors landed and brought the guns away.

On August 15th we bid good bye to Harrison's Landing, and after a march of some four miles, were left on picket, or rather as rear guard of the army. The next day we moved on as far as Charles City Court House. On the following morning we started at sunrise, and, although the day was hot and the road dusty, we made good time. The country we passed through was very good, with large mansions and fine plantations. Near sunset, after a march of about twenty miles, we crossed the Chickahominy river at its junction with the James, on one of the best pontoon bridges we ever saw; it was so strong that a train of artillery or wagons went in the center with two ranks of infantry on each side.

On the 17th we passed the former residence of ex-President Tyler, that was protected by a safe guard from our army, and soon after reached Williamsburg. On leaving the city we passed the fortifications that cost us so many to capture last May, and on the following day reached Yorktown. We remained at this historical place one day, and then by easy marches traveled on down the peninsula and reached Newport News on the 20th, and from here we went by transport to Alexandria, where we arrived on the 23d.

McClellan was now relieved from command of the Army of the Potomac, and Gen. John Pope placed at its head.[*] The latter was busy marshaling his forces for the disastrous battle of Chantilly, or the second Bull Run,[†] which will be remembered in history for the frothy orders of Gen Pope, that were prefaced with "Picks and shovels to the rear"; "No more lines of retreat"; "Honor is at the front"; "Shame and disgrace is at the rear." These orders, with the jealously of the subordinate officers, of which Fitz John Porter was made the "scape goat", have given this campaign a prominent place in the history of the rebellion. Pope blazed forth like a meteor and disappeared about as quick, and as complete. "His star set, never to rise again."

---

[*] This is not totally accurate—McClellan was directed to cooperate with Pope and send him help. The popular belief was that Pope had replaced McClellan as Westervelt believed.

[†] Second Bull Run and Chantilly were two separate battles—the first on August 27-30; the second on September 1.

THE BATTLE OF GAINES' MILL

Notes — Chapter 7

1. Fairchild, *History of the 27th Regiment, N.Y. Vols.*, p. 49.

2. Shelby Foote, *The Civil War* (New York: Vintage Books, 1986), Vol. I, p. 477.

3. Johnson and Buel, *Battles and Leaders of the Civil War*, Vol. II, p. 180.

4. Ibid., p. 328.

5. Foote, *The Civil War*, Vol. I, p. 483.

6. Bruce Catton, *Terrible Swift Sword* (New York: Doubleday & Co., 1963), p. 318.

7. Fairchild, *History of the 27th Regiment, N.Y. Vols.* p. 52.

8. Johnson and Buel, *Battles and Leaders of the Civil War*, Vol. II, p. 337.

9. Fairchild, *History of the 27th Regiment N.Y,. Vols.*, p. 66.

10. Johnson and Buel, *Battles and Leaders of the Civil War*, Vol. II, p. 339.

11. Ibid.

12. Ibid., p. 340.

13. Foote, *The Civil War*, Vol. I, pp. 490-491.

14. Fairchild, *History of the 27th Regiment, N.Y. Vols.*, p. 53.

15. Guernsey and Alden, *Harpers Pictorial History of the Civil War*, p. 367.

16. Fairchild, *History of the 27th Regiment, N.Y. Vols.*, pp. 52-53.

17. Johnson and Buel, *Battles and Leaders of the Civil War*, Vol. II, footnote, p. 339.

18. Headley, *The Great Rebellion, A History of the Civil War in the United States*, Vol. I, p. 487.

19. Freeman, *Lee's Lieutenants*, Vol. I, Chapter XXXII, p. 517.

Chapter 8

THE ANTIETAM CAMPAIGN — AN OVERVIEW

As Westervelt indicates in the preceding chapter, "Pope's star set, never to rise again." Events in Pope's downfall involved McClellan and Franklin and his VI Corps. They are noted here for they ultimately played a part in McClellan's exit and probably contributed to Franklin's exile from the eastern theater of the war.

When McClellan was ordered to return to Washington after the Peninsular Campaign, he was also ordered to cooperate with Pope.[1] He sent Porter and the V Corps to join Pope in facing Lee, but found several reasons for delaying sending Franklin and the VI Corps, including the 27th New York and Westervelt. By the time he did send them, Lee, Jackson, and Longstreet were upon Pope at Bull Run.[2] Thus, the only role the VI Corps played was to stem the tide of retreat and defend Fairfax against Jeb Stuart's raid.[3] When Halleck pressured McClellan to send Franklin earlier than he did, McClellan wired Halleck that one option was "to leave Pope get out of his scrape."[4] This, of course, was interpreted in Washington as reflecting McClellan's attitude about helping Pope and did not set well with Lincoln or Halleck. Along with all of McClellan's other actions, that telegram played a part in his departure from service after Antietam.

Pope brought charges against Porter and made him a scapegoat. He also accused Franklin of disobedience and dilatoriness. On September 5, an order was prepared relieving Porter, Franklin, and Reynolds from their commands.[5] McClellan saved his friends then; ultimately Porter would be cashiered, and Franklin would be banished to the West. For the time being, throughout the Antietam Campaign and the First Battle of Fredericksburg, Franklin would continue to have the 27th New York as part of his command.

With the Federal defeat at Second Bull Run, Lee was free to invade Maryland—leading to the Battles of South Mountain and Antietam. He moved into Maryland, crossing the Potomac at fords near Leesburg, Virginia between September 4 and 7. His purposes were to:

- make the North defend both Washington and Baltimore
- give the people of Maryland a chance to join the South as he was sure they would do
- draw the Federals to Western Maryland away from their base where they could be defeated by Lee and his army.[6]

As Lee moved into Maryland, he expected the Federals to evacuate Harpers Ferry and Martinsburg, thus clearing his line of communications to the Shenandoah Valley and the South.[7] Since this did not happen, he divided his army west of South Mountain sending Jackson, McLaws, and Walker to capture Martinsburg and Harpers Ferry, while D.H. Hill held South Mountain, and Longstreet went on to Hagerstown to get some supplies. Instructions to do this were in Special Orders 191, dated September 9, 1862—commonly known as the famous "Lost Order."[8]

Back in Washington, Lincoln and Halleck went to see McClellan and asked him to take command of the army and the defenses of Washington.[9] McClellan proceeded to leave Banks in charge of the capital city fortifications and went after Lee in Maryland. He called his organization the Army of the Potomac, but it was not the same organization he had in the Peninsular Campaign. This army's units were as follows:

The Confederates Crossing the Potomac

THE ANTIETAM CAMPAIGN — AN OVERVIEW

- three from his old organization; II Corps under Sumner, V Corps under Porter, and VI Corps under Franklin
- two from Pope's Army; I Corps under Hooker, and XII under Mansfield
- plus Burnside's independent unit, IX Corps; and Cox's Kanawha Division.[10]

Knowing that Lee was near Frederick and not sure whether he might be planning to attack Washington or Baltimore, McClellan sent the Army of the Potomac toward Frederick on three roughly parallel roads—the farthest southwest was near the Potomac River and the farthest northeast near the railroad to Baltimore.[11]

The Union army reached Frederick on September 13, 1862, and there two Union soldiers found a copy of Lee's Special Orders 191 in a field where Lee's army had camped.[12] The copy was quickly forwarded to McClellan, who received it by 12:00 noon on September 13. Now McClellan was elated for he said he had "all the plans of the rebels."[13] He proceeded to order attacks on the Confederate units holding the gaps of South Mountain. The main efforts were at Turner's Gap and Fox's Gap near Boonsboro with Hooker and Burnside carrying out those attacks. Franklin was assigned the job of breaking through Crampton's Pass (or Gap) in order to attack McLaws and Anderson on Maryland Heights and relieve the pressure on Harpers Ferry.[14]

Franklin found the Confederates behind a wall at the base of South Mountain just west of Burkittsville.[15] The battle started in mid-afternoon with the 27th New York in a lead position, and ended by nightfall. Harpers Ferry was surrendered at 7:30 A.M. the next day, September 15, and Franklin and the VI Corps remained where they were until September 17, when they were ordered to the Battle of Antietam.

Lee had retreated to Sharpsburg and had his troops in a defensive position on high ground near the town and in a line so they covered all the bridges across the creek in that area—the Rohrbach Bridge to the south (now called Burnside's Bridge); the Middle Bridge near the Pry House; and the Upper Bridge or Hitt Bridge to the north. The battle started early in the morning of September 17, 1862, with the Union attack of the Confederate left above the Upper Bridge and ended near Burnside's Bridge. The VI Corps arrived on the field at about 10:00 A.M. and promptly prepared to attack, but were held back. The 27th New York occupied the Cornfield for the rest of the day after the terrible fights there were over. They saw no real action in the battle. At the end of the day, there were nearly 23,000 casualties, and this figure may be understated by as much as 2,000.[16]

Both armies were exhausted as a result of the battle. They remained quiet the following day, September 18. Lee took his tired army back across the Potomac the night of the eighteenth. McClellan made a feeble attempt to follow, without success and with some additional losses.[17]

Lincoln came to visit McClellan and the Army of the Potomac in early October. He urged McClellan to pursue Lee, which McClellan finally did, starting October 26, 1862.

THE ANTIETAM CAMPAIGN — AN OVERVIEW

Notes — Chapter 8

1. Stephen W. Sears, *Landscape Turned Red* (New Haven and New York: Ticknor & Fields, 1983), p. 2.

2. Ibid., pp. 6-7.

3. Johnson and Buel, *Battles and Leaders of the Civil War*, Vol. II, p. 540-541.

4. Guernsey and Alden, *Harpers Pictorial History of the Great Rebellion*, p. 386.

5. *O.R.*, Vol. XII, Part 3, p. 811.

6. *O.R.,* Vol. XIX, Part 2, pp. 144-145.

7. Ibid.

8. Palfrey, *Campaigns of the Civil War*, Vol. V, The Antietam and Fredericksburg (New York: Scribners & Sons, 1882), pp. 20-21.

9. Ibid., p. 4.

10. Dr. Jay Luvaas and Harold W. Nelson, eds., *The U.S. War College Guide to the Battle of Antietam, The Maryland Campaign of 1862* (Carlisle, Pennsylvania: South Mountain Press, 1987), pp. 285-293.

11. Sears, *Landscape Turned Red*, p. 98.

12. James V. Murfin, *The Gleam of Bayonets* (New York: Thomas Yoseloff, 1968), pp. 132-134.

13. *O.R.*, Vol. XIX, Part 2, pp. 270-281.

14. Johnson and Buel, *Battles and Leaders of the Civil War*, Vol. II, p. 592.

15. Murfin, *The Gleam of Bayonets*, p. 182.

16. Luvaas and Nelson, *The U.S. Army War College Guide to the Battle of Antietam*, Appendix III, pp. 301-302.

17. Murfin, *The Gleam of Bayonets*, pp. 304-306.

Chapter 9

CRAMPTON'S PASS / SOUTH MOUNTAIN

Background

Franklin's Corps had the route from Washington to Frederick, Maryland, nearest the Potomac River, and on September 13, 1862, it moved into Buckeystown, which is about six miles south of Frederick. After McClellan came into possession of Lee's Order 191, he sent orders to Franklin to move by the way of Jefferson and Burkittsville through Crampton's Pass to cut off, destroy, or capture McLaw's command and relieve Harpers Ferry. Franklin was also ordered to protect Rohrersville in Pleasant Valley in the process.[1] He was directed to march at daybreak on the fourteenth. A Division of the IV Corps under Major General Darius N. Couch was attached to Franklin's command for this assignment.

And so, the VI Corps started its march to relieve Harpers Ferry at daybreak on September 14. About noon, it waited for Couch to come up and join the march.[2] This break gave Westervelt a chance to get a good meal under his belt before he went into battle; an incident he describes in detail in this chapter.

When the lead regiment, the 96th Pennsylvania, could not find the enemy, General Slocum ordered Bartlett to take the lead with his (Slocum's) old organization, the 27th New York, and take the enemy and the mountain pass.[3] The regiment moved into a skirmish line at 3:00 P.M. and shortly thereafter led a line of battle up the mountain.[4]

The Confederates had six regiments (an estimated 2,200 men)[5] and a few pieces of artillery to face Franklin's Corps of 12,300.[6] However, they had the advantage of terrain and made the most of it. The chapter in the *Regimental History of the 27th N.Y.* covering the Battle of Crampton's Pass states, "On went our line, up the side of the steep mountain—so steep in many places that the men had to pull themselves up by taking hold of the bushes."[7]

After three hours of fighting, the Federals were victors at the top of the mountain. By this time, McLaws realized he had a real problem on his hands and brought six of his brigades back to the western base of the mountain near the Pass and set up a line of defense. At nightfall, the Federals held the mountain, and the Confederates held Pleasant Valley and the road to Harpers Ferry.

The 27th New York lost a total of 33; 6 men and 2 officers killed, and 25 men wounded in the Battle of Crampton's Pass. The total Federal losses were 531. The Confederate losses in killed and wounded were about the same, plus an additional 400, who were taken prisoner—a total loss of 930-950.[8]

Franklin took a look at McLaw's line of defense very early in the morning of September 15, and felt that it was too formidable for his tired troops to attack.[9] Shortly thereafter, Harpers Ferry was surrendered by the Federals trapped there and the VI Corps was ordered to remain in Pleasant Valley until the morning of September 17.

President Lincoln appreciated the work done by the 27th New York and the VI Corps at Crampton's Pass. Franklin states, "In October, 1862, when Mr. Lincoln visited the army, he came

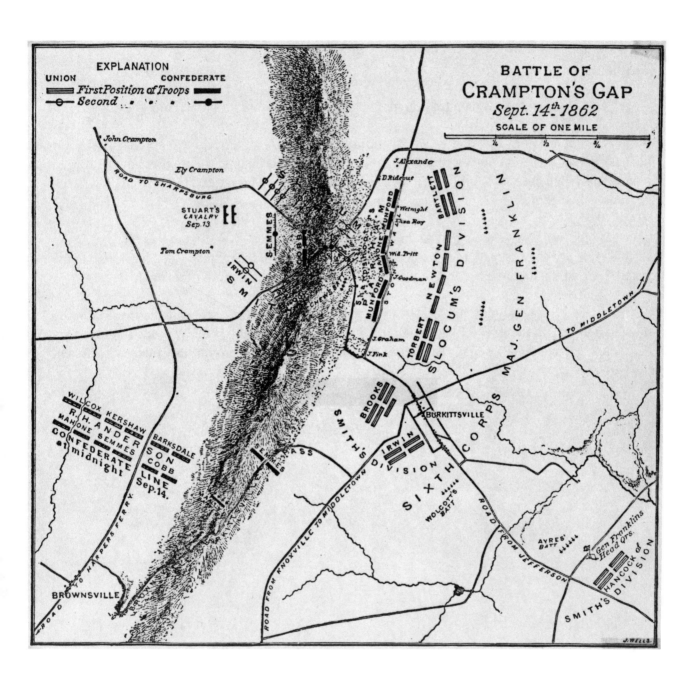

EXPLANATION

UNION   CONFEDERATE

First Position of Troops

Second

BATTLE OF
CRAMPTON'S GAP
Sept. 14th 1862
SCALE OF ONE MILE

¼   ½   ¾   1

John Crampton

Ely Crampton

ROAD TO SHARPSBURG

STUART'S CAVALRY Sep. 13

Tom Crampton

J. Alexander

D. Rideout

Wetnight

Thos Roy

W.d. Pritt

J. Goodman

BARTLETT

NEWTON

TORBERT

SLOCUM'S DIVISION

MAJ. GEN FRANKLIN

SEMMES

IRWIN

COBB

KERSHAW'S

MAHONE

MUNFORD

STO...MAINE

J. Graham

J. Fink

TO MIDDLETOWN

BROOKS

SMITH'S DIVISION

IRWIN

BURKITTSVILLE

SIXTH CORPS

WILCOX

KERSHAW

R.H. ANDERSON

MAHONE SEMMES

BARKSDALE

COBB

CONFEDERATE LINE Sep. 14.

CONFEDERATE at midnight

ROAD TO HARPERS FERRY

BROWNSVILLE

ROAD FROM KNOXVILLE TO MIDDLETOWN

WOLCOTT'S BATT

ROAD FROM JEFFERSON

AYRES' BATT

Gen Franklins Head Qrs.

HANCOCK of

SMITH'S DIVISION

J. WELLS.

through Crampton's Gap; he told me that he was astonished to see and hear of what we had done there. He thanked me for it, and said that he had not understood it before. He was in all respects very kind and complimentary."[10]

Highlights

Three incidents warrant attention in this chapter; they are highlighted below.

1. Food, Glorious Food!: All of the available information on William B. Westervelt indicates that he was a proper Victorian gentleman. Yet, in this chapter, he reports how he barged in as an uninvited guest at a family Sunday dinner in Jefferson, Maryland on September 14, 1862. Obviously, his stomach took precedence over his manners on that occasion!

2. Skirmishing as a Game: As indicated earlier, Westervelt's regiment had the lead in the skirmish line and the attack. His description of skirmishing from the relative safety of a shed at the eastern base of the mountain sounds more like a game than the beginning of a deadly battle.

3. The Surgeon in the Field: Westervelt has high praise for Surgeon Stuart, who did the unusual and was in the thick of battle helping alleviate the suffering of the wounded **before** they were sent back to a field hospital. This action set a precedent for modern military medical treatment in a battle.

CRAMPTON'S PASS / SOUTH MOUNTAIN

McClellan was once more placed in command, and the first part of September found us moving through Maryland, trying to intercept Lee's army, who had followed up their victory at Chantilly by an attempt to transfer the fighting ground from Virginia into the northern states, and now seemed to be somewhere between Rockville and Hagerstown. McClellan moved very slowly, as after our defeat it took time to get our army well in hand, and in proper position for a decisive blow. On Saturday night, Sept. 13th, after a short march from Sugar Leaf Mountain,* where our cavalry had had a skirmish the day before and lost a few men, we camped at Buckeyesville.†

Sunday, Sept. 14th. — At daylight reveille sounded, and after a hurried breakfast we packed up, and just as the sun came up, we moved out of camp. The morning was all we could ask for in regard to weather—cool and pleasant—while the country had more the appearance of northern thrift, than the portions of Virginia through which we had been campaigning during the summer. There were fine, large peach and apple orchards, while the wheat that was in stacks, or in the buildings, would have been creditable to any New York state farmer. About noon we reached Jefferson, just as the people were returning from church. As our line halted a few minutes, I slipped into one of the houses just as the family were sitting down to their noonday meal, and with the modesty that characterizes an old campaigner, I took the only vacant chair at the table, and invited myself to dinner. It was well I did, for the old

gentleman failed to invite me, and even seemed to ignore my presence after being seated. After waiting patiently until he had helped the whole table including himself, I quietly exchanged my empty plate for one he had just filled and placed in front of a dudish-looking young man who seemed to be the guest of his daughter. Picking up a knife and fork I commenced my dinner. A smile passed around the table at my monumental cheek; but with perfect gravity and without speaking a word, I continued to devour everything eatable that came within my reach, knowing that minutes were precious. I listened for our bugle to sound the advance, and took no notice of the muttered imprecations from the "nice young man" on my right, who seemed to have lost his appetite at the time he lost his plate. I did not even notice the muttered sounds that came from the old gentleman at the head of the table, that I imagined sounded very much like "hog." Having no time for anything but the work before me, it received my undivided attention for about fifteen minutes. As my breakfast had been taken at daylight, and had consisted of one hard tack and a quart of coffee, I was then in good condition to astonish the old gentleman and his family with my gastronomic feat. In fact, I almost astonished myself.

However, as all things must come to an end, so did this dinner, and as I left the house I felt inspired with fresh courage, and did not care how soon the fight came. Now, as I look back over my four years' experience, this was, I believe, the only time in the sixteen engagements in which it was my lot to take part, that I went into a fight with a full stomach.

On leaving Jefferson on Sept. 14th we came to an open rolling country, with mountains a few miles distant. Looking off to our

---

* Sugar Loaf Mountain

† Buckeystown

right several miles we could see our troops fighting this way up the side of South Mountain. We pushed on towards Burketsville*, a small village about seven miles southeast of where we had seen the fight going on. When we reached the village our regiment, the 27th, was called out and deployed as skirmishers and sent forward, as we evidently expected to find the enemy holding the road that crosses the mountain at this place, known as Crampton Pass, a few miles from Harper's Ferry. We moved slowly through the village, keeping our alignment as correct as possible. We soon reached the foot of the mountain, when a battery opened fire on us from a point about halfway to the summit, while from the stone walls, directly in our front, came such a fusilade of musketry that we were ordered to rally by fours, halt, and wait for our line of battle to come up. Our squad, consisting of four and a corporal, halted in a barnyard, with the barn between us and the enemy. Going to an adjoining shed we opened a door to see what was in front of us. Our curiosity was soon satisfied, as we received a volley that dropped two of our squad—one W.H. French, now living at Susquehanna, Pa., was shot through the arm; the other, David Keeler, who I believe is now dead, was shot through the body just above the heart. Fearing they would bleed to death, two of our squad took them to the rear to our surgeons. This left me alone, and realizing that it would be inconvenient to be disabled while there alone without help, I concluded to keep away from that door.

In looking around for a better position, I ascended a rickety stairway from the basement to the main floor of the barn, where was piled a quantity of wheat in bags. With these it was but little trouble to build a barricade about breast high, across one of the doors, and when everything was ready the door was thrown open, and in came a perfect volley from the enemy, who were behind a stone wall not more than one hundred yards distant. Carefully keeping below the danger line until the firing ceased, I would raise and place my rifle in a loophole between two of the bags, take careful aim and fire, and then drop out of harm's way. While loading they would pour volley after volley into the door. By the time my gun was loaded they would stop firing. That would give me another chance, when we would repeat our little game.

Soon our main column arrived, when joining with them, we charged across the field, receiving a sharp fire from the enemy, until we were within a few yards of the wall, when some of them tried to retreat up the side of the mountain, but being exposed to our fire all the way up, but very few of them reached the summit. Some of them, when they saw their comrades retreating, dropped down behind the wall and as we came over the top of it threw down their guns, and surrendered. Leaving these prisoners in charge of a few of our men, we continued our advance, and soon had their second line on the retreat, that we drove over the top of the mountain, when looking off to the right we saw Gen. Bartlett, with his staff and orderlies, charging one of their cannon that they had placed in a good position to defend the road, but in a very poor position for a hurried retreat, so joining with Gen. Barlett we soon surrounded and captured the piece. This was lively work and we lost quite a number, but our loss was not as heavy as that of the enemy, even with all their shelter of stone walls, while we were exposed most of the time from first coming

---

* Burkittsville

under fire until the fight was over; but they committed the common error of all troops, that of shooting too high, and they being above us on the mountain side, sent most of their shots over our heads, while we, on the contrary, were shooting up, so our fire had much more fatal effect.

In looking down the line I saw our newly appointed assistant surgeon, W. H. Stuart, now of Norwich, N.Y., close up with our line of battle, and whenever a man was hit he would help place him on a stretcher, straighten out a shattered limb, or hastily staunch a bleeding wound, before sending him to the rear, where our field hospital was established. Although this is the place where a surgeon can do a world of good, and alleviate a great deal of suffering and often save life, yet it was such an unusual sight to see a surgeon right up in the thickest of the fight, and exposed the same as one of the soldiers, that the boys were astonished, and we concluded that the Doctor, though a stranger, was a capital good fellow, which opinion we never had occasion to change.

While this was going on, quite a different scene was being enacted at Harper's Ferry. Here our garrison had surrendered without firing a gun[*] and the enemy after quietly taking possession, heard of the fight at Crampton Pass, and taking all the men they could spare, ran them from Harper's Ferry to where we were engaged. After a run of five miles they arrived just as we came up over the top of the mountain, and we had the pleasure of running them all the way back with our cavalry, while our infantry camped upon the mountain side and occupied the ground we had fought over.

After the fight at Crampton Pass we remained two days in camp, near the top of South Mountain, where we buried the dead of our army and the enemy's, and on the evening of Sept. 16th we received orders to move the next morning.

---

[*] Harpers Ferry was surrendered at 7:30 A.M. on September 15, 1862.

CRAMPTON'S PASS / SOUTH MOUNTAIN

Notes — Chapter 9

1. Sears, *Landscape Turned Red*, pp. 119, 146.

2. Ibid., p. 145.

3. Fairchild, *History of the 27th Regiment, N.Y. Vols.*, p. 91.

4. Ibid., p. 101 (Slocum's report).

5. Johnson and Buel, *Battles and Leaders of the Civil War*, Vol. II, p. 596.

6. Sears, *Landscape Turned Red*, p. 146.

7. Fairchild, *History of the 27th Regiment, N.Y. Vols.*, p. 91.

8. Sears, *Landscape Turned Red*, p. 149.

9. Johnson and Buel, *Battles & Leaders of the Civil War*, Vol. II, p. 596.

10. Ibid.

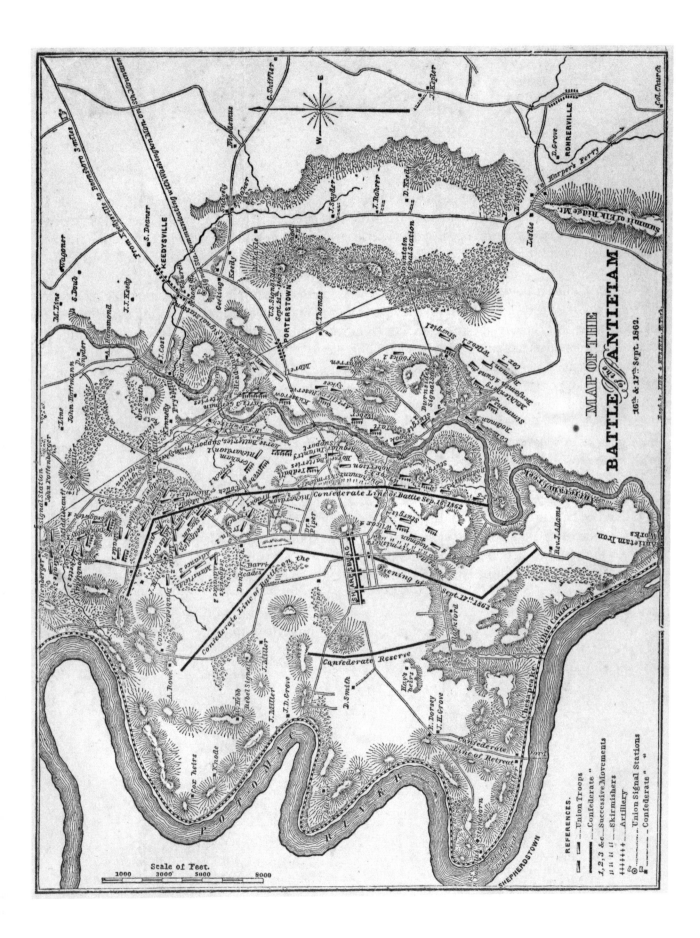

MAP OF THE
BATTLE of ANTIETAM
16th & 17th Sept. 1862.

REFERENCES.
⊏ .....Union Troops
⊏ .....Confederate "
1,2,3 &c...Successive Movements
ıı ıı ıı .....Skirmishers
+++++++ ....Artillery
.....Union Signal Stations
— " — ....Confederate "

Scale of Feet.
1000   3000'   5000   8000

Chapter 10

ANTIETAM

Background

After the Battles of South Mountain and Crampton's Pass on September 14, 1862, Lee retreated to the hills around Sharpsburg. His front was covered by the Antietam Creek, his line of retreat across the Potomac was open, and he was in an excellent position to have Jackson return from Harpers Ferry and join him there.[1] This was a fine defensive position, the kind that Longstreet liked.[2]

McClellan followed Lee and massed his corps on the eastern side of the Antietam Creek on both sides of the Sharpsburg Road.[3] The Union corps were not in their positions until the morning of September 16. Then, on the sixteenth, Lee shifted his defenses and McClellan spent the morning making adjustments in order to prepare for the attack.[4] McClellan states, "My plan for the impending general engagement was to attack the enemy's left with the corps of Hooker and Mansfield, supported by Sumner's, and if necessary by Franklin's; and as soon as matters looked favorably there, to move the corps of Burnside against the enemy's right, upon the ridge running to the south and rear of Sharpsburg, and having carried their position, to press along the crest towards our right; and whenever either of these flank movements should be successful, to advance our center with all the forces then disposable."[5]

The numbers of men available to both Lee and McClellan are, and probably always will be, a matter of controversy. Murfin, one of the most highly regarded experts on the Battle of Antietam, says that Lee had 35,255 effectives on the morning of the seventeenth and McClellan had 87,164.[6] Despite this, McClellan believed that Lee outnumbered him two to one and this belief very much affected the way McClellan conducted the battle.[7]

The actual battle turned into a situation where the North attacked piecemeal, one corps at a time (or at best parts of two). With his interior lines and his willingness to commit all his forces to action, holding back no reserves, Lee was able to match the Union attacks on an equal or better than equal footing. A reconstruction of the Federal attacks shows the following:

Timing	Forces Attacking	Strength	Casualties
Daylight -7:00 A.M.	Hooker's I Corps	9,438	2,590 Hooker wounded; corps totally disorganized
6:00 A.M. -8:30 A.M.	Mansfield's XII Corps	7,631	1,765 Mansfield killed; green troops barely able to hold line
9:00 A.M. -10:30 A.M.	Sumner's II Corps; Sedgwick's Division	5,437	2,210 Sumner demoralized; Sedgwick's troops decimated

ANTIETAM

(Figures and times are from "The Battle of Antietam" published by *The Civil War Times*, Harrisburg, Pennsylvania, 1962, 31 pages.)

The VI Corps was ordered to leave Crampton's Pass at daybreak on the seventeenth. Franklin writes, "Slocum's Division arrived in the field about 11:00 o'clock. Immediately after its arrival, two of his brigades (Newton's and Tolbert's) were formed in column of attack, to carry the wood in the immediate vicinity of the white church. The other brigade (Bartlett's) had been ordered by General Sumner to keep near his right. As this brigade was to form the reserve, I waited until it came up. About that time, General Sumner arrived on the spot and directed the attack to be postponed...." "Shortly afterwards, the commanding general came to the position and decided it would not be prudent to make the attack..."[8]

Both Sumner and McClellan apparently reasoned that Franklin's Corps was the only organized corps on that part of the field and should be held in reserve.

And so, Westervelt and the 27th New York left Crampton's Pass in the early morning, came on the battlefield prepared to fight, only to be halted by the senior officer on the field, Sumner, and the commanding general (McClellan). The regiment remained there in the cornfield in the midst of dead and dying men and horses and other remnants of the battle for the rest of September 17 and the next two days.

During the afternoon of the seventeenth, Franklin suggested that he place artillery on a hill to the right of the cornfield (on the Poffenberger Farm) early in the morning of the eighteenth, and that after shelling the West Woods, the entire VI Corps should attack the Confederates. McClellan agreed to this proposal and then, during the night of the seventeenth, countermanded the order.[9] Again, the 27th New York was denied the opportunity for action. As a result, the 27th New York had no casualties at Antietam.

With the advent of Slocum's stabilizing the Federal line near the cornfield and the West Woods, the battle at that end of the field was over. Jackson lost about 6,000 in the morning's fight while the Federals lost about 7,000.[10]

The Federal attack now shifted to the middle of the field and Bloody Lane where two of Sumner's Divisions (French's and Richardson's) assaulted Longstreet's troops under D.H. Hill. The Federals lost about 3,000 men in this attack and the Confederates lost more. At the end of this fight, the Confederates still held their retracted original line.[11]

Then the battle shifted to the far right of the Confederate line where Toombs with about 600 men had been keeping Burnside's 13,000 from crossing the Antietam.[12] Finally, the bridge (now called Burnside's Bridge) was crossed and by 3:00 P.M. Burnside was on the way to clearing the area behind Sharpsburg and near the Potomac River. Shortly after 3:00 P.M., A.P. Hill's 3,000 men returned from Harpers Ferry, many wearing Federal uniforms, and entered the fray. Confusion reigned in Burnside's ranks, and his attack stalled before it reached the village of Sharpsburg. For all practical purposes, the Battle of Antietam was over.

Both sides remained in position on September 18, exhausted antagonists unable or unwilling to start the fight again. Lee retreated to Virginia the night of the eighteenth. McClellan's troops made a feeble effort to follow and then settled down to recoup.

ANTIETAM

Highlights

Instead of reporting on fighting, as at Crampton's Pass, Westervelt's picture of the Battle of Antietam is one of hospitals, the wounded and dead on the field, truces, perceptions of actions on other parts of the battlefield, and preparation for winter quarters. Each of these is covered below.

1. Hospitals: Westervelt comments on the number of houses used as hospitals as he marched through Keedysville. When a battle was imminent, Federal medical officers selected in advance of the battle houses and barns that would be used as hospitals. Such was the case at Antietam. The casualties at Antietam were so high that John Schildt, a current-day author whose specialty is Antietam, is of the opinion that every house and barn then in Washington County was a hospital after the battle.

2. Dead and Wounded in the Cornfield: The carnage on the cornfield at Antietam was mind-boggling. The soldiers of the 27th New York had to hold their positions for almost three days where the heaviest fighting had occurred. They undoubtedly had to hold their noses also to survive in a field bloodied with the remains of humans and horses and made worse by the September heat on the seventeenth and eighteenth. The scenes Westervelt portrays in writing can be viewed in pictures taken after the battle and contained in Volume II of Miller's *The Photographic History of The Civil War*.[13]

3. Truces: Westervelt was critical of the truces on September 18 which he saw as Lee's way of buying time to cover his retreat. He was even more critical of the Confederates firing on stretcher bearers and taking some prisoners the minute the truce expired. This issue is not found in standard reports on Antietam, but it is found in the *Regimental History of the 27th New York*.[14] Thus, Westervelt is supported on this point by his comrades and by Generals Slocum and Bartlett.

4. Perception of Activity on Other Parts of the Battlefield: Westervelt tells about Burnside holding Monocacy Bridge (actually this was the Rohrbach Bridge over the Antietam) and meeting the charge of the enemy. His perception of events was somewhat fanciful and too complimentary to Burnside when one considers how long it took the IX Corps and its 13,000 men to cross a bridge held by less than 600 of the enemy, and that he was later held in check by A.P. Hill's 3,000 men returning from Harpers Ferry.

Westervelt also felt that the Confederates started their retreat during the truces of September 18. The first truce, by his account, lasted from early morning on the eighteenth until morning on the nineteenth. Generals Walker and Longstreet both indicated that the retreat was not started until night of the eighteenth.[15]

In both instances, Westervelt's perceptions of actions on other parts of the battlefield were inaccurate.

5. <u>Winter Quarters</u>: In the winter of 1861-62, the Army of the Potomac was in winter quarters from September until April. Westervelt and his comrades assumed this practice would continue in the winter of 1862-63. Such was not the case for that winter or any subsequent one of the Civil War, as Westervelt found out to his chagrin.

Battle of Antietam

ANTIETAM

Wednesday, Sept. 17th. — At daylight reveille sounded through the camps of our division on the mountain sides, and as the clear notes of the bugle went forth, it brought back thousands of echoes from the rocks and hillsides. Soon the camps were astir. Water was scarce, as it had to be carried in canteens from the foot of the mountain about a mile distant. So after making our coffee, it is needless to say our morning ablutions were not very extensive. Soon after daylight heavy cannonading commenced, and not long after we were packed up and in line, with the head of the column turned in the direction of the firing. A short march brought us to the west side of the mountain, and while descending we had a view of a well cultivated valley, with fine buildings, put up more in the style of farm buildings of the north, and in fact, we found the mode of farming all through this state more after the manner of New York and Pennsylvania than in the states further south; but we spent little time in looking at the land or buildings, as something of more importance claimed our attention. A few miles in advance we could hear the continual boom of cannonading, with a steady roar of musketry, and was very plain to the ear of the veteran that it was not the popping of the picket, or a skirmish line, but the sharp engagement of a heavy line of battle, well supported with artillery. And every mile was bringing us nearer to the ominous sounds. About noon we reached Keedysville, and found many of the houses in possession of our surgeons, and fast being filled with our wounded.* The streets were almost blocked with ambulances waiting to unload their mangled suffering burdens, while the surgeons and assistants with coats off and sleeves rolled up—with hands and amputating instruments covered with blood— looked more like butchers in the shambles, than like professional men in hospitals. It was not a pleasant sight. I would gladly turn my eyes in some other direction, and my thoughts to some other subject more pleasant to dwell upon, as I always found this worse than going right into a fight.

On we went through the village, when, on coming to the open country beyond, the order was given, by the right flank, that placed us in line of battle. Our pieces were then loaded, and we moved forward across fields, through bits of wood, over fences, stopping occasionally to correct our alignments, continually passing dead—in blue, or gray—and meeting stretcher carriers with wounded, on their way to the rear. By this time the firing in front of us had nearly ceased, the boom of cannon was heard at intervals on different parts of the field, and sometimes the sharp rattle of musketry would come, lasting for a few minutes, when it would stop and all become quiet. Still we kept on advancing, and finally reached a cornfield about the center of our lines, where the heaviest fighting had taken place some two hours before. The dead lay so thick we had to pull them out of our way to make room for us to form our lines. This ground had been fought over twice before we reached it, each side holding it in their turn; the corn was trampled to the ground, while some bushes that were left standing were completely riddled with bullets—one could not place the hand on a bush but what it wuld cover a number of bullet marks. Where they offered

---

* Franklin's Report indicates that Slocum's Division arrived on the field about 11:00 A.M.

sufficient resistance they were cut off; others that swayed to and fro, were splintered in every direction, and entirely stripped of leaves. Here we formed our line, while a battery was put in position on a slight elevation just in our rear. One of our companies was deployed a short distance in front, as a skirmish line by day and a picket line at night, and we quietly sat down to await results. Here we remained all day; but little fighting took place in our immediate front. Two or three times the enemy's skirmishers advanced and exchanged a few shots with our line and then retired. Once, for some reason, our artillery opened fire, and sent a few rounds of shot and shell over our heads into the woods where the enemy were supposed to be. This made us hug the ground close, while each man held his Springfield in his hand ready to spring into his place in ranks at the word of command.

This little diversion over, all quieted down, and we would get in as comfortable positions as possible, and while away the time wondering where they would strike next. Just before sunset, after some hours of almost undisturbed quiet, the fight opened on our left, and for two hours raged furiously. They were out of sight of us, but we could hear them plainly and see the smoke and dust rise, as a continual roar of musketry was kept up, with a lively accompaniment of artillery. This was Burnside holding Manocacy Bridge.* It had been captured by our men during the day, and Gen. Lee, seeing the importance of regaining it, hurled brigade after brigade of his best troops against it. But it was no use; Burnside and his corps had come there to

---

* This was the Rohrbach or Lower Bridge, now called "Burnside's Bridge."

stay, and met every charge of the enemy, with a counter charge, not only holding their own but each time advancing until they at length occupied the heights beyond. Darkness now settled upon the field and we unrolled our blankets, and lay down behind our stacks of guns, ready to "fall in" at the slightest alarm. Nothing disturbed our slumbers but some slight picket firing, and we enjoyed a very fair night's rest.

Thus ended the first and principal day of Antietam battle, and although we took but little part in the fighting, it was the hardest fought battle of the war up to this date.

Thursday, Sept. 18th. — Just before daylight we were called in line, as that is considered the favorable time to surprise a camp, and we did not intend to be caught napping. Here we stood, leaning on our guns, while in the rear of us were the artillerymen with guns shotted and lanyard in hand ready to attach to the prime, and send death and destruction into the ranks of an advancing foe. All remained quiet, however, and soon after sunrise we were ordered to stack arms and break ranks. Soon scores of small fires were kindled with cornstalks and small twigs, and the coffee cup—that inseparable companion of the soldier—was steaming, and meat frying, and we soon sat down to our morning meal right among the dead that, already in the hot September sun, began to give forth a very unpleasant odor. This only shows to what extent we could adapt ourselves to our surroundings. A few months before I could not have taken a mouthful of food and swallowed it in the presence of a corpse. Now, although they showed unmistakable signs of decomposition, we did not mind it, even though they lay so thick we were obliged to lift some of them out of our way to make room for our lines of battle.

ANTIETAM

Soon after sunrise Gen. H.C. Rogers,[*] adjt. general for Gen. Slocum, accompanied by some other officers, rode to the front to meet a flag of truce from Gen. Lee, where, after a short parley, it was agreed to cease hostilities until 5 P.M., in order to bury the dead and carry off the wounded that lay uncared for between our lines. In agreeing to this McClellan made the mistake of a life—time, as Lee's army was retreating, part of them being already south of the Potomac, and this was a well laid plan to gain time and get over with his supply train and artillery. But McClellan fell in with this scheme and granted the armistice.

Stretcher carriers now came up, and while they carried off scores of wounded we turned in with pick and shovel, in the capacity of grave diggers, and like most everything else done by the army, our grave digging was on a wholesale scale. We first dug a grave six feet wide and about sixty feet long. In this grave, or rather trench, were placed side by side, forty of a South Carolina regiment. A few rods from this was another that contained thirty more.. This disposed of all that lay close to our lines, and as we had but few tools for digging, it took most of the day to complete our wholesale interments. As we were looking about for a good place to dig another trench to gather some forty more that were scattered about between our lines, 5 P.M. arrived, and the time of the armistice had expired. Promptly to the moment the enemy opened fire, wounding some of the stretcher bearers and taking several more of them prisoners. This anxiety to commence

hostilities was but the carrying out of the scheme of Gen. Lee to safely retreat to the south bank of the river.

We quickly sprang to arms, and had the order been given we would soon have found the strength of our foe, but no, a repetition of the blunder of the morning here took place. General Rogers was once more sent out with a white flag, and the time of the armistice was extended until morning. We did not relax our vigilance, however, knowing we were faced by a wily foe, who would stop for nothing, allowed in honorable warfare to gain an advantage, and would even strain a point, as was shown by the firing on our stretcher bearers, consequently our advance line of pickets were kept on the "qui vive," while we a few rods in their rear lay down behind our stacks of guns, each man with cartridge box buckled on, and ready to spring into his place at the first sign of alarm. Nothing, however, disturbed us, the stretcher carriers continued their ghastly work, and after the wounded were carried off, the dead were removed to give us clear ground to fight over in the morning, while we, after the excitement and fatigue of the day, slept soundly.

Friday, September 19th. — At daylight we were again under arms, when our picket line reported no signs of the enemy in our front. At sunrise they were ordered to advance, when it was discovered they had made good use of their time during the cessation of hostilities, and were safe with their supply trains, and artillery south of the river leaving most of their wounded, however, in our care. About noon got orders to move, and as we crossed the battle field the stench from the unburied dead almost took our breath away. We soon crossed the Sharpsburg Pike, where the dead lay in every

[*] Rogers is listed as a major in Slocum's report on Crampton's Pass, not a general.

conceivable position; one with his rammer half drawn from his gun, as he had finished loading his piece, having his gun in one hand and the rammer in the other, with a small, round hole through his forehead, his countenance being but slightly disfigured, but more expressive of surprise than pain. Others noticed his look as well as myself, and as Bogart expressed it, "he was astonished at how quick we killed him." Another was killed in the act of biting off the end of a cartridge, and lay with his hand still at his mouth. One of them had been killed just as he was climbing a fence, and in his death grip had caught the top rail where, in his half standing position he looked like one in the act of leaping over, and our men had fired repeatedly at him, thinking him still alive and trying to escape. I counted sixteen bullet holes in the lower part of his back that had been made after he was dead. Guns and equipments by the thousand lay scattered about the field representing every manu-

factory of Europe, showing how well our neutrality laws were respected.

We soon reached the bank of the Potomac and saw the last of the enemy disappearing over the hills on the Virginia side of the river, as Lee had finished his first attempt at carrying the war into the Northern states. Here we camped two days, when it was rumored the enemy were attempting to cross the river near Williamsport, and we were sent on a night excursion to receive them. It proved a false alarm, and two days after we moved back to Baker's Mills, near the field of Antietam, where we camped until November, and were flattering ourselves that we were to spend the winter here. Some of us built log huts in place of tents, Sergeant Trusdell and myself finishing ours on the evening of October 31st, and when we turned in for the night were congratulating ourselves on our comfortable quarters, when orders came to move at sunrise the next morning.

ANTIETAM

Notes — Chapter 10

1. Palfrey, *Campaigns of the Civil War*, Vol. V, "The Antietam and Fredericksburg," p. 49.

2. Johnson and Buel, *Battle and Leaders of the Civil War*, Vol. II, p. 665.

3. House of Representatives, Letter of the Secretary of War transmitting McClellan's Report, 1st Session, Ex. Document 15, Washington, D.C., Government Printing Office, 1864, p. 201.

4. Ibid.

5. Ibid., pp. 201, 202.

6. Murfin, *The Gleam of Bayonets,* p. 198.

7. Ibid., p. 205.

8. Fairchild, *History of the 27th Regiment of New York Volunteers*, p. 108.

9. Johnson and Buel, *Battles and Leaders of the Civil War*, Vol. II, p. 597.

10. Edward J. Stackpole, *Showdown at Sharpsburg — Story of the Battle*, Civil War Times Special, Harrisburg, Pennsylvania. (August 1962), p. 30.

11. Ibid.

12. Ibid., p. 31.

13. Francis T. Miller, *The Photographic History of The Civil War* (New York: Castle Books, 1911), Vol. II, pg. 63.

14. Fairchild, *History of the 27th Regiment, N.Y. Volunteers*, p. 96.

15. Johnson and Buel, *Battles and Leaders of the Civil War*, Vol. II, pp. 672, 682.

Chapter 11

THE FREDERICKSBURG AND CHANCELLORSVILLE CAMPAIGNS

AN OVERVIEW

After Antietam, Westervelt spent seven out of eight of the final months of his first enlistment in the area around Fredericksburg, Virginia. During this period (September 18, 1862-May 17, 1863), he served under three different commanding generals of the Army of the Potomac (McClellan, Burnside, and Hooker). He was in two campaigns and one aborted campaign (the Fredericksburg Campaign, the Chancellorsville Campaign, and the Mud March). His writing reflects the changing and inept leadership of the army during this period and its effect upon the regiment and its men.

Lincoln and Halleck prodded McClellan after Antietam and he finally moved to follow Lee into Virginia. McClellan left Sharpsburg on October 27, 1862; Westervelt and the 27th New York moved out on November 1.

McClellan's plan apparently was to travel south on the east side of the Blue Ridge Mountains hoping to catch Lee with part of his army east of the Mountains and part in the Shenandoah Valley. Most historians feel that McClellan did not tell Lincoln of his plans. However, Longstreet understood what McClellan was trying to do and was concerned that he might succeed.[1]

The VI Corps went south via Berlin, Maryland (now Brunswick),[2] crossed the Potomac there and arrived in New Baltimore, Virginia on November 9.[3]

McClellan was in Rectortown, Virginia on November 7, and it was here that he received Lincoln's order which removed him from command and ended his military career.[4]

General Ambrose P. Burnside replaced McClellan. He had twice before refused the command of the Army of the Potomac and accepted the assignment in November 1862 with great reluctance. His concern was that he doubted his own ability.[5] This became a self-fulfilling prophecy at Fredericksburg.

Burnside reviewed McClellan's plans for the campaign against Lee and then came up with his own—to seize Fredericksburg and, from there, move on Richmond.[6] The key to the success of Burnside's plan was to beat Lee to Fredericksburg by crossing the Rappahannock on pontoons. Halleck did not like the plan; the president gave his consent but thought it would work only if Burnside moved rapidly.[7]

Burnside moved fast enough; the Federal advance arrived in Falmouth opposite Fredericksburg on November 17. The VI Corps reached Stafford Court House on the eighteenth.[8] Fredericksburg was virtually unoccupied by the Confederates. But pontoons were the essential ingredient for success and the first pontoons didn't arrive until November 25, and an adequate supply was not available until several days later.[9] By that time Lee had massed his troops in and around Fredericksburg in strong defensive positions, and the element of surprise was gone. Burnside and Halleck each blamed the other for this fiasco, but it was the Union army that suffered from it.

Burnside organized his army into three grand divisions under Franklin on the left, Sumner in the center, and Hooker on the right. This and other events meant changes in leadership for the VI Corps. Franklin, the corps commander, was replaced by Smith; and Slocum, the division commander, was replaced by Brooks (Slocum had been promoted to command the XII Corps after Mansfield was killed at Antietam).

THE FREDERICKSBURG AND CHANCELLORSVILLE CAMPAIGNS

AN OVERVIEW

The Army of the Potomac crossed the river on December 12 and 13, 1862, and carried out its attack on December 13. Burnside did exactly what his opponent wanted him to do.[10] The results were disastrous. The Federals lost 13,771 men in the attack; the Confederates lost 5,409.[11] Burnside wanted to personally lead a renewed attack the next day but was dissuaded from doing so. The army retreated back across the Rappahannock the night of the fifteenth.

The senior officers of the army lost all confidence in Burnside, and the leaders of this falling out were Hooker and several associated with the VI Corps—Franklin, Smith, Brooks, Cochrane, and Newton. Franklin and Smith wrote President Lincoln on December 20 and proposed a plan of action totally different from that of Burnside.[12] A week later, Generals Newton and Cochrane went to see the president in Washington. The result of these actions was that on December 30, an attack Burnside had started was cancelled by the president.[13]

On January 20, 1863, Burnside resolved to attack again. He proposed to make the attack above Fredericksburg with a feint below it.[14] This time the elements took over and rain turned the ground into a morass. The troops had to return to their old quarters on January 23. They dubbed this expedition "The Mud March."

These events and the well-known dissension among the senior officers then led Burnside to prepare orders dismissing Hooker, Brooks, Newton, and Cochrane from the service (General Orders No. 8) and relieving Franklin and Smith from duty with the Army of the Potomac.[15] The president disapproved this order and replaced Burnside with Hooker on January 25, 1863. He also relieved Franklin who was eventually assigned elsewhere in the West.

As a result of all these moves, Westervelt was again under new leadership. Hooker was now commanding general of the Army of the Potomac and Sedgwick was named the new commander of the VI Corps.[16]

It appears that Bartlett was almost caught up in the maelstrom, too, for Congress failed to approve his appointment as brigadier general. Bartlett was in civilian clothes and about ready to return to civilian life when the president wired Hooker, "Tell General Bartlett to put on his clothes again and return to his command. A. Lincoln."[17]

Hooker, the new commanding general, was a man who had both marked strengths and weaknesses. One weakness was described by a fellow officer who knew Hooker before the Civil War. He said, "Hooker could play the best game of poker I ever saw until it came to a point where he should go a thousand better, and then he would flunk."[18] This was the way he performed at Chancellorsville.

His strengths as commander of the Army of the Potomac were that he reorganized the army and restored its morale. He disbanded the Grand Divisions, and instituted a system of badges which improved both recognition and pride. (The VI Corps' badge was a plain or Greek cross, and the 27th New York wore a red one since it was in the First Division.) He also greatly improved the food that the soldiers ate, and he started a system of furloughs. He drilled the troops incessantly.

By April, the 27th New York troops were thinking of going home. All of the companies forming the regiment and all of the men had entered service in early May 1861. They expected that their two years of service would be up in early May 1863. But the Federal government had a

THE FREDERICKSBURG AND CHANCELLORSVILLE CAMPAIGNS

AN OVERVIEW

different idea; the 27th New York had been accepted into Federal service on May 21, 1861, and would not be mustered out until May 21, 1863, or later.[19]

Hooker started his Chancellorsville Campaign on April 27. The main portion of the Federal army was sent up the Rappahannock north of Fredericksburg where they were to cross the river and strike south through Chancellorsville to attack Lee's army. The VI Corps, along with the I and III, were sent south of Fredericksburg to confound Lee and create a diversion. Lee then surprised Hooker when he had Jackson attack Hooker's right flank where he mauled Howard's XI Corps. Hooker then went on the defensive and called upon Sedgwick and the VI Corps to make an all-out attack on Fredericksburg to come to Hooker's relief. Then, without waiting for Sedgwick to join him, Hooker withdrew all the rest of the army and retreated back across the river. Lee now turned all his attention to Sedgwick who just barely was able to make it back across the river, also.

Between April 28 and May 5, 1863, the 27th New York fought at Franklin's Crossing, Second Fredericksburg (Marye's Heights), Salem Church, and Banks' Ford. Nineteen men who had expected to go home in early May were killed, wounded or missing (3, 13, and 3 respectively).

THE FREDERICKSBURG AND CHANCELLORSVILLE CAMPAIGNS

AN OVERVIEW

Notes — Chapter 11

1. Johnson and Buel, *Battles and Leaders of the Civil War*, Vol. III, p. 85.

2. Victor, *History of the Southern Rebellion*, Vol. III, p. 332.

3. Fairchild, *History of the 27th Regiment, N.Y. Vols.*, p. 111.

4. Long, *The Civil War Day by Day,* p. 285.

5. Victor, *History of the Southern Rebellion*, Vol. III, p. 369.

6. Ibid., p. 370.

7. Williams, *Lincoln and His Generals*, p. 196.

8. Fairchild, *History of the 27th Regiment, N.Y. Vols.*, p. 114.

9. Col. Vincent Esposito, *The West Point Atlas of the Civil War*, Map 72.

10. Palfrey, *Campaigns of the Civil War, the Antietam and Fredericksburg*, p. 141.

11. Guernsey an Alden, *Harper's Pictorial History of the Civil War*, p. 416.

12. *O.R.*, Vol. XXI, pp. 868-870.

13. Ibid., p. 900.

14. Guernsey and Alden, *Harper's Pictorial History of the Civil War*, pp. 416-417.

15. *O.R.*, Vol. XXI, pp. 998-999.

16. *O.R.*, Vol. XXV, Part I, pp. 156-164.

17. Fairchild, *History of the 27th Regiment, N.Y. Vols.*, p. 153.

18. Bruce Catton, *Glory Road* (New York: The Fairfax Press, 1984), p. 306.

19. Fairchild, *History of the 27th Regiment, N.Y. Vols.*, p. 163.

Chapter 12

PRELUDE TO FREDERICKSBURG

Background

Westervelt and his comrades assumed that after remaining in the Sharpsburg area through October 1862, they would spend the winter there. To their chagrin, they were on the move south into Virginia on November 1.

The 27th New York retraced its steps back over South Mountain at Crampton's Pass, down into Burkittsville, and on to Berlin. They crossed the Potomac River at Berlin on November 3. The regiment proceeded through Loudoun County east of the Blue Ridge Mountains and parallel to them, then east near the Thoroughfare Gap of the Bull Run Mountains and on into New Baltimore, Virginia on November 8. Here McClellan visited the VI Corps on November 10 and took his final leave of the Army of the Potomac.[1]

Burnside's new plans for the army involved a rapid march from the area around Warrenton, Virginia to Falmouth, opposite Fredericksburg on the Rappahannock River. Orders were issued on November 14,[2] and the VI Corps reached Stafford Court House on the eighteenth. All of the army's stores at Warrenton had to be sent back to Alexandria and then sent down the Potomac River to Belle Plain on Aquia Creek and thence overland to Fredericksburg.[3]

To be successful, Burnside had to have both supplies and pontoons before Lee had a chance to erect his defenses.[4] The pontoons were at Berlin and Harpers Ferry where they had been used by the army in crossing the Potomac and into Virginia early in November. Burnside requested Halleck to send the pontoons, and then communications totally broke down. Contemporary writers place the blame on Halleck.[5] Victor, another contemporary writer, presented both Burnside's and Halleck's versions of the pontoon debacle and then added, "And this is the whole story of the wretched mistake which defeated the movement upon Fredericksburg and cost the country over two thousand precious lives."[6]

From November 19 until December 6, the 27th New York was either in camp or on picket duty. From December 7 through December 9, the men were unloading the ships at Belle Plain.[7] Then on December 11, Westervelt and his comrades marched to the lower pontoon bridge on the Rappahannock River and crossed over at dark.[8] No sooner had they gotten across and into position when they were ordered to recross.[9] This loss of the element of surprise by this movement was a portent of the disaster that followed.

Highlights

Several highlights are worth noting in this chapter.

1. McClellan's Departure: Westervelt simply writes, "The next day McClellan rode through our camp, bidding good bye to the troops, he having been relieved from command." This is slight reference to a general who was supposed to be the idol of his men. Was it because of Westervelt's personal feeling or did it reflect the current attitude of the army? The answer will probably never be known.

PRELUDE TO FREDERICKSBURG

2. <u>Counterfeit Confederate Money</u>: After evading the pickets, Westervelt and his buddy walked into the country and purchased food for their Thanksgiving dinner. This was done with Confederate money which they purchased at one cent per bill regardless of denomination! This is an amazing revelation about the army and counterfeit Confederate money; one not found in any standard reference on the Civil War! On the surface, it would appear that Federal authorities were making bogus Confederate bills readily available to the troops in order to help undermine the Rebels' economy.

3. <u>Captain Brainard</u>: The absconding of Captain Brainard with the enlisted men's borrowed money is another illustration of the problem with officers in the Army of the Potomac. It is interesting to note that this is the only place in Westervelt's book that the denigrating term "nigger" appears and here its thrust was against the captain and not the black man who accompanied him.

4. <u>The Weather</u>: It is difficult to realize how bad the weather was in the Winter of 1862-1863, and how much it affected the operations of the army. Clearly the weather was much more severe then, than it is today. Its impact upon the men and the operations is a theme that runs through the Fredericksburg Campaign and later "The Mud March."

PRELUDE TO FREDERICKSBURG

Saturday, Nov. 1st. — *Three o'clock A.M. found us busy packing our household effects and personal property, and just at sunrise we bid good bye to the improvements we had made, and gazed regretfully at the remains of the log hut that we had finished but yesterday, and marched away. Our road took us to the left of Antietam battle field, through the village of Keedysville, and after a pleasant march of about ten miles we camped near Crampton Pass, on the opposite side of the mountain from where the fight took place on September 14th. The next morning we crossed the mountain, passed over the battle field and to the right of Burketsville [sic], where we halted a few minutes, and while here several of our wounded that were left at the village on the day of the fight, came to see us. I was pleased to meet with W.H. French, and found that his arm had been saved from amputation, and although to this day he has but little use of it, yet it is much better than none.*

We continued our march through Maryland two days more and then crossed the Potomac on a pontoon bridge at Berlin, that brought us into London* county, Va., the richest part of the Shenandoah Valley. On the 7th, while camped at White Plains, we had a slight snow storm. The next day we came to Thoroughfare Gap, when our officers, seeing smoke on the opposite side of the mountain, thought it the enemy. A battery was hastily put in position, our lines of battle formed, and skirmishers sent to the front, who soon returned and reported Gen. Siegel on the opposite side with twelve thousand of our men, when we took up our line of march, and at night camped at New Baltimore. The next day McClellan rode through our camps,

bidding good bye to the troops, he having been relieved from command. We remained here several days, which gave me an opportunity to visit Thoroughfare Gap, and although it cost me a walk of some six miles, I felt well paid for my visit.

It is a natural cut through the mountains, just wide enough for a small stream, a railroad, and wagon road — all as level as though graded; while on either side the rocks rise almost perpendicularly hundreds of feet, and as smooth as though cut by hand.

Thursday, Nov. 27. — *This was Thanksgiving in N.Y.; we had no turkey, but we tried to be thankful for our salt pork and hard tack. About nine A.M. we were sent on picket, and being left with the reserve, we took possesion† of a big house where, in the open fire place, we soon had a large comfortable fire, when as our dinner did not come up to orthodox Thanksgiving, I proposed to my tent mate that we take a walk out into the surrounding country, and see if we could improve it some. To this he agreed and off we went. By using a little strategy we soon passed our picket lines, and struck off through the open country some five or six miles, when we came to a farm house, with a poultry yard that evidently had not yet been visited very severely by the soldiers. We soon selected a pair of fine roosters, and going to the house purchased some bread, eggs, milk, and sweet potatoes, that we paid for in Confederate money, of which we always kept a supply, it being very cheap, as it was printed in Philadelphia, and sold to the soldiers at one cent a bill—no matter what the denomination was. Although it was counterfeit, it was better*

---

* Loudoun

† possession

86

made than the genuine, and proved to be just as valuable. We always paid cash and were not very particular about the change.

With our load we hurried back to the picket reserve and commenced our dinner. The fowls were first boiled until tender, and then suspended in front of a hot fire by a string that kept them turning, and soon were done to a nice brown. While this was progressing the sweet potatoes were roasting in the ashes, and as soon as the fowls were out of the pot, by means of a tin pail it was transformed in a double kettle in which boiled custard was bubbling.

At the fashionable dinner hour of six P.M., we pronounced it ready, and sat down to a bill of fare equal to that of many a northern home. Just as we commenced out meal Jim Bogart came in, and depositing his gun in a corner of the room, remarked, "I guess I will have to contribute something to this "lay out." "Certainly, Jim; if you will contribute something we will go shares, and ask you to sit by." "That's a go; you find the grub, I will furnish the appetite," and suiting the action to the word, he seated himself on a box at our improvised table, and fell to with us. He was none the less welcome, however, as his good nature was contagious, and never failed him under any circumstance, and looking back now, over the many Thanksgiving dinners enjoyed since this one, there has, I am sure, never been one that offered the same amount of real enjoyment or relish, no matter if our table was made of a door, and innocent of a table cloth, our plates and cups of tin, and spoons of iron, no matter if the fowls were eaten without Worcestershire or jocky club sauce, our sweet potatoes came on the table covered with ashes, our bread taken without

butter, our boiled custard minus vanilla or other flavoring—it was good, and the meal as a whole was pronounced par excellence, and we doubted if Delmonico could beat it with the same facilities.

We remained on picket until the 29th. During this time one of the captains whose resignation had been accepted took advantage of our absence, and started for home. On our return we found he had borrowed money from all the enlisted men he could, holding out to them dazzling promise of advancement, that were never to be realized. In the evening a number of victims, came around the fire at our tent. The result was, the next morning there appeared on the regimental bulletin board this notice. It was written large, and plain, and was left up several hours before the adjutant saw it, and tore it down—long enough for most of the men to read it, some of whom took copies, to send for publication in the papers published in their immediate neighborhood. The negro spoken of was his cook, whom he persuaded to go home with him, and then turned him adrift in New York, penniless.

"NOTICE - ONE CENT REWARD."
"Ran away from the camp of the 27th Regt., near Stafford Court House, Va., Nov. 27th, 1862, Capt. W. Brainard, and another nigger. The former is about six feet high, has a guilty hang-dog look, and was dressed in a borrowed suit of clothes and stolen gloves. The latter had an honest, intelligent look, was cleanly clad and is supposed to own the clothes he wore. The above reward will be paid for his capture or for information that will enable his many victims here to collect the sums of money he borrowed, and ran away without paying."

PRELUDE TO FREDERICKSBURG

We remained in camp near Stafford Court House several days, during which time Gen. Burnside was placed in command of the army, and determined to attack Fredericksburg, on the Rappahannock, opposite Falmouth. On Dec. 4th we broke camp, and after a tiresome march of about ten miles through the mud, we camped on the top of a high hill where the wind blew cold, and we passed a very uncomfortable night. The next morning we moved our camp a short distance and put up our tents in a piece of woods that was more sheltered. We soon fixed our tent very comfortable, when it began to rain; but as we lay in our tent on a bed of pine boughs, with our feet to a roaring fire of logs, that the rain could not extinguish, enjoying an after dinner smoke, we congratulated ourselves on the fact that we were in camp instead of being on the march. But our comforts were of short duration. About 2 P.M. the "General" sounded (a call to strike tents), and in half an hour more we were on the road. The rain continued to fall, and soon we were about as wet as we could be, while the mud became so deep we could scarce get along. Just so before dark the rain changed to snow, which did not add to our comfort; still we pushed on, and finally reached Belle Plains on the Potomac. By this time it was so dark and the snow so deep we could get no wood, so we just sat down on our knapsacks, and wrapping our blankets about us, shivered until morning. About midnight the storm ceased and sky cleared. Soon after there was a partial eclipse of the moon, but I can't say that I enjoyed looking at that eclipse very much. In the morning the snow was about three inches deep; the day was warm, but the nights were cold, and not being very well supplied with blankets, we suffered from the cold.

The following day, Dec. 7th, we had the coldest day we ever experienced in Virginia. It froze all day, while the ice in the Potomac river was so thick near the shore the boats had great difficulty in landing. Four days after we reached the Rappahannock river just below Falmouth, and found our engineers trying to put down a pontoon bridge, but the enemy's sharpshooters on the other side of the river, were picking them off and giving them a great deal of annoyance. Some of them were sheltered in an old house near the bank and our riflemen could not succeed in dislodging them. Soon Upton's battery was put in position and a volley fired. The old building was badly torn to pieces, and no more shots came from it; we saw no one retreat from it. The next day when we crossed the river, we found three dead soldiers, which showed we had some "sharpshooters" even in our artillery. About dark the bridge was completed and sixty pieces of our artillery were placed in line on high ground, half a mile back from the shore. Our brigade was then marched to the front of them, to a level plain near the bank. Suddenly all the batteries opened fire and sent a continual stream of shells over our heads across the river to the plain beyond. It was the most beautiful display of pyrotechnics we ever witnessed. Just then the order forward was given, and with our regiment in the lead, we crossed the pontoon bridge and advanced about a mile across the plain, where our advance encountered the enemy's pickets. We were ordered to "about face," and returned over the river. What this move was for has always looked mysterious. Why we were sent over and then called back, leaving the ground we had so easily obtained, still remains a conundrum, which I would not attempt to solve.

PRELUDE TO FREDERICKSBURG

Notes — Chapter 12

1. Fairchild, *History of the 27th Regiment, N.Y. Vols.*, p. 111.

2. Wilson, *Pictorial History of the Great Civil War*, p. 339.

3. Victor, *History of the Southern Rebellion*, Vol. III, p. 370.

4. Ibid., p. 372.

5. Wilson, *Pictorial History of the Great Civil War*, p. 339.

   Palfrey, *Campaigns of the Civil War, the Antietam and Fredericksburg*, p. 137.

6. Victor, *History of the Southern Rebellion*, Vol. III, p. 372.

7. Fairchild, *History of the 27th Regiment, N.Y. Vols.*, pp. 115-116.

8. *O.R.*, Vol. XX, p. 526.

9. Ibid.

Chapter 13

THE BATTLE OF FREDERICKSBURG

Background

On December 12, 1862, the pontoon bridges were in place and Burnside moved his forces across the Rappahannock River. The Battle of Fredericksburg was about to begin.

Pollard, in *The Lost Cause*, eloquently describes the scene of the impending engagement:

The Confederates numbered abut eighty thousand men. They were drawn up along the heights in the rear of Fredericksburg, which, retiring in a semi-circle from the river, embrace within their arms a plain six miles in length and from two to three in depth. It seemed as if nature had prepared here an arena for one of the grandest conflicts of arms that had yet been witnessed in the war. The landscape, stretching from the hills to the river, was like an amphitheatre; the intrenched Confederates holding an upper tier of seats, and the stage being the valley in which were placed the red-brick building of Fredericksburg. Outside the town a few houses were scattered here and there over the scene, and leafless woods added to the bleak aspect of the country.[1]

The Confederates had their men on the hills and behind them. Artillery was well placed. On the left at Marye's Heights, Longstreet says he had "an almost unapproachable defense."[2] Longstreet's chief of artillery said of the artillery coverage of the field in front of the Heights, "A chicken could not live on that field when we open on it."[3] Twenty years after the battle, when asked if Burnside could have won at Fredericksburg, Longstreet replied, "Such a thing was hardly possible."[4]

The Federal army crossed the river on pontoon bridges; the Left Grand Division at the lower bridges two miles south of Fredericksburg and the Center and Right Grand Divisions on bridges at Fredericksburg. Franklin had over 40,000 men;[5] the remainder of the army under Sumner and Hooker brought the Federal total up to 113,000.[6]

Franklin expected to carry the weight of the attack. On December 12, he understood that he was to assail the enemy in "columns of assault on the right and left of the Richmond road, carry the ridge and turn Lee's flank at any cost."[7] He did all the preliminary work possible and then awaited further orders, which Burnside had promised. The orders he received at a relatively late hour, 7:30 A.M., on the thirteenth, were not compatible with the plan that had been discussed and presumed approved the night before. The orders called for the positioning of the VI Corps so that it could not move without danger of losing the bridges. They, also, called for the seizing of the heights near Captain Hamilton's using a single division.[8] Burnside's orders were delivered by General Hardie, a member of Burnside's staff, who remained with Franklin all day and served as an interpreter for and conduit to Burnside. Palfrey, highly respected as an officer and historian on Fredericksburg, writes, "It seems to be true that Burnside formed no definite plan of battle at all."[9]

Obeying the new orders, Franklin ordered a division forward, Meade's of the I Corps supported by Gibbon's, and later Birney's. Brooks' Division of the VI Corps (formerly Slocum's), including the 27th New York, held the Richmond Road on the right and Deep Creek (Deep Run).[10]

90

Pontoon Wagons on Their Way from Aquia Creek to the Rappahannock

Franklin's Grand Division Crossing the Rappahannock

THE BATTLE OF FREDERICKSBURG

Meade's Division went forward around noon, broke through Jackson's lines, and then was thrown back by 2:15 P.M.[11] At 3:00 P.M., General Brooks ordered Colonel Torbert and his First New Jersey Brigade, supported by other regiments, to advance and drive out the enemy in their front. The fighting became difficult for these Northern troops for the Confederates had a stronger force than supposed. Finally, Torbert was ordered to break off the engagement and fall back and hold his original position.[12]

While all this was occurring, the 27th New York remained in the ravine of Deep Run, ready for action but never called.[13] Brooks, in his report of the battle, wrote, "Although not directly engaged with the enemy, the troops of the other brigades of the division were exposed for four days to much shelling from the enemy's batteries that were located on the heights all around us. In this trying situation they displayed great fortitude, patience, and endurance."[14]

On the army's right, Couch who commanded the II Corps of Sumner's Right Grand Division, ordered French and Hancock to attack at 1:00 P.M. and "carry the enemy's works by storm."[15] "The attack of the Second Corps had spent its force by 2:30 P.M."[16] The valiant attempts by these troops against an impregnable hill, wall, and sunken road are the basis for most of the memories and impressions people have about Fredericksburg. Hancock lost 2,000 men in that short time, French, 1,200; and Howard, who was sent in later, lost 877.[17]

At about 2:30 P.M., Burnside sent orders to Franklin "to make a vigorous attack with his whole force; our right is hard pressed."[18] Franklin did not respond to this order. Reasons given for his lack of action are the lateness in the day and the question as to whether the order, as understood, could be effectively carried out.

Both Confederate and Federal reports indicate that there was active skirmishing on December 14. Burnside wanted to renew the attack and lead it personally, but his senior officers, particularly the old veteran Sumner, talked him out of his rash proposal.[19] And so, the army remained in place on the fourteenth and fifteenth. It retreated back across the Rappahannock River after dark on the night of the fifteenth. The Confederates made no effort to follow.

In the battle, the Confederates lost about 5,400 men.[20] The Federals lost 12,653, and the breakdown for this latter figure shows the following:

Organization	Losses
Left Grand Division	3,787
(VI Corps)	(446)
(27th New York)	(0)
Center Grand Division	3,555
Right Grand Division	5,444
Miscellaneous Units	59
Total Federal Losses	**12,653**

THE BATTLE OF FREDERICKSBURG

<u>Highlights</u>

Two items bear mentioning here.

1. <u>Confederate Artillery</u>: Every report on Fredericksburg makes mention of the Confederate artillery. Westervelt talks about it, as does the *History of the 27th New York*. In addition, Brooks, in his report of the battle, cites the stress his troops were under from the Rebel barrage.

2. <u>Perceptions—December 14</u>: As indicated above, reports of both sides indicate skirmishing on December 14. Franklin, in his report, states, "A desultory cannonading and a brisk skirmish fight long the whole line were carried on during the day, with, I presume, about equal loss on both sides."[21] The men of the 27th New York saw it a little differently. Their history reports, "About 8 o'clock, we were sent up to the front to relieve the 8th Jersey regiment on picket, and were ordered close up to the enemy's works, ..."[22] From this vantage point, both Westervelt and the Regimental History report two desperate attacks on the right before the wall. None of the reports of the senior officers on the right mention an attack on the fourteenth; only that the IX Corps was ordered to prepare for attack and then the order was suspended.

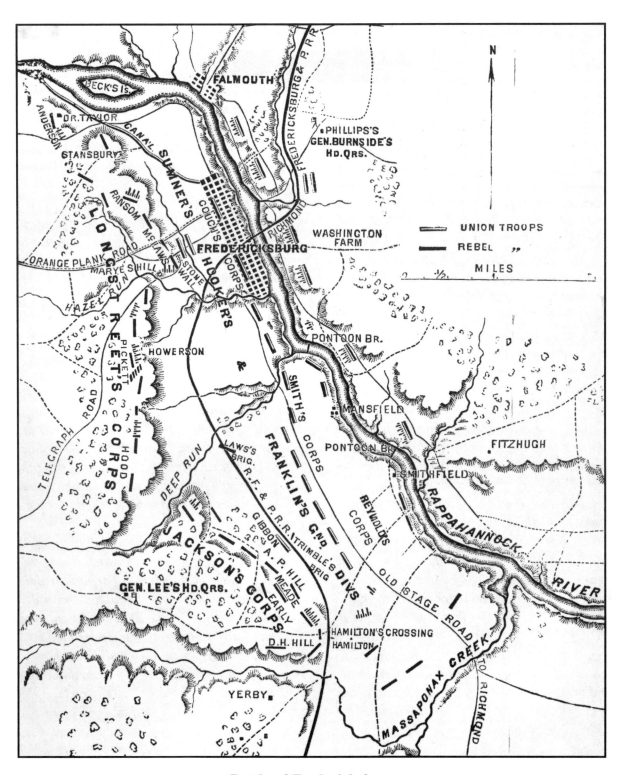

Battle of Fredericksburg

THE BATTLE OF FREDERICKSBURG

On the following morning we got up at our own convenience and leisurely preparing our breakfast remained in camp, seeing no signs of a move until about eight A.M., when our troops began to move across the bridge. Soon we were called up and followed. We first moved to the right near Fredricksburgh;* we then moved to the extreme left, some three miles below, and again moved to near the centre of our line. The enemy were posted on a range of hills in the form of a half circle, reaching from above Fredricksburg,[sic] southwest some four miles, while we were manoeuvering on a level plain, extending from the river back some two miles to the food of the hills. A dense fog very conveniently hid our movements, until about 11 A.M., when it suddenly lifted, and the enemy caught sight of us and opened fire. Fortunately, at the time we were near a deep ravine, in which we took shelter. Here we were protected from the enemy's fire, and found plenty of wood and water; so we stacked arms, and while the shot and shell were flying over our heads and striking the opposite bank, we leisurely cooked our dinner.

Soon all became quiet, and remained so until about 3 P.M., when they opened on us again, and by the way of variety, fired over some pieces of railroad track iron. It was cut in pieces of about two feet, and wrapped in oakum, so as not to injure the gun, and as it went tumbling through the air it sounded as though the infernal regions had broken loose, and the demons of disorder were trying which could produce the most horrible sounds. I have listened to shot and shell from different guns, both large and small, and thought that the fifteen-inch shot from the Monitor, that

were sent over our camp at Harrison Landing to dislodge an enemy's battery that had followed us, had a demoralizing effect, but I found that when it comes to the double concentrated essence of infernality, a piece of railroad iron passing through the air, about thirty feet above one's head, can discount them all.

About this time firing commenced in the streets of Fredricksburg[sic]. It was our troops trying to carry the heights. To give the reader an adequate idea of the work laid out for our men, just picture yourself a street a trifle wider than South street, Newburgh, with a rise of ground of about a mile, and on the heights a strong earthwork with guns in battery as close together as they could be worked, and each one commanding the approach for nearly a mile, and no way of getting to them but marching directly up in front. If it don't require some nerve to face that kind of music when they are fairly belching forth double charges of grape and canister, why, I am no judge of human nature. Three times our men went up the hill, only to be driven back. Once they reached the fortification, but with no way of crossing the ditch of scaling the earthwork, there they stood, under the murderous fire until ordered to withdraw, strewing the hillside with dead on their retreat worse than on the advance. At dark all became quiet and remained so all night, but was so cold we could not sleep.

Saturday, Dec. 13th. — At daylight as usual, when in front of the enemy, we were called in line, and stood under arms for an hour; we were then dismissed and got breakfast. About noon our batteries on the right commenced to shell the heights, which brought on an artillery duel, and was kept up at intervals all day. Just before sunset the First Jersey brigade, composed of the first

---

* Fredericksburg

four regiments from that state, engaged the enemy in front of us, and soon carried two lines of their works, some two miles south of Fredricksburg,[sic] but our men could not hold them, and were driven back with heavy loss. Then all became quiet, and we stacked arms for the night.

Sunday, Dec. 14th. — Before daylight we were on the alert. Soon after the first gun was fired on our right, and almost immediately the fight became fast and furious, as our men were making another desperate effort to carry the heights; but it was no use; human courage was of no avail. Entirely regardless of danger, our men moved up to the works, leaving a trail of dead behind them. Twice they reached the outer works, but with their numbers reduced to such an extent, they could not carry the works before them, so they had to retreat.

This was their last effort, but after their repulse our corps, the 6th, who with the exception of the First Jersey Brigade, did but little of the fighting since crossing the river, asked permission to try the works just once, and from the feeling of esprit de corps that was infused throughout the rank and file, I believe we would have been successful.

About 8 A.M. we were sent on picket, and stationed in front of the works that gave the Jerseymen such a warm reception yesterday. Gen. Bartlett, of our brigade, wished to try them again, but Gen. Burnside, seeming disheartened by his repulse at Fredricksburg,[sic] refused to let him attempt it; but we did the next best thing. We crawled up as near their works as we were allowed, and every head that came above their line of works, would receive a volley. At first they would answer us by one in return; soon, however, they found it did not pay to expose themselves, when they got down in their trenches and kept out of sight as much as possible. At dark our firing ceased and we remained quiet all night.

Monday, Dec. 15th. — Just before daylight the 96th Pennsylvania relieved us, when we moved back to the ravine and cooked our breakfast. Here we remained quiet all day. There was but little firing anywhere along our lines. At dark we put up our tents, and made ourselves as comfortable as possible, expecting to have a good night's sleep. Just at midnight, as we were quietly passing off to the land of dreams, orders came to move, and we packed up lively and moved back across the river, and camped near the bank. This ended the first battle of Fredericksburg[sic] under Gen. Burnside, that for dashing courage, stubborn bravery, and reckless sacrifice of life, had not been equaled from the commencement of the war up to this time.

Note: Westervelt depicts action at Fredericksburg as occurring on December 12. Actually, the main battle was on December 13; however, his report is picked up in the *History of the 27th Regiment.*

THE BATTLE OF FREDERICKSBURG

Notes — Chapter 13

1. Edward Pollard, *The Lost Cause* (New York: E.B. Treat & Co., 1866), pp. 341-342.

2. Johnson and Buel, *Battles and Leaders of the Civil War*, Vol. III, p. 78.

3. Ibid., p. 79.

4. Ibid., p. 84.

5. Ibid., p. 133.

6. Palfrey, *Campaigns of the Civil War, The Antietam and Fredericksburg*, p. 143.

7. Johnson and Buel, *Battles and Leaders of the Civil War*, Vol. III, p. 133.

8. Ibid., p. 134.

9. Palfrey, *Campaigns of the Civil War, the Antietam and Fredericksburg*, p. 143.

10. Ibid., p. 155.

11. Ibid., pp. 157-159.

12. *O.R.*, Vol XXI, p. 528.

13. Fairchild, *History of the 27th Regiment, N.Y. Vols.*, pp. 119-121.

14. *O.R.,* Vol. XXI, pp. 526-527.

15. Palfrey, *Campaigns of the Civil War, the Antietam and Fredericksburg*, p. 168.

16. Ibid.

17. Ibid.

18. Ibid., p. 174.

19. Guernsey and Alden, *Harper's Pictorial History of the Civil War*, p. 415.

20. Ibid., p. 416.

21. *O.R.*, Vol. XXI, p. 451.

22. Fairchild, *History of the 27th Regiment, N.Y. Vols.*, p. 121.

Chapter 14

WINTER QUARTERS NEAR FREDERICKSBURG

Background

From December 16, 1862, until January 20, 1863, the army was in winter quarters near Fredericksburg. During this time, the senior officers were bickering with each other; the men in the ranks were trying to make themselves as comfortable as possible.

Burnside states that he spent the initial period after the Battle of Fredericksburg refitting the Army of the Potomac and preparing for another movement against Lee. He ordered the movement on December 26.[1] However, Franklin and Smith had written Lincoln and their letter had reached him. Generals Cochrane and Newton had visited Lincoln, also. The VI Corps' officers had things in an uproar. On December 30, 1862, Lincoln wired Burnside and cancelled the attack.[2]

Perplexed and concerned about the situation, Lincoln wrote to Halleck on January 1, 1863, and directed him to go to Fredericksburg, gather information from all the senior officers, and approve or disapprove Burnside's plans.[3] Halleck's response was to resign.[4] Lincoln then withdrew his letter and Halleck stayed.[5]

Burnside then wrote to Halleck and asked for permission to attack Lee again.[6] Halleck responded with general advice on options plus a plea for action. He left it up to Burnside to decide the specific course of action to be taken.[7] Halleck's letter was dated January 7. The next day, Lincoln sent a letter to Burnside approving Halleck's advice. Thus the stage was set for Burnside's next move. He issued orders on January 19 for the army to move out on the twentieth.[8]

While these high-level activities were taking place, the men were doing their best to be comfortable and make the best of their situation. They constructed huts, boned up on their culinary arts, and visited with friends in the Army of the Potomac and even with the enemy troops across the river.

Highlights

There are three interesting highlights in this chapter of Westervelt's; one historic and two humorous.

1. Friendly Enemies: Westervelt was one of the first to fraternize with the enemy pickets across the Rappahannock River. The event is historic in that it led to friendships that were important during and after the war. Bruce Catton, in *Glory Road*, cited similar fraternizations between the 24th New Jersey and the 17th Mississippi.[9] He credits these meetings with helping the two sides reunite after the conflict was over.

2. Love Letters: The incidence of illiteracy among the troops in the Civil War was extremely high. Westervelt's story of the "friends" who helped the illiterate bridegroom write to his bride and Westervelt's rescue of the poor fellow is funny, but it wasn't funny to the victim.

3. <u>Crullers</u>: The story of the crullers is another example of Civil War humor. It illustrates what can happen when you have an idle soldier with an active mind.

Tuesday, Dec. 16th — The enemy having got a battery in position, began to shell our camp as soon as they could see. This caused us to pack up lively and move back out of range. Here we put up our tents and had a good day's rest. At dark we went on picket, on the bank of the river, and relieved the 2nd Regt. Pennsylvania Reserves, who cautioned us not to show ourselves, as the enemy would pick off anyone they could get a shot at. During the night we threw up some breastworks to protect us, and patiently waited for daylight.

Wednesday, Dec. 17th. — As soon as it was light enough, we found the enemy on the opposite bank, and by looking through a loop-hole in our breastworks, we could see they were carefully watching us, when without exposing myself I called out "Hello! Johnnie." The answer came back, "Hello! Yank." "Say, Johnnie, we won't fire if you won't!" "All right, we won't fire, unless the officer of the day comes and tells us to, and then we will fire high until you get under cover." Taking them at their word, we stepped from behind our works, when they did the same, and we both walked down close to the shore, where the river was not more than three or four rods wide, and commenced talking. We found they were the Texans whom we had fought at West Point in May, and Gaines' Mill in June. Soon we invited them to come across the river, and have a social time, with a promise that it should be all friendly, and they should return when they wished, without hindrance from us. They gave us the same invitation, and promise, and on both sides of the river a search was made for a boat. Soon one was found, and pushed off from the opposite side filled with Texans. On reaching our side of the river, we cordially shook them by the hand, and while some of our squad entertained them, some of our men got in the boat and crossed over to the rebel side, where we met with just as friendly a reception as we had given their comrades. While we could treat them to coffee, they could treat us to tobacco. The boat went back and forth all day. We had already found them brave men, and now found them to be of more intelligence than the ordinary southern soldier. We traded knives, pipes, rings, and other trinkets, and what was better we took the names of many of them, and they took our names, with a promise that if either were taken prisoners, we would either of us do what we could for the other, and before the war closed, there were several cases, where the promises made that day were faithfully carried out.

Just before dark we parted, after a general handshaking, as each one betook themselves to their own side of the river, ready to shoot each other at the word of command. Soon after dark we were relieved from picket, and moved back to our camp, where we remained two days, when we moved off to the left some five miles, and camped in a wood near White Oak Church. On the following day, the ever welcome paymaster put in his appearance, and soon disbursed four months' pay to the command. This was followed by the usual amount of drunkenness and gambling, that the officers did not make any effort to restrain, in fact so many indulged in these vices, that the minority who kept clear, were so few, that had they made any effort to stop it, such would have proved futile.

However, let each one speak for themselves. For my part I can say, what few can who wore the blue, and that is, I never touched a card for fun or money the whole four years I was in the service, and feel quite

Constructing Winter Quarters

positive my tentmate Truesdell, could say the same thing. Neither of us ever indulged in whiskey for the fun of drinking, but we sometimes took it when worn out by fatigue, or by the advice of our surgeon, during the first two years, but during the time I was with Sherman on all his marches, I never touched either wine or liquor. On those campaigns we suffered as much hardship as any part of our army, and I enjoyed as good health as ever before in my life; much better than those who drank whiskey, whenever they could get it, and today, I am just enough prohibitionist, to believe the Government should prohibit whiskey from the rank and file of the army, and navy, and in place of which, improve the rations of the private soldier; and the death rate from disease, and losses from desertion will decrease.

Soon after camping at White Oak Church, we received orders to make ourselves comfortable for the winter, as this would be our winter quarters. We had now sufficient experience to know about what was needed. We first selected a building site in our company street, where the ground rose quite abruptly, on a line with the street. Here, as there was a chance for good drainage, we dug into the bank, making a cellar the size we wished for our tent, digging it about a foot deep on the lower side and two and a half on the upper side, where we dug into the bank two feet square. That gave us a fire-place ready-made and a good start for a chimney, which we carried up a few feet further with split sticks, well plastered inside and out, with the tough Virginia clay, which is a good substitute for mortar. We next built a foundation of logs fitted together nicely, about two feet high, on the upper side, and brought up at the ends and lower side, even with it.

This gave us walls about four and a half feet high, and they were covered with shelter tents, that let in plenty of light; we then banked the logs and plastered them with clay that made them wind proof. Our cabin was abut six by seven feet, which any old soldier will say was an abundance of room for two. Our bed was just high enough from the ground to make a comfortable seat in front of the fireplace, as it took up about two-thirds of the cabin. It was made of pine, split thin enough to make a good spring bottom. We then gathered enough gunny bags from the forage train to make ticks, which were filled with straw. Our knapsacks and overcoats were our pillows and our two blankets our covering, that we thought then, was a bed good enough for a brigadier.

By the time our cabin was built and furnished, Christmas was close to us, and as the day drew near, we began to discuss the momentous questions of the ways and means of providing a Christmas dinner. We knew there was no show of anything to be had in the way of foraging, so we had to depend entirely on the commissary and sutler for the wherewithal. An inventory of our kitchen department showed that we possessed one pot, one frying pan, one cast iron bake oven, such as are common in the South, and are used by putting coals under and on the lid. This one we had borrowed from a farm house, and promised to return at the close of the war. In these, one can, with a little practice, bake pie or biscuit, or roast meat as well as in a range.

My chum was called away the day before, and on his return about noon on Christmas Day, I had a few choice friends invited and dinner ready. On each of the tin plates was a bill of fare that announced the following:

MENU
Roast Beef.   Dried Apple Sauce.
Pickles   a la Sutler.
Pod Vegetables.
Baked Beans - dressed with Saline
Rooter.
Berry Liquid.
Maracaibo Juice - hot and cold.
Dessert.
Dried Apple Pie, flavored with Commissary
vinegar and molasses.
EXTRAS.
Baked Clay Bowls - stuffed with
Virginia weed.
Wind Pudding.   Yarn Sauce.

Our dinner did not quite come up to the one we set out on Thanksgiving, but it had had more style, and what it lacked in grub, was more than made up by the good nature of our guests. Of course our tent was so small we could set no table; so each one curled himself up in one corner as small as possible, with his plate in his lap, while I, as master of ceremonies, occupied the center, and dispensed hospitality all around. How often now, as I look back over those rollicking days of the past, even when seated by a well-filled table and surrounded by friends, cultivated and refined, I wonder why I don't get the same amount of real, hearty enjoyment I had in the times of which I am writing. Then, heart and fancy free, with no family ties to bind me to life; no wife or children whose welfare, support and education is sure to rise up as the paramount object of life; nothing of the kind to trouble me, but with a determination to extract all the pleasure possible out of life as I went through it. I tried to look on the bright side of everything, and it was a dark day that did not afford some pleasure.

We remained quietly in this camp several weeks with nothing to disturb the monotony of camp life. We visited our friends in the different regiments, within a radius of ten miles of our camp, read all the books and papers we could get, wrote to all the girls we left behind us, and such letters—breathing eternal and everlasting constancy to them all —but that was one of the soldier's prerogatives. Well, if they believed it all, I am sorry for them. One job I had put upon me was not enviable. A private of our company went home and got married. On his return he of course wanted to hear from his new wife, but unfortunately he could not write, so he went from one to another to write for him. Some of them with an inexcusable love of mischief, would write one thing and read another to him, and soon got both him and his wife jealous of each other. Although I loved mischief as well as anyone, I thought this was going too far; so I set to work to straighten out this family tangle, and soon succeeded, but not until I had learned more of married life than I ever knew before. My chum, one of the best fellows living, resigned the culinary department to me, while he, always willing to do his part, would provide wood and water, or do any-thing else required. At one time during this winter we, growing tired of government rations, put our heads together to study up something new. I suggested crullers, and then, as in many other new dishes, we both tried to remember what we had seen our mothers use and how they were put together. We knew flour, sugar, and lard were three indispensable articles; the two former we got from the commissary, while the third was got by procuring a lot of fat salt pork and extracting the grease. We then remembered we had seen milk and eggs used; these we could not get, but the omission of these trifles were of no account to a soldier, and one day while alone in the tent I deteremined to try my hand. So mixing up a batch of flour, sugar, water and soda, I concluded I had about the proper thing. I left out the shortening, thinking that cooking them in grease would make them short enough. Then, taking a long black bottle, such as we generally found plenty of about the officers' quarters, for a rolling pin, with a board on our bed for a table, I soon had things in working order, and in a short time had quite a box full of them done, and taking up one to try it I found that in leaving out the shortening I had the toughest lot of cakes that was possible to make. By taking one end in my teeth and the other in my hands they would stretch like a piece of gutta percha. To say I was disappointed and chagrined, would not half express it. I felt like a woman who prides herself on cooking, and when company comes to tea finds the biscuits soggy and cake heavy; but as Truisdell said, there's no use grieving, so let's have what fun we can out of them. So opening the door of our cabin, with a plate of them in my hand, I called to the men in our company street to come and we would treat them all to crullers. Soon each of them had one, vainly trying to tear it apart. They looked all right and the men came to me to explain why they were so tough. That I gravely accounted for from the fact that in the hurry of putting them together, I got the shortening in lengthwise, which made all the trouble. But the comparison as "tough as the corporal's crullers," stuck to me as long as the regiment was together.

Our quiet camp life at White Oak Church was not disturbed by any great amount of duty. All sorts of rumors filled the air—of a raid here, or a flank movement in some other direction; but we continued to enjoy ourselves in our snug winter quarters until the night of January 19th, when, just as we were undressed for the night—that is, our caps, shoes and coats off, as this was the extent of our disrobing— orders came to move the next morning. We lay awake a long while discussing what the intended move would be, and finally fell asleep with the question still unsolved.

Notes — Chapter 14

1. *O.R.*, Vol. XXI, p. 95.

2. Ibid., p. 96.

3. Ibid., p. 940.

4. Ibid., pp. 940-941.

5. Ibid., p. 941 (footnote).

6. Guernsey and Alden, *Harper's Pictorial History of the Civil War*, p. 416.

7. *O.R.*, Vol XXI, p. 954.

8. Ibid.

9. Catton, *Glory Road*, pp. 263-264.

Chapter 15

THE MUD MARCH

Background

On the morning of January 20, 1863, the army started to move. Burnside directed Franklin's and Hooker's Grand Divisions to lead the attack; Franklin crossing the Rappahannock just below Banks' Ford, and Hooker crossing just above it.[1] The crossings were to take place at 7:30 A.M. on January 21.[2]

The troops were marched up the river by parallel roads and were screened from the enemy across the river by the intervening heights.[3] The march on the twentieth went well; the weather was cold but pleasant. The *History of the 27th N.Y.* states, "Scarcely had night arrived, when a storm arose, a storm in earnest. The wind blew a gale and rocked the trees spitefully. The night was very dark. The rain soon dissolved the crust that had borne us up all day. The tent-pins would not hold, and down came the tents. The wheels of the artillery and wagons settled into the oozing muck, hours before an attempt was made to move them."[4]

By the twenty-first, two things had happened; first, the mud made it impossible to move the army, and second, the element of surprise was gone for the enemy was fully aware of the army's movements. On that day, General Woodbury of the Engineers was telling Burnside, "The rain has prevented surprise...It seems to me the part of prudence to abandon the present effort, not only because the enemy must be aware of our intention, but because the roads are everywhere impassable."[5] Lee was, in fact, well aware of Burnside's attempt for in his report he states that on the nineteenth he knew Burnside was massing troops for a move and he promptly "strengthened and re-enforced" his positions at Banks' and United States Mine Fords.[6]

Finally Burnside saw the light, and on January 22, he issued orders to Franklin and Hooker to "withdraw their commands."[7] Franklin was ordered to detail a division to guard the pontoon trains; the job was given to General Brooks' Division, including, of course, the 27th New York.[8]

By the twenty-third, the weather had improved some; the men were in fine spirits—rations were in short supply and whiskey was substituted for rations.[9] The men were beginning to laugh at their predicament, and they were also being ridiculed by the Confederates across the river.[10]

The 27th New York spent Saturday, the twenty-fourth, pulling pontoons out of the mud. An incident in the Regimental History tells it all:

At one time, when we were all tugging away at the ropes, a spruce young officer rode up, dressed in bright uniform, with white gauntlets, and, in a preemptory tone, ordered some of the men to pull harder, — when a man who had hold of one of the ropes, and was dressed in an old blouse, with a slouch hat, looked around over his shoulder, and said "Who are you, any way?" "I am Lieut. Hunter, in command of the engineers." "Well, I am Major-Gen. Brooks, in command of this division, and I order you to get down from that horse and take hold of the rope with these men." And down he had to come, saluted by a derisive cheer from the men; and the boys soon had his new uniform well spattered with mud.[11]

THE MUD MARCH

At dark Sunday night, January 25, Westervelt and his comrades were back in their old quarters, glad to be released from the grip of the cold, the wet, and the mud.

Highlights

Two items are of note in this chapter.

1. <u>The Weather</u>: To repeat, it is difficult to imagine today the weather the troops encountered in Virginia during that winter of 1862-63. It was so cold that Confederate sentries froze on the picket line. Then the rains of January 21 and 22 turned the ground into a sea of mud. It is possible to find this situation in northern New England now at the end of March or the first of April; but in eastern Virginia in January—never!

2. <u>The Confederates' Attitude</u>: Westervelt resented the ridicule of the Confederates, and this posture is found in most Northern reports of "The Mud March." Just how much this contributed to a resolve on the part of Westervelt and others to "get even" we'll never know, but it must have had some effect upon his re-enlisting in the fall of 1863.

THE MUD MARCH

Tuesday, Jan. 20th. — As soon as our breakfast was over we dismantled our cabin of its canvas roof, as it had to serve us for a tent on our march, and about noon bid a sorrowful adieu to our comfortable quarters and started on a march. From the direction we traveled it looked as though we intended to once more strike Fredricksburg, but were taking a roundabout way, as though a flank movement was contemplated. After going some twelve miles we camped in the woods, and tried to make ourselves as comfortable as possible; but as it rained all night we wished ourselves back to our comfortable cabins at White Oak.

Wednesday, Jan. 21st. — When we got up we found that the ground, which the night before was so hard we could scarce drive a tent pin, from the effects of the night's rain, was now like an immense bed of mortar. As soon as the teams attempted to move the mud grew deeper. Soon after daylight we packed our wet tents and blankets, which made a load heavy enough to discourage a mule. With these loads on our backs, and the mud over the tops of our shoes, we marched about five miles and camped. The rain continued to fall all day and night.

Thursday, Jan. 22d. — Storm still continued; we remained in camp; heard the intended move was given up, and an effort was now to be made to get the pontoon train and artillery on some high ground out of the mud. Rations grew short, and the men were each given a gill of whiskey in place of food.

Friday, Jan. 23d. — Clear and warm. We made some large log fires and dried our clothes and blankets for the first time since the night of the 20th. In the afternoon we packed up and moved about a mile, to a place where our pontoon train was stuck in the mud. Here the wagons were sunk in the mud to the axles,

and the drivers were vainly trying to get them out. The more mules they attached to them the worse they were off, as the animals would sink down to their bodies, and there floundered about in this semi-liquid, while the drivers, who were noted the world over for their proficiency in profanity, would get off their whole catalogue of oaths, with many new combinations invented for the occasion; but it was no use. Twenty pair of mules could not start one of them, and finally, in despair, the mules were unharnessed. Some of them had to be pulled out of the mud, for they could not extricate themselves. As the weather was clear we did not put up our tents, but spread them on the ground under us, which made a comfortable bed, and we enjoyed our first good night's sleep since starting.

Saturday, Jan. 24th. — Our whole division was detailed to pull the pontoons out of the mud. It was done by fastening a long rope on each side of the wagons, and from one to two hundred men would take hold of each rope, and at a given signal we would start and draw them up a hill to some high ground where they were parked and left for the mud to settle. This gave us a hard, dirty day's work. About dark the last boat was drawn out, while we, looking as though we had been buried in the mud and dug out again, went into camp. It rained most of the night.

Sunday, Jan. 25th. — Just before daylight the rain ceased, and we made some roaring fires and dried our tents and blankets, for we expected to march, and wished to reduce the weight as much as possible. About nine A.M. we started on our way back to our old camp at White Oak Church. The roads were very muddy, but we went right across the country, keeping on high ground as much as

The Campaign in the Mud

possible, while the men were allowed to march at will, and pick their way as well as possible. Still it was hard traveling, and when we reached our cabin at dark we were very tired. Here, through a mistaken kindness, the men were given all the whiskey they could drink, that instead of doing them good set some of them fighting, and they committed acts that they would have gladly recalled the next day. My tentmate and myself were so tired we thought a good bed better than whiskey, and we were soon wrapped in our blankets and dreaming of drawing pontoon canal boats through a canal of mud, with mules as drivers, who were cracking their whips over our backs and visiting us with all the oaths in a canal driver's vernacular, while we with heavy knapsacks on our backs were trying to escape over a muddy, slippery towpath.

This ended the march that has gone down to history under the name of "Burnside's Stick in the Mud." It was the second unsuccessful attempt to capture Fredricksburg, that still held out against us, while the enemy's pickets would tauntingly call across the Rappahannock to our pickets and ask, "When are you coming over again?" "Have you got your mules out of the mud?" But we quietly bided our time knowing the place would eventually fall into our hands; but we knew, too, that there was some hard fighting to be done to capture it, and many of us would lose the number of his mess before we occupied it.

THE MUD MARCH

Notes — Chapter 15

1. *O.R.*, Vol. XXI, pp. 78-79.

2. Ibid.

3. Guernsey and Alden, *Harper's Pictorial History of the Civil War*, p. 417.

4. Fairchild, *History of the 27th Regiment, N.Y. Vols.*, pp. 134-135.

5. *O.R.*, Vol. XXI, p. 989.

6. Ibid., p. 755.

7. Ibid., p. 994.

8. Ibid., p. 999.

9. Fairchild, *History of the 27th Regiment, N.Y. Vols.*, p. 135.

10. Catton, *Glory Road*, pp. 274-275.

11. Fairchild, *History of the 27th Regiment, N.Y. Vols.*, p. 136.

Chapter 16

IN WINTER QUARTERS AGAIN

Background

From January 25, until April 27, 1863, the 27th New York was back in winter quarters doing all the routine things soldiers do when in camp. In the upper echelons of the Army of the Potomac, events were hardly routine; the leaders were erupting and changes were being made.

Burnside had had enough carping from his senior officers. On January 23, he prepared Orders No. 8, dismissing Hooker from the service and ordering Franklin to report to Washington for reassignment elsewhere. VI Corps officers also affected were:

Smith, VI Corps Commander — Reassignment
Brooks, First Division — Dismissed from service
Newton, Third Division — Dismissed from service
Cochraine, First Brigade, Third Division — Dismissed from service

In addition, three IX Corps officers were to be sent to Washington for reassignment.[1]

Burnside took the order to the president for approval, saying in effect, "They go or I go." The president reacted by making Hooker head of the Army of the Potomac and relieving both Burnside and Franklin from duty with that army.[2]

Plaintively writing in his report of his service as commander of the Army of the Potomac, Burnside said:

> I made four distinct attempts, between November 9, 1862, and January 25, 1863. The first failed for want of pontoons; the second was the battle of Fredericksburg; the third was stopped by the President, and the fourth was defeated by the elements and other causes.[3]

Major General John Sedgwick was named the new commander of the VI Corps; Brooks remained as head of the First Division, Bartlett as head of the Second Brigade, and Adams as head of the 27th New York Regiment. Westervelt, at this time, had two new leaders (Hooker and Sedgwick) and three old ones (Brooks, Bartlett, and Adams).

One of the improvements Hooker initiated was a system of furloughs. Westervelt went on ten days' leave (or furlough) on February 11. He did not enjoy his time off and returned to camp before his leave expired.

The other events in this period of time were routine for Westervelt, except for participating in a review (parade) for President Lincoln. Westervelt had seen Lincoln three times before: first at Bailey's Cross Roads in Virginia on November 20, 1861;[4] second, at Harrison's Landing in Virginia on July 8, 1862;[5] and third, at Sharpsburg, Maryland on October 4, 1862.[6] As Westervelt indicates, the review at Fredericksburg was the last time he saw the president.

IN WINTER QUARTERS AGAIN

<u>Highlights</u>

Three additional items are worthy of note in this chapter.

1. <u>Firewood</u>: The soldiers used firewood for cooking, for heat, and for light. To them, firewood meant survival. With 120,000 men requiring the necessity over a period of time, wood became scarce, and the supply became farther and farther away from camp. Small wonder then that Westervelt made such a issue of the theft of his firewood and that he developed an ingenious way to catch the thief who was stealing it.

2. <u>Going Home</u>: Near the end of April, the men of the 27th New York were thinking about going home. Their two years of service would be up on May 21, 1863. The report of their discussions about fighting or refusing to fight after that date reveals the tenor of the thoughts of the men at that time. Their reactions are significant when considered in the light of events involving the 1st New York which are reported in the next chapter.

3. <u>Baseball</u>: Westervelt refers to organizing "a baseball nine" in March. Another New Yorker, Major General Abner Doubleday, is credited with originating the game.[7] The Civil War was the starting point for the game as we know it today. "Both Rebs and Yanks played early versions of baseball."[8]

On our return from Burnside's mud march we spent a few days fixing up our cabin and putting things in order for housekeeping once more. About this time my tentmate, Truisdell, received a box of provisions and clothing from home, and when it was opened in our cabin, I found myself not forgotten, there being the same for me as for him— flannel shirts, woolen mittens and socks. This may seem like a trifling thing to mention, but it was these trifling remembrances that brightened the soldiers' lives more than anything else, and these coming from his folks, whom I had never seen, showed at least that my name was known in his far off northern home.

On February 11th I started for Washington on a ten days' leave, and the next night found me at the Central Hotel, where I undressed and slept in a bed for the first time in twenty months. I remained in the city five days, and getting homesick returned to camp. This was the first and only furlough I had while in the service. We now settled down to the routine of camp life, doing as little duty as possible and spending our time in keeping up our large correspondence, playing back-gammon and visiting among our friends in the different regiments and in receiving company at our cabin. The latter afforded us more amusement than anything else. Our invitations were sure to be accepted, and often added to the invitation would be—and bring your plate, knife and fork with you. Sometimes we went out for a four days' tour of picket duty, and if the weather was fine it would vary the monotony of camp life quite pleasantly.

About the first of March the weather began to be more pleasant, and we organized a baseball nine. Nearly every day we would measure our strength with some other nine of the brigade, and of course we met our share of defeats; but it was a good thing for us. We had sat idly in our tents and cabins all winter, until we had become fleshy, our muscles softened, and our strength weakened, and were in poor shape generally for a spring campaign. We therefore needed just such sharp exercise to put us in condition. Another thing gave us considerable exercise, and that was providing ourselves with wood. When our camp was formed in December, it was in a heavy pine wood, extending for miles in every direction.

We used a good many trees building our cabins and winter quarters, and for a while would build huge log fires in our streets each night. Soon wood began to get scarce and had to be carried some distance, and this distance gradually increased until now, about the middle of March, all we used had to be carried at least two miles. This made us practice economy. In some places where the trees had been cut high, we took the second crop off the stumps and even dug out the roots where it was easy digging. We got but little at a time, as it was not safe to leave any out doors at night, for some found it easier to steal it than carry it from the woods.

After suffering from the depredations of the wood fiends for some time, we thought to set a trap for them, and did, that they walked right into. A small pile of wood was cut up and partly concealed behind a tent, but hid away so it could be easily found. In the pile was one stick that looked like any of the others, but had any one examined it very closely a plug would have been found in the end that was smoothed off, it being very hard to detect. Beneath this plug, or in the centre of the stick, was the powder from about a dozen cartridges. In the morning the wood was gone, and having a strong suspicion of

The Grand Review at Falmouth during President Lincoln's Visit

which cabin it went into, we waited results, and they came sooner than we expected. As we stood in the company street at morning roll call, there came a loud report, with a concussion in the air, that was instantly filled with sticks, clay and other parts of a cabin chimney, with a frying pan and half cooked breakfast; and looking round we found the whole chimney and one side of a cabin entirely demolished, while inside still greater havoc had been wrought. Perhaps half of our company were in the street, and as the stick exploded a shout went up, "that's the man who stole the wood," and the unenviable sobriquet, "wood thief," hung to the man the remainder of our term of service.

General Hooker had now re-lieved General Burnside as commander of the Army of the Potomac, and was followed by the usual number of reviews. On the 3d of April our division was reviewed on our parade ground by Generals Hooker and Slocum. On the 8th our whole corps, the 6th, marched to General Hooker's headquarters and were reviewed by General Hooker and President Lincoln. That was the last time I ever saw President Lincoln. On the 14th orders came to move and we received sixty rounds of cartridges and ten days' rations; but for some unknown reason the move was postponed.

The first thirty-eight regiments of New York state troops were enlisted for two years, and their time had now nearly expired. Most of them were in the Army of the Potomac, and there was considerable discussion among the men whether they would be asked to do any fighting after their time was out. Men who had never flinched from duty or danger declared that they would do no duty after their time expired, and it was very clear that the Government had no right to ask it. Our regiment, the 27th, being among the number, we began to count the days that intervened between us and home.

Saturday, April 25th. — Pay-master arrived and disbursed four months' pay to the men.

Sunday, April 26th. — The usual amount of gambling that always followed pay day took place, and was carried on openly in our company streets; the officers made no effort to stop it, and in fact some of them took a hand at the game. Before night some of the men had lost all their money. For the men themselves we had no pity; but for their families who needed all they could send them, we felt really sorry, and often wondered what flimsy excuse they could get up to write in place of sending money.

IN WINTER QUARTERS AGAIN

Notes — Chapter 16

1. *O.R.*, Vol. XXI, pp. 998-999.

2. Ibid., pp. 1004-1005.

3. Ibid., p. 96.

4. Fairchild, *History of the 27th Regiment, N.Y. Vols.*, p. 26.

5. Ibid., p. 82.

6. Ibid., p. 97.

7. Warner, *Generals in Blue* (Ann Arbor, Michigan: Louisiana University Press, Cushin-Mallory, Inc., 1964), pp. 131-132.

8. Bell I. Wiley, *The Common Soldier of the Civil War* (Jamestown, Virginia: Eastern Acorn Press, 1987), p. 47.

Chapter 17

CHANCELLORSVILLE

Background

April 1863 saw the Army of the Potomac on the march again. Hooker's plan 1) was to attack Lee's right below Fredericksburg with three corps: Sedgwick's VI, Sickles' III, and Reynold's I, 2) attack Lee's left by crossing the upper fords of the Rappahannock River with four corps: Couch's II, Meade's V, Howard's XI, and Slocum's XII, thereby fighting the battle on ground of Hooker's choosing, and 3) send the cavalry under Stoneman to destroy the railways, trains, and supplies to cripple Lee's retreat.[1]

To carry out this assault, Hooker had 110,000 infantry and artillery, plus 11,000 cavalry against Lee's estimated 55,000-60,000, excluding cavalry.[2]

The Federal cavalry under Stoneman started out on April 13, 1863, to carry out the first phase of the operations. It returned to its camps after two days—the rains wrecked that part of the plan.

Then, on April 27, the march against Lee's left started.[3] The following day, the twenty-eighth, the VI, I, and III Corps moved to Franklin's Crossing (named for the location of General Franklin's pontoon bridges during the Battle of Fredericksburg in December 1862). The VI Corps was opposite Deep Run; the I Corps was a mile farther down the river, and the III Corps was in the rear between the two.[4]

Sedgwick's move was intended to lead Lee to think that the main attack would come from below Fredericksburg. Brook's Division crossed the river in boats on April 29, led by the Third Brigade under Russell, and the 27th New York and 16th New York of the Second Brigade.[5] Others crossed later on the pontoon bridges.

This was one of four engagements the 27th New York was in from April 28-May 5. The first was Franklin's Crossing on April 28-30; the second was Marye's Heights or Second Fredericksburg on May 3; the third was Salem Church or Salem Heights on May 3, also; and the fourth was Banks' Ford on the night of May 4.

After the 27th New York crossed the river on April 29, it spent most of its time until May 2 in the first or second line facing the enemy.[6]

The move across the upper fords was made without opposition and was completed by nightfall on the thirtieth. Hooker and his senior officers were elated—they had Lee caught between the two Federal forces; one at Chancellorsville and the other at Fredericksburg.[7]

On the thirtieth, also, Hooker detached Sickles' III Corps from Sedgwick and moved that organization up the river to join the major part of the army.

Lee correctly discerned that Sedgwick's move against his right was a feint and that the main attack would come from near Chancellorsville. He left Early's Division and Barksdale's Brigade (about 10,000 men) to watch Sedgwick while he moved the rest of his army to face Hooker.[8]

After advancing past Chancellorsville on May 1, Meade, Howard, and Slocum were ordered back. Hooker had gone on the defense and had given up high ground and open space.[9] At this point, Couch who commanded the Second Corps concluded, "My commanding general was a whipped man."[10]

CHANCELLORSVILLE

Lee then went on the offensive. He split his army again in the face of the enemy, and with only a token force in front of Hooker, sent Jackson with about 30,000 men around Hooker's right flank to fall upon Howard's XI Corps.

On May 2, Hooker withdrew Reynold's I Corps from Sedgwick; now Hooker had more than 90,000 men and Sedgwick had 22,000.[11]

Jackson attacked Howard on May 2 and routed his corps. The rest of the army near Chancellorsville was essentially intact. That night at 11:00 P.M., Sedgwick received an order from Hooker directing him to cross the Rappahannock at Fredericksburg and to be in the vicinity of Hooker near Chancellorsville at daylight![12] This involved rousing 22,000 men, getting them in line of march including crossing the river for some, brushing aside the 10,000 Confederates in their way, and traveling 12 miles in 7 hours!

When he received the order, Sedgwick and his command group plus some of his men, including the 27th New York, were actually across the river below Fredericksburg. Part of his corps had to cross the river to join him. Thus, on May 3, the VI Corps fought its way through Fredericksburg, taking Marye's Heights by storm and moved to Salem Church. When it reached that point, Early's men moved in behind it. Lee held Hooker at bay with a small part of his force and turned his full attention to Sedgwick. The fighting was furious and the losses severe.

The 27th New York acted as rear guard as the VI Corps moved through Fredericksburg.[13] Near Salem Church the regiment was drawn up across the road to stop stragglers from the battle and to enable the broken lines coming from the fighting to reform.[14]

On the morning of the fourth, Sedgwick received a dispatch from Hooker telling him, in effect, that he was on his own. Hooker had withdrawn all of the rest of his forces to a place of safety and by 2:00 A.M. of the fifth had the major portion of the Army of the Potomac back across the river.[15] At 11:45 P.M. on the fourth, Hooker ordered Sedgwick to "Withdraw. Cover the river..."[16] Sedgwick crossed the VI Corps over the river before daylight on the fifth, lucky to have escaped. The 27th New York had the job of holding the line until the rest of Brook's Division was well on its way to Banks' Ford.

Westervelt's account reveals the feelings of the enlisted men about Hooker's lack of support to the VI Corps. Hooker's trait of fading at the wrong moment in a poker game carried over into his generalship at Chancellorsville. Even the enlisted men knew that Hooker had failed when he could have won.

The Federal losses at Chancellorsville were staggering—a total of 16,735[17] or 14% of its strength. The VI Corps lost 4,590 or 21%; Bartlett's Brigade lost 612 or 39%. The 27th New York was fortunate in that its assignments kept it out of the major part of the attack at Salem Church. Its loss was only 19.

The crowning insult was for Hooker to attribute his defeat at Chancellorsville to the failure of Sedgwick to join him on Sunday morning, May 3. Swinton, a noted correspondent and author on the Civil War, called this "a cruel charge to bring against a commander, now beyond the reach of detraction, whose brilliant exploit in carrying the Fredericksburg Heights, and his subsequent fortitude in a trying situation, shine out as the one relieving brightness amid the gloom of that hapless battle."[18] (Note: General Sedgwick was killed in battle on May 10, 1864.)

CHANCELLORSVILLE

Highlights

Four things are worthy of note in this chapter:

1. The Boat Ride: The 27th New York was one of the few regiments sent across the Rappahannock in boats on April 29 to establish a bridgehead so that two pontoon bridges could be built. Westervelt's company was one of the first to row across the Rappahannock and capture the breastworks. He tells what it felt like to cross the River and clamber up a steep bank, all in the face of enemy fire.

2. Competition — Regulars vs. Volunteers: Two bridges were built at the crossing; one by regular army men and one by volunteers. The competition was hot and heavy; the volunteers won —to the satisfaction of the onlookers, most of whom were volunteers also.

3. The First New York: Westervelt describes in detail the plight of the First New York Volunteers whose members initially refused to fight because their enlistments, according to Westervelt, had expired. This incident is not covered in standard histories of the Civil War. Hayman, the brigade commander, states in his report, "The First New York was brought into action under peculiar circumstances, and its conduct more than realized my expectations."[19] Lieutenant Colonel Leland, who commanded the First New York, wrote in his report, "I would respectfully call attention to the fact that the regiment was on the eve of being mustered out of the service when the movement commenced, its term of service having nearly expired, and that it fought well and lost heavily in all the battles and skirmishes in which the brigade was engaged."[20] The brigade lost 3 killed, 18 wounded, and 59 missing or captured at Chancellorsville, a total of 80.[21] Westervelt saw the situation from an enlisted man's point of view and judged it on the basis of fairness as he perceived it. The other side of the coin was that Hooker was motivated by the fact that the terms of enlistment of 40,000 of his army were about to expire.[22] His situation was similar to McDowell's in July 1861. Had the First New York refused to fight and the remainder of the 40,000 followed, Hooker would have been certain to fail.

4. Tactics: This is one of the few places that Westervelt discusses tactics—in this case, falling back to Banks' Ford under enemy fire. His comments must have met his comrades' and superiors' acceptance for they are repeated verbatim in the *Regimental History of the 27th New York*.[23]

The next day orders came to move on the day following. I therefore sent most of my funds North, as it was evident a fight was close at hand and if I fell into the enemy's hands I did not mean to be a very rich prize to my captors.

April 28th. — Part of our regiment went on picket, and the remainder of us marched at 3 P.M. After going about five miles we halted near Falmouth until midnight, when the picket party joined us, and we were promised some warm work in the morning.

Wednesday, April 29th. — At 1 A.M. we were called in line and marched to our pontoon train. Here, as many as could take hold of the side of a boat, were placed on each side, and picking up the boat we started for the river. A short march brought us to the bank, where by some misunderstanding of orders, we were halted and kept waiting until daybreak, when we were ordered to launch the boats, row across and drive the enemy from their rifle pits on the opposite side, that would enable our engineers to put down the pontoon bridge. I don't pretend to know where rests the responsibility of delaying us until it was light enough for the enemy to use us for target practice; but it looked like criminal imbecility somewhere, for we were all ready to go several hours before we were ordered, and with darkness to favor us our task would have been comparatively easy and our loss light.

Finally, just as daylight tinged the eastern sky, the order was given, and quickly the boats were pushed into the water, filled with men, the oar manned, and we started. No sooner did we start than the enemy opened fire, and we being packed so close in the boats could hardly return it; but if we ever pulled an oar we did then, and in less time than it takes to write this, we reached the opposite side of the Rappahannock river. Here a new difficulty presented itself. A bank about twenty feet high was before us, and so steep we could only ascend by catching hold of some small trees and bushes and pulling ourselves up, and this we had to do in the face of the sharpest fire the enemy could deliver. By the time we reached the top we were the maddest set of men the Army of the Potomac ever turned loose, and made very short work of capturing the enemy's works and about all the troops it contained. Very few tried to escape, and those who did had a long, level plain to cross, and were exposed all the way to our fire; consequently not many of them got away.

The engineers now came up, and as there were two bridges to put down one was given to the regulars and the other to the 15th N.Y. Vol. Engineers. There always was a strife between these two branches of the service—the volunteers and the regulars—and here was a chance to test their skill. Each bridge was about the same length and the facilities for working about as near equal as could be. So from the start it was a race to see which could complete their work first. They had plenty of spectators, as the army on either bank were watching their movements, and this served as an incentive for them both to do their best. Boats were quickly anchored, and the men who carried the string pieces and plank would not think of walking; but while carrying their load, or returning empty, would run their best. The morning was cool, but the sweat ran off their faces. Still they kept on, willing to make this a test case—of the regulars or volunteers.

CHANCELLORSVILLE

In one hour and ten minutes the first bridge was completed, and the volunteers had won the day by nearly six minutes. This was received with hearty cheers by thousands who lined the banks on either side. The troops and artillery now began to pass over and move off to the left, where cannonading soon commenced and continued at intervals all day. In front of us it was very quiet and during the afternoon we had some showers. Toward dark we threw up some rifle pits and remained behind them all night.

Thursday, April 30. — We remained quietly behind our rifle pits all day, and while the troops were moving to the right, preparing for a desperate fight at Chancellorsville, we were drawn up in line and mustered as quietly as though we were in camp. After dark we were sent on picket, as it was deemed unsafe to change the pickets in daylight. Our company was placed on the outpost, and were very keenly alert all night. At daylight the next morning we could see the enemy moving about on the heights in front of us, where they were partly hidden by the bushes and trees; but as they showed no disposition to fire upon us we showed them the same respect, and remained very quiet all day. Soon after dark the 32d New York relieved us and we moved back to the rifle pits and spent the night.

Saturday, May 2d. — About 8 A.M. the enemy got a battery in position and got good range of us where we lay behind a bank. This made us pack up lively and move to a more sheltered position. Soon the troops on our left recrossed the river and moved off to the right to join Gen. Hooker, who was now fighting the battle of Chancellorsville, some six miles distant "air line," but was twice that distance the way the troops had to move. We could plainly hear the continual roar of artillery,

and sometimes when the air was favorable the sound of musketry would reach us, and convinced us of the fact that some hard fighting was going on, and we anxiously awaited results. Looking back to the north side of the Rappahannock we could see a regiment with a guard around them. At first we thought they were rebel prisoners, but on inquiry we found they were the 1st New York, whose time of enlistment having expired, had refused to cross the river. And now, after the lapse of nearly a quarter of a century, we can look back and quietly judge whether the 1st New York did right or not. They had volunteered to serve two years and had served their time; had never flinched from duty or danger; had taken part in the battles of Big Bethel, Peach Orchard, Glendale, Malvern Hill, Bull Run and Chantilly; they had faithfully performed their part of the contract, and now only asked the government to perform their's, and for asking this were put under guard, with orders to feed them on bread and water until they gave up.

I don't know what general officer gave this order, but whoever it was attached to his name a worse disgrace than the stigma of traitor that accompanies the name of Jeff Davis; and then, finding they could not be starved into submission, a resort was made to deception, and the regiment was promised that if they would cross the river the only duty they would be asked to perform would be guarding rebel prisoners. To this most of them agreed, but no sooner did they reach the front than they were ordered to charge a battery—which was another black spot upon the escutcheon of some officer—while those who refused to go were sent to the Dry Tortugas, and kept at hard labor nearly a year, in company with the worst and vilest felons that were ever sent from our army.

Is it any wonder that draft riots followed a few weeks after, and the streets of New York ran red with innocent blood, when the officers, representing the government, would stoop to violating the contract with the men and then punish them for asking for their rights?

It is fortunate that I am writing this in '86 instead of '63, or Fort Lafayette would be waiting for me.

About dark the firing in the direction of Chancellorsville nearly ceased, and we quietly went into camp and slept soundly until midnight.

Sunday, May 3d. — At one A.M. we were called and ordered to pack up ready to march, and we soon moved to the front. About four A.M. the troops on our right moved up and charged the works at Fredricksburg,* or as it is known, Marye's Heights. As the garrison had been reduced to aid Lee at Chancellorsville, it was not found as impregnable as when our men tried them in December last; still with but a small force to hold them they proved hard to capture. Once our men were driven back, but rallying they charged again, and after some desperate fighting and a heavy loss, our men succeeded in getting inside. Even then they had to fight the rebel artillerymen away from their guns, who seemed determined not to surrender, and did not until they were actually overpowered and out-numbered by our men, who finally got possion† of their works.

About sunrise the enemy opened on us with shell from their fortifications, south of Fredricksburg [sic], and we moved forward into the same ravine that sheltered us when

---

* Fredericksburg

† possession

here on the 13th of last December. Here we hurried through our breakfast, as we were told there was some work waiting for us. Soon after we again fell in and moved to the front. On our way out the enemy opened on us with shell, which went tearing through the air overhead, and made us do some lively dodging. Gen. Bartlett and staff stood near us, and the enemy tried to train one of their guns on the group; soon they had range but their shots were a trifle high. Gen. Bartlett stood watching the guns with his glass, and as the shells came over, but a few feet about their heads, the staff officers would involuntarily get down close to the ground, but the general, with his glass to his eyes, would not seem to move an inch, and showed a perfect control of his nerves and muscles.

We soon reached the front, and occupied the first line, when the enemy opened on us, and we replied, keeping up a lively firing until about 3 P.M., when the enemy, having evacuated Fredericksburg, soon withdrew from our front. We then fell in, and marched to Fredericksburg, and up through the town, where the dead and wounded showed the desperate fighting that had taken place before the heights were captured. We passed the fortifications, and went about three miles in the direction of Chancellorsville, and arrived just as our Division engaged the enemy. Here the fighting was furious, but from some misunderstanding of Col. Adams, our commanding officer, we did not get into the thickest of the fight.

It was here the 121st New York, of our Brigade, received their first fiery baptism, and nobly did they acquit themselves. Col. Upton, their commander, had spent the winter previous making a regiment of them. He had weeded out all the waste timber among the officers, and made many promotions from the

The Stone Wall at Marye's Heights

ranks, until he prided himself on having as good a regiment of volunteers as there were in the service. He led them into the heaviest of the fight; his horse was killed under him, and even the visor of his cap was partly cut off by a rifle bullet. His regiment suffered heavily, and finally withdrew a few rods, when he, having procured another horse, rode over to a battery he had formerly commanded, and amused himself until dark sending shot and shell into the woods, where the enemy were supposed to be massing their troops. As the slaughter had been terrible, the stretcher bearers were busy all night caring for the wounded, and as we lay down behind our stacks of guns, ready to spring into line at a moment's notice, our sleep was light, and all night long we could hear the grinding of the ambulance wheels on the roads, as they moved back and forth, filled with their bleeding, suffering loads of wounded. The dead were left unburied on the field.

Monday, May 4th. — At four A. M. we were called in line and stood until daylight. We then cooked breakfast and soon after moved off to a ravine. It was not long before the enemy caught sight of us and sent over a few shells that made us hug the ground. They came uncomfortably near, but we suffered no casualties. At ten A.M. we went on picket. No sooner had we taken our positions than the enemy advanced and we had a lively skirmish; they then withdrew and all remained quiet until about five P.M. when they advanced on our left, recaptured the heights of Fredericksburgh [sic]; and nearly surrounded us. Soon word was passed down our line that the enemy were advancing on us in line of skirmishers, with sharpshooters in their lead. We were then ordered to fall back, which we did in line of skirmishers, fighting as we went. The front rank would fall back while the rear

would load and fire; then the rear rank would pass to the rear of the front rank. Thus we fell back, fighting our way for two or three miles above Fredericksburgh [sic]. Here we found the troops crossing on a pontoon bridge.

Soon after midnight we crossed over, and after marching some five miles we went into camp near the river, and thus ended the second attempt to capture Fredericksburgh [sic], that cost the lives of many hundred brave men, and while it always seemed in poor taste to criticize, from the standpoint of a private, the doing of the generals, yet it has always looked as though Fredericksburgh [sic] might have been held. After the works were captured a few hours labor would have turned them, and made them very unpleasant to approach from the south. Instead of doing this the main body of our army moved on to join Hooker at Chancellorsville, and even then, when the weight of Lee's whole army was hurled against us, although within but a few miles of Hooker's army, we received no help from them, and the result was we were beaten in detail. Hooker must have heard the sharp fighting that we were subject to, and had his army crowded up on Lee's flank, the result could not have failed to have been different from what it was. This ended the last battle in Virginia in which our regiment took part.

Tuesday, May 5th. — We remained in our camp on the north bank of the Rappahannock. In the morning the enemy shelled us some from their batteries on the south side of the river, but as they did not seem to have a definite idea of the location of our camp, that was concealed by the woods, they did us no damage; in fact we did not deem them of sufficient importance to change our camp. Being tired out with the fatigue and excitement of the past four days we slept

Sedgwick's Position

most of the time. At night it commenced to rain, which generally follows within twenty-four hours of an engagement. This continued for the next three days, while the weather was very cold and unpleasant, that made us wish ourselves back to our winter quarters.

Friday, May 8th. — At 9 A.M. we marched leisurely, taking our way right across the country. In fact the roads, fences and woods, and all other landmarks, were almost entirely obliterated. It seemed a mystery to me how the land-owners could ever establish the boundary lines of their estates. At 3 P.M. we had traveled about eight miles, when we reached our old camp at White Oak Church, and took possession of our old quarters. The next day we fixed up our cabin so that it would be comfortable for our short stay, as we expected to leave for home in a few days.

Notes — Chapter 17

1. Victor, *History of the Southern Rebellion*, Vol. IV, pp. 20-21.

2. Johnson and Buel, *Battles and Leaders of the Civil War*, Vol. III, p. 157.

3. Ibid., p. 156.

4. *O.R.*, Vol. XXV, Part 1, p. 557.

5. Ibid., p. 587.

6. Ibid.

7. Johnson and Buel, *Battles and Leaders of the Civil War,* Vol. III, p. 157.

8. Guernsey and Alden, *Harper's Pictorial History of the Civil War*, p. 489.

9. Johnson and Buel, *Battles and Leaders of the Civil War*, Vol. III, p. 159.

10. Ibid., p. 161.

11. Guernsey and Alden, *Harper's Pictorial History of the Civil War*, p. 486.

12. *O.R.*, Vol. XXV, Part 1, p. 558.

13. *O.R.*, Vol. XXV, Part 1, p. 588.

14. Fairchild, *History of the 27th Regiment, N.Y., Vols.*, p. 169.

15. *O.R.*, Vol. XXV, Part 1, p. 560.

16. *O.R.*, Vol. XXV, Part 2, p. 418.

17. *O.R.*, Vol. XXV, Part 1, pp. 174-193.

18. Wilson, *Pictorial History of the Great Civil War*, pp. 480-481.

19. *O.R.*, Vol. XXV, Part 1, p. 434.

20. Ibid., p. 440.

21. Ibid.

22. Guernsey and Alden, *Harper's Pictorial History of the Civil War*, p. 486.

23. Fairchild, *History of the 27th Regiment, N.Y., Vols.*, p. 171.

Chapter 18

MUSTERING OUT

Background

The 27th New York had entered Federal service on May 21, 1861. Its two years of service ended on May 21, 1863, and its men were mustered out on May 31, 1863.[1]

The regiment had been in fourteen engagements:[2]

Bull Run, Va.	July 21, 1861
Pohick Church, Va.	Oct. 3, 1861
West Point, Va.	May 7-8, 1862
Near Mechanicsville, Va.	May 20, 1862
Gaines' Mill, Va.	June 27, 1862
White Oak Swamp, Glendale, Va.*	June 30, 1862
Malvern Hill, Va.*	July 1, 1862
Crampton's Pass, Md.	Sept. 14, 1862
Antietam, Md.	Sept. 17, 1862
Fredericksburg, Va.	Dec. 12-15, 1862
Franklin's Crossing, Va.	April 28-May 2, 1863
Marye's Heights, Va.	May 3, 1863
Salem Church, Va.	May 3-4, 1863
Banks' Ford, Va.	May 4, 1863

(* Westervelt not involved due to injury)

Of these, only four could be called successes—Crampton's Pass, Antietam, Franklin's Crossing, and Marye's Heights. The last two, of course, were wiped out by the failure of the

131

MUSTERING OUT

Chancellorsville Campaign. Small wonder, then, that the troops went home with a feeling that the work was not completed.

Many of the men, as did Westervelt, decided to help finish the job by reentering service. The Regimental History states, "After a few weeks' rest, we find that nearly every man who was able-bodied had reentered the service and was again found fighting the battles of his country."[3]

The regiment furnished a large number of the officers and men of the First New York Veteran Cavalry. The comradeship started during the Civil War carried on afterward and The Survivors Association of the 27th New York Regiment and the 1st New York Veteran Cavalry held fourteen annual reunions for which there are printed reports starting in 1876 and continuing through 1897.[4] The bonds among the men were strong and continued as long as they lived.

These reunions and similar reunions of regiments throughout the country led to forming more permanent organizations, predecessors to the American Legion and the Veterans of Foreign Wars. Westervelt was one of the founders of the Ellis Post of the Grand Army of the Republic, located in Orange County, New York.

Highlights

In this last chapter on his first enlistment, two things come through clearly:

1. Missing the Old Corps: Despite his feeling that he had seen all the service he wanted, Westervelt missed the VI Corps and all about it. He says, significantly, "The hardships we had endured seemed to dwarf when looked at in the past, while our pleasures were correspondingly magnified." This perception of his earlier experiences undoubtedly contributed to his reentering the army.

2. Serving to the End of the War: After he had wrestled with himself as to the right course of action, Westervelt finally decided to commit to serve again "until the war closed unless disabled by wound or failing health." As an optimist, he doesn't even suggest that he might be killed; as a practical person, he recognizes that wounds or ill health could end his commitment.

MUSTERING OUT

On the 11th the 16th N.Y. started for home; that made us feel very lonesome, as we had always camped right beside each other, and had seemed more like one regiment than two distinct commands; and when in action, no difference which regiment were crowded, the other was always ready to come to its relief.

For the next four days we made our farewell calls among the regiments where we had acquaintances. Our camp seemed very dull, our minds were so fully occupied with the thoughts of going home, and meeting with the loved ones, that we could not settle ourselves to any employment or amusement.

On the 14th, at evening parade, orders were read for us to start for home the next morning. We were then addressed by Generals Slocum and Bartlett, and when the parade was dismissed the men gave three of the heartiest cheers they had given in many months. There was but little sleeping that night, as the men were determined to make their last night in Virginia a lively one, and I guess they did. At 3 A.M. on the 15th the drums sounded the reveille, which was almost superfluous, as scarce a man was asleep. At five we were packed up and on our way to Falmouth.

The different regiments of our brigade turned out to wish us good bye, and as we said adieu to these weather-beaten veterans we heartily wished the war was over, and that we were all going back together. It is needless to say there was no straggling to the rear on that march, but every man was up in his place.

Arriving at Falmouth we loaded on the cars, and a short run took us to Aquia creek, where we were soon on board a steamer for Washington. About dark we reached the capital and were quartered in the Soldier's Retreat.—The next day we spent in Washington, as there seemed a lack of cars to send us north. About 5 P.M. we loaded on the cars and ran as far as Baltimore, where we unloaded to change cars, and remained the rest of the night.

Sunday, May 17th. — At daylight we started, and ran very slowly. About noon we passed Harrisburgh, and at midnight reached Elmira, where we unloaded from the cars and slept the remainder of the night on the platform of the depot. The next morning we marched to the barracks, but finding them very dirty, and fairly alive with vermin, I took board in a private family and remained until June 5th, when our regiment was mustered out, and we received our discharge, pay, and bounty of $100, having been in the service two years and twenty-eight days.

The remainder of the summer I spent in Orange County, and tried to convince myself that I had seen all the service I wanted, but in spite of myself I would often find a longing to sit around the camp fire once more, and to take a part in the stirring events of active service. When I read of what our old corps, the 6th, were doing at Gettysburg, and in following Lee's army through Maryland, and down through the Shenandoah, I felt that I was losing time, and that the hum drum of civil life was not the thing. The hardships we had endured seemed to dwarf when looked at in the past, while our pleasures were correspond-ingly magnified. I lost all taste for business, and, although solicited by my friends to keep out of the army, the attraction that way was so strong as to appear almost irresistible. Finally I determined to enlist, and when I did, it was with the intention of remaining in the army until the war closed, no difference how many years it lasted, unless *disabled by wounds or failing health. But the "Lights and Shadows" of the next two years,* *while with Sherman, will be reserved for future papers.*

END OF BOOK FIRST

FLAG OF THE 27TH REGIMENT.

MUSTERING OUT

Notes — Chapter 18

1. Fairchild, *History of the 27th Regiment, N.Y. Vols.*, pp. 293-294.

2. Dyer, *A Compendium of the War of the Rebellion*, Vol. II, pp. 1414-1415.

3. Fairchild, *History of the 27th Regiment, N.Y. Vols.*, p. 178.

4. Reports in the editor's private collection.

Chapter 19

THE SECOND ENLISTMENT — A DIFFERENT WAR

Although Westervelt was out of the army a little more than three months, he returned to a different war. The War in the East through the Battle of Gettysburg had been essentially a gentleman's war with armies fighting armies. After Gettysburg that changed, particularly in the West, and the changes are reflected in Westervelt's activities from September 8, 1863, to April 26, 1865, when General Joseph E. Johnston surrendered all the remaining Confederate armies to General William T. Sherman.

After the Federal victories of Gettysburg and Vicksburg in July 1863, leaders in the North felt that the war would end soon. Sherman's biographer, Lloyd Lewis, states that after Vicksburg, the Confederacy, instead of recognizing the hopelessness of further warfare elected to revive it.[1]

Edward Pollard, the noted wartime editor of the *Richmond Examiner* explains. Writing in his book, *The Lost Cause*, Pollard said, "She [the South] had, also, on her side the single advantage which should have been decisive of the contest—an advantage which no numbers could really surmount, or skill effectively circumvent. That advantage was space...."[2] Pollard went on to say that the South should have been expected to win "unless the management of her affairs should become insane, or her people lose the virtue of endurance."[3]

The question for the North was how to convince the South to cease hostilities. The original concept of the North in fighting the war was based on General Scott's Anaconda Plan. This plan was developed by General Scott and endorsed by McClellan and Halleck. "It contemplated the surrounding of the insurgents at all points by a cordon of troops, cutting off their supplies by a land as well as a sea blockade, and a gradual contraction of its lines, hemming them in and crushing them, as the Anaconda by the contraction of its coils, crushes its prey."[4]

Grant and Sherman saw this policy as being defensive in nature requiring an inordinate number of troops to carry it out; usually with small numbers in each location, making them inviting targets for guerrillas such as Forrest, Morgan, and Roddey.

Grant and Sherman believed in destroying the South's ability and will to wage war through the destruction of factories, railroads, and food supplies. Theirs was the concept of what today is known as "total war."

And so we see Westervelt, in his second enlistment, being governed by one plan and then the other, back and forth. Finally he was under Grant's and Sherman's plan to the end of the war.

Specifically, we see Westervelt:
  -being placed in garrison at Eastport, Tennessee (Anaconda Plan)
  -chasing Forrest when he went recruiting in Western Tennessee (product of the Anaconda Plan)
  -going with Sherman on his first expedition to Meridian (the beginning of total war)
  -in garrison again at Decatur, Alabama and chasing Forrest, Roddey, and their guerrillas (Anaconda Plan)
  -joining Sherman in the Atlanta Campaign (total war)
  -going with Sherman to the Sea (total war)
  -marching with Sherman through the Carolinas to the end of the War (total war)

THE SECOND ENLISTMENT — A DIFFERENT WAR

The first enlistment of Westervelt's involved a struggle between armies in the classic pre-1860s sense; the second involved a fight to the finish under a new concept in which armies and all the means of supporting armies were affected.

Two other things were different for Westervelt in his second enlistment: 1) the nature of the troops in the 17th Veteran New York, and 2) the perspective he had about the last two years of the war.

The soldiers of the 17th New York were not the comrades and "chums" of his first tour of duty. In fact, in his "Book the Second," Westervelt refers to only one friend, C.S. Crist, a boyhood pal from Orange County. After the war, Westervelt's total association was with the veterans of the 27th New York, where he was an officer in the Survivors Association and a participating author in its Regimental History.

In contrast, the 17th New York consisted of a hardened group of veterans. A picture of them is provided by one Union soldier, Lucius Barber, who was with them on the Meridian Expedition. He writes of the 17th New York, "This regiment was composed of Wilson's old zouaves and roughs from New York City and they were a rough set...but yet there was not a better fighting regiment in the whole division than the 17th N.Y."[5]

Westervelt's perspective changed, too. This is reflected in the tone of his second book which is different from the first. The lilt in his writing is gone; war was no longer associated with frolic; it was serious business. He was the senior noncommissioned officer in his company and he had to control the troops and maintain discipline in and out of battle. He had a job to do and he did it until the war was over.

THE SECOND ENLISTMENT — A DIFFERENT WAR

Notes — Chapter 19

1. Lloyd Lewis, *Sherman, Fighting Prophet* (New York: Harcourt, Brace, and Co., 1932), p. 304.

2. Edward A. Pollard, *The Lost Cause* (New York: E.B. Treat & Co., 1866), p. 133.

3. Ibid.

4. Samuel M. Schmucker and L.P. Brockett, *The History of the Civil War in the United States* (Philadelphia: Jones Brothers and Co., 1865), p. 672.

5. Margie Riddle Bearss, *Sherman's Forgotten Campaign: The Meridian Expedition* (Baltimore, Maryland: Gateway Press, 1987), pp. 182-183.

Chapter 20

TO THE WEST

Background

On September 8, 1863, after a three-month period out of service, Westervelt joined Company A of the 38th New York Veterans Volunteers where he was appointed first sergeant (the highest ranking noncommissioned officer in the company).

Several regiments of veterans were being formed in New York from the ranks of the disbanded two-year regiments. Some were unable to fully staff their new organizations and, as a result, were combined with others. Major W.T.C. Grower, formerly of the 17th New York, recruited for the 17th New York Veteran Regiment and he received Westervelt and others by transfer. The total transferees came from the 9th New York and 38th New York second or veterans organizations.[1]

On October 17, 1863, the 17th New York Veteran Regiment was formally mustered into service with Grower as colonel and Westervelt as first sergeant of Company K.[2] The regiment was moved immediately to Washington, D.C. where it was assigned to the defenses of the capital.

The situation in the East was that Meade and Lee maneuvered for position and this action ended in a stalemate.

In the West, Rosecrans, the Union commander, had driven Braxton Bragg, the Confederate commander, out of Chattanooga. Then Bragg received reinforcements—Longstreet from Lee's army; Johnston with parts of two divisions; contingents from Georgia, North Carolina, and South Carolina.[3] Bragg turned on Rosecrans, beat him decisively at Chickamauga on September 19 and 20 and bottled his army up in Chattanooga. Rosecrans was shocked by Chickamauga and lost his ability to lead. Lincoln described him as "confused and stunned like a duck hit on the head."[4] Washington was in an uproar, and on Wednesday night, September 23, Stanton sent John Hay, one of Lincoln's secretaries, to fetch Lincoln from Soldier's Home for a council.[5]

The council, attended by Lincoln, Stanton, Halleck, and Hooker, decided to send reinforcements to Rosecrans immediately. Hooker was to take Howard's XI Corps and Slocum's XII Corps.[6]

What happened then was "the first mass railroad movement of troops in history, and it has been a model for every one since."[7] In the period from September 26, 1863, to October 6, 1863, approximately 15,000 troops were moved from Washington, D.C. via Baltimore, Harpers Ferry, Cincinnati, and Louisville to Chattanooga.[8]

Westervelt was not in this initial movement but his regiment was sent west approximately three weeks later (October 31, 1863). The 17th New York Veteran was to replace troops sent to Rosecrans by General Hurlbut from his XVI Corps.[9] Westervelt describes in detail the trip from Washington, D.C. to Louisville which was essentially the same as that involving the transfer of the two corps. It is a remarkable account.

Upon leaving Louisville, Kentucky, Westervelt went by boat to Evansville, Indiana; Paducah, Kentucky; and then into the Tennessee River (see Map on page 150).

TO THE WEST

<u>Highlights</u>

1. <u>Officers of the Regiment</u>: The 17th New York had 34 officers exclusive of staff officers such as the quartermaster, the chaplain, and the surgeons. These included 1 colonel, 1 lieutenant colonel, 1 major, 1 adjutant, 10 captains, 10 first lieutenants, and 10 second lieutenants. A major criticism of the North's organization during the Civil War was that it created new regiments rather than fill existing ones which were depleted. One reason for this practice was that it created new officer positions.

Of the initial officer cadre, 11 out of 34 had no previous military experience (despite the fact that it was a veteran regiment), 20 had had previous experience as officers, and 3 as enlisted men. Eight of the 20 had served as officers in the first 17th New York and five had served in the 9th New York, a two-year regiment known as the Hawkins' Zouaves.[10]

2. <u>The 17th New York Zouave Uniform</u>: As Westervelt indicated, the uniform of the 17th New York Veteran Regiment was the same as that of the 9th New York or Hawkins' Zouaves. The number of officers and men from the two-year regiment must have influenced the choice of uniform for the new regiment which Westervelt describes in part. The full description for the uniform is as follows:

> ...scarlet wool fez with blue tassel, dark blue wool serge short jacket, vest, and full trousers. Their sashes were turquoise blue. They had a black leather cartridge box sliding on their waist belt, and oval U.S. brass plate and white canvass gaiters. The blue jacket and trousers had elaborate crimson magenta lace and piping. Officers wore French-style caps.[11]

(The Hawkins' Zouaves are shown on page 142 at Fredericksburg.)

3. <u>Westervelt's First Commander, Henry Slocum, also moves west</u>: Westervelt's first commanding officer, Henry W. Slocum, was promoted to major general in July 1862 and was appointed to lead the XII Corps after Antietam, replacing Joseph Mansfield, who was killed in that battle. Slocum was extremely critical of Hooker's leadership at Chancellorsville and stated so publicly. Thus, when Hooker was assigned to lead the XI and XII Corps in the West, Slocum resigned, saying, "My opinion of General Hooker as an officer and a gentleman is too well known....The public service cannot be promoted by placing under his command an officer who has so little confidence in his ability as I have."[12] Lincoln refused to accept the resignation; Slocum was assigned to a division of the XII Corps and charged with the protection of the Nashville and Chattanooga Railroad.[13] Therefore, Slocum's military career continued; Westervelt would serve under him again in the March to the Sea and in the Carolinas Campaign.

4. <u>Discipline</u>: As first sergeant, Westervelt was responsible for the discipline of the enlisted men in Company K. He writes extensively in this Chapter about his efforts, as well as that of others, to keep the men away from whiskey. This must have been a pervasive problem, for in his orders to

Hawkins' Zouaves at Fredericksburg

Slocum relating to the transfer west, Hooker directed "The troops will not be permitted to leave the cars in the large towns and nowhere else except by the authority of the commanders of regiment or battery."[14]

5. <u>Steamboats in the West</u>: Westervelt was fascinated with steamboats in the West. He had lived on the Hudson River in New York and was familiar with the steamboats there. They had paddle wheels amidship in the sides and were deep-draught for the Hudson is a deep river.

In contrast, many of the steamboats in the West had their paddle wheels in the stern; they were designed to operate in the shallow waters of the Tennessee and the Mississippi Rivers (see page 144).

Throughout his experience in the West from November 1863 to August 1864, Westervelt indicates he traveled on the following steamboats:

Navigator - November 4, 1863, Cincinnati, Ohio to Eastport, Tennessee
>November 25, 1863, Eastport, Tennessee down river and then return to Eastport, Tennessee

Mariner - December 6, 1863, Eastport, Tennessee to Paducah, Kentucky

Perry - January 18, 1864, Columbus, Kentucky to Vicksburg, Mississippi

Sir William Wallace - March 9, 1864, Vicksburg, Mississippi to Memphis, Tennessee

Olive Branch - March 19, 1864, Memphis, Tennessee to Cairo, Illinois

S.R. Pringle - March 26, 1864, Cairo, Illinois to Crumps Landing, Tennessee

His travels indicate the extent to which the North relied upon water transportation to move troops from one location to another.

Government Steamboat Used on the Upper Tennessee

TO THE WEST

BOOK THE SECOND.

After spending the summer of '63 in civil life I felt a desire to once more get into service. About the first of September I visited N.Y. city, and enlisted for three years in an organization known as the 38th N.Y. Veteran Volunteers. A few days after I was sent to their camp on Staten Island, and assigned to duty as 1st Sergeant of the company. We remained here doing camp duty and drilling until about the middle of Oct., when our company with several others was formed into a regiment that was known as the 17th N.Y. Veteran Zouaves. Our uniforms were dark blue, with red trimmings, the same as had been worn by the 9th N.Y. (Hawkin's Zouaves) during the two years of their service. In fact one of the largest companies of our regiment was composed of men who had served in the 9th. Our regiment was commanded by Col. W.T.C. Grower a veteran of the 17th N.Y.

On the 21st of October State Paymaster Van Burn arrived, and paid the men their state bounties. That night we packed our personal property in our knapsacks, and taking the cars at our camp at New Dorp, soon ran to the landing, where we embarked on a steamboat, that landed us at Camden about midnight. We now crossed the river to Philadelphia and took breakfast at the celebrated "Cooper Shop," and soon after loaded on the cars and arrived safely in Washington about midnight of the 22d, where we were quartered in the barracks at the Soldiers' Retreat. They were dirty enough to make a soldier or any one else with any regard for cleanliness wish to retreat without unnecessary delay. The following day we received shelter tents, and about noon crossed the Long Bridge into Virginia and camped near Fort Albany. The weather soon became cold and rainy, and our camp muddy. Two days after we moved our camp about a mile, to higher ground, and were quartered in Sibley tents. Here we remained until Oct. 30th, when we broke camp and returned to Washing-ton, and slept once more at the Soldiers' Retreat. On the following day we loaded on the cars and ran as far north as the Relay House, then turned west on the Baltimore & Ohio road.

About midnight we reached Harper's Ferry, where hot coffee and rations were served us. This road being under contract of the govern-ment, and continually in use transporting troops, east and west, the commissary department had established cooking stations at each place where the trains stopped to change engines or take water. When a train loaded with troops were coming, those in charge were notified by telegraph and bread and coffee was ready and commencing with the first car, they would serve as far as their time and material would go. When the train started they would telegraph the next station "We have served so many cars." When the train arrived at the next stop, the cooks would commence where the others left off, and go on through the train, or as far as possible, so there was no doubling rations until all were served.

The cars we occupied were freight cars, and were packed so close we could not lay down, or make fire in the stove, so we suffered from cold and want of sleep. As soon as daylight appeared, I took some of the men from our car, which gave us room to make a fire in the stove, and added greatly to our comfort. About noon we reached Cumberland, where we were detained near two hours and got our supper. On leaving

145

here we climbed the Blue Ridge, and as the grade was heavy, two engines were attached to our train, and even then we ran very slowly. For seventeen miles the grade was sixty feet to the mile. About midnight we reached the top of the mountain, where we stopped and took coffee, then ran on until daylight.

Monday, Nov. 2d. — At daylight we found we were stopping at Belmont, where the officers got breakfast, and the men got whiskey, with the usual results. We next stopped at Littleton, where the men got more whiskey and became very troublesome. We soon found that many of the laborers' shanties contained a jug, or demijohn, of the vilest liquor that could be bought, and was sold to the soldiers at from three to five dollars a canteen. Some of us determined to spoil the jug tavern the rest of the way, so, whenever the train stopped, we would join with the men and run to the shanties, and as soon as the jug appeared from its hidden receptacle under the bed, we would seize it and run, and when the old woman, with her mouth full of curses, would run after us, we would let it fall on the railroad track and break. At the next stop, after leaving Littleton, one of our cars jumped the track, injuring one of our company, so he is crippled for life.

Five miles further another drunken man fell from the cars, and about half the train passed over him, killing him instantly. We gathered up his remains in a blanket and ran on to Benwood, where we unloaded from the cars, buried the dead man, and sent the wounded one to the hospital, from which he never returned to our company.

We now crossed the Ohio river, on a small boat, with a wheezing, puffing, asthmatic engine, that seemed to be in the last stage of consumption, and was continually catching on the centre, and had to be coaxed along by the use of poles. But little more than one company could cross at once, so it was well along into the night before we were all across. We then loaded on the cars. Here, by using a little strategy, I managed to get a good supper at a hotel. During the night it rained hard, but we being comfortably quartered, did not mind it. We remained here one day, when we once more loaded on the cars and reached Columbus about noon on Nov. 4th.

Here the penitentiary is located, and at that time the guerilla John Morgan was confined here, having been captured a few weeks previous, while attempting a raid through the states of West Virginia and Ohio. Our next stop was at a place called Xenia, where we had a very pleasant reception. As we ran up to the station, we found it surrounded by several young ladies, from the neighboring boarding schools, each with a well filled basket of provision and delicacies, that we did not need much persuasion to accept. This gave us a very pleasant delay of about an hour, and as we started it was mid the waving of handkerchiefs and wishes of "God speed" us on our way. At ten P.M. we reached Cincinnatti.* This was the end of our railroad journey, so we unloaded from the cars, and after some delay went on board the steamboat Navigator, where we turned in and had the first good night's sleep since leaving Washington.

Thursday, Nov. 5th. — When we awoke in the morning we found our steamboat still moored to the bank at Cincinnati [sic]. Seeing no signs of starting I hurried through my morning reports, and then went on shore

---

* Cincinnati

to see the city. I would have enjoyed this very well, but soon found whiskey was plenty and the men were getting drunk and troublesome, so I had to come back to the steamboat and stay there, to keep the men on board from fighting. A patrol guard was then sent out to gather in the drunken ones, about the city. At dark we had most of them aboard when we moved out into the river and anchored.

The next morning at sunrise we started down the river, and were obliged to run slow, as the river here is narrow and crooked, and at this time the water was low, making navigation difficult. In the afternoon the boat was run to the bank, and while our crew carried several cords of wood on board, our cooks went on shore and cooked rations.

At dark we were once more under way and ran all night. The steamboat looked rather odd to those of us who were used to the fine vessels of the Hudson. It was very large and flat, was driven by a paddle-wheel that, instead of being amidship on the sides, was placed at the stern and covered the whole afterpart of the vessel. The motive power was furnished by a double engine on the main deck. Steam was supplied by two long tubular boilers, that were arranged for either wood or soft coal; these with the engines took up about all the deck. The troops occupied the remainder, that was generally used for freight. The hold was from two to four feet deep, as it was necessary that the bottom should be flat to run in shoal water. Some of the largest of them, even when loaded will run in two and a half feet of water, or as a facetious pilot answered me when I asked "What is the lightest draft vessels on the western rivers?" "Why," said he, as he shifted a small cargo of Lynchburg fine cut from the starboard to port side of his cheek, and expectorated something less than a half pint of the juice, "Why, some of them will run right across the country when there is a heavy dew." I don't vouch for the truth of this statement, but give it to the public the same as this weather-beaten wheelsman tried to give it to me.

At daylight of the 7th we arrived at Louisville. There we entered the canal and were locked through past the city, as the falls rendered the river impassable at this time of the year. At nine A.M. we again entered the river and soon passed Fort William, at the mouth of Salt river, and the following day reached Cannelton, where the hold of the boat was partly filled with coal, that the troops had to help load. This delay gave me a chance to go on shore and see something of the place, and although it is a noted coal depot, it had a sort of "starved to death" look during the war.

On the 9th we reached Evansville, and stopped another day, that I was fortunate to spend on shore.

TO THE WEST

Notes — Chapter 20

1. Phisterer, *New York in the War of The Rebellion 1861-1865*, Vol. III, p. 1935.

2. Ibid., pp. 1935-1946.

3. Victor, *The History of the Southern Rebellion*, Vol. IV, p. 155.

4. Benjamin P. Thomas, *Abraham Lincoln* (New York: Alfred A. Knopf, 1952), p. 395.

5. Fletcher Pratt, *Stanton — Lincoln's Secretary of War* (New York: W.W. Norton and Co., 1953), p. 320.

6. Ibid., pp. 320-321.

7. Ibid., p. 323.

8. *O.R.*, Vol. XXIX, Part 1, p. 150.

9. Ibid., pp. 150-151.

10. Phisterer, *New York in the War of the Rebellion*, pp. 1935-1946.

11. Bearss, *Sherman's Forgotten Campaign*, p. 327.

12. *O.R.*, XXIX, Part 1, p. 156.

13. Warner, *Generals in Blue*, p. 452.

14. *O.R.*, XXIX, Part 1, p. 152.

Chapter 21

THE TENNESSEE RIVER / EASTPORT, MISSISSIPPI

Background

On November 13, 1863, Westervelt sailed on the Tennessee River for the first time. The Tennessee was one of the most important rivers in the Civil War for, in a sense, it was the back door to the Confederacy. It led to Alabama and Mississippi and it separated Western Tennessee from the rest of the South that was east of the Mississippi (see Map on page 150). (Note: The map does not show Eastport, Mississippi which is almost on the Alabama line directly east of Corinth.)

The river runs from south to north, contrary to the direction of flow of other major navigable rivers in the United States. Hence, when Westervelt said he sailed up the river to Eastport, he was correct. It was navigable for gunboats, transports, and supply ships from Paducah, Kentucky to Eastport in the northeast Mississippi.

The area in which the 17th Veteran New York would spend the next month was shaped like a triangle with Paducah, Kentucky at the apex, the Mississippi River as the left side, the Tennessee River as the right side, and the Tennessee-Mississippi line as the base. Along the Mississippi and Ohio Rivers, the North had major installations at Cairo, Illinois; Paducah and Columbus in Kentucky; and Island Number 10, Fort Pillow, and Memphis in Tennessee. Across the base and protecting the important Memphis and Charleston Railroad were troops at Colliersville, LaGrange, Moscow, and Pocahontas in Tennessee and Corinth in Mississippi. On the Tennessee River, Northern forces occupied Eastport, Mississippi and Hamburg Landing, Tennessee while gunboats patrolled the river.

In November 1863, Sherman wrote, "...I attach importance to the region of the country at the head of the navigable part of the Tennessee, say Eastport, as it is a fine point from which to pierce Alabama in the rich district from Russelville to Decatur..."[1] As troops were drawn from Hurlbut's XVI Corps to take part in the Chattanooga Campaign, Sherman directed Hurlbut to hold Eastport and fortify it.[2] Thus, we find Westervelt and his regiment assigned to that important post replacing others who had gone to join Grant and Sherman at Chattanooga. Organizationally, the 17th Veteran New York was assigned to the XVI Corps under Major General Stephen A. Hurlbut whose headquarters was at Memphis, and specifically to its Sixth Division led by Brigadier General Andrew Jackson Smith, headquartered at Columbus, Kentucky.

By mid-November 1863, Grant had taken charge of the Western armies and was trying to break Bragg's siege at Chattanooga. Longstreet was pursuing Burnside trying to bottle him up at Nashville. Even though Hurlbut expected an attack from the south along the base of the triangle, Grant was more concerned about Burnside. On November 21, 1863, Grant wired Admiral David Porter that there were seven or eight regiments at Eastport and he wanted all but three sent to Burnside's relief.[3] Therefore, on November 25, Westervelt was on the way to relieve Burnside. While he may not have known his destination, General John D. Stevenson at Corinth did, for he reported to Hurlbut on that date, "...the New York brigade at Eastport is embarking on transports today, destination Burnside."[4] (Note: There was no New York Brigade in the XVI Corps at that time; Stevenson must have meant regiment.)

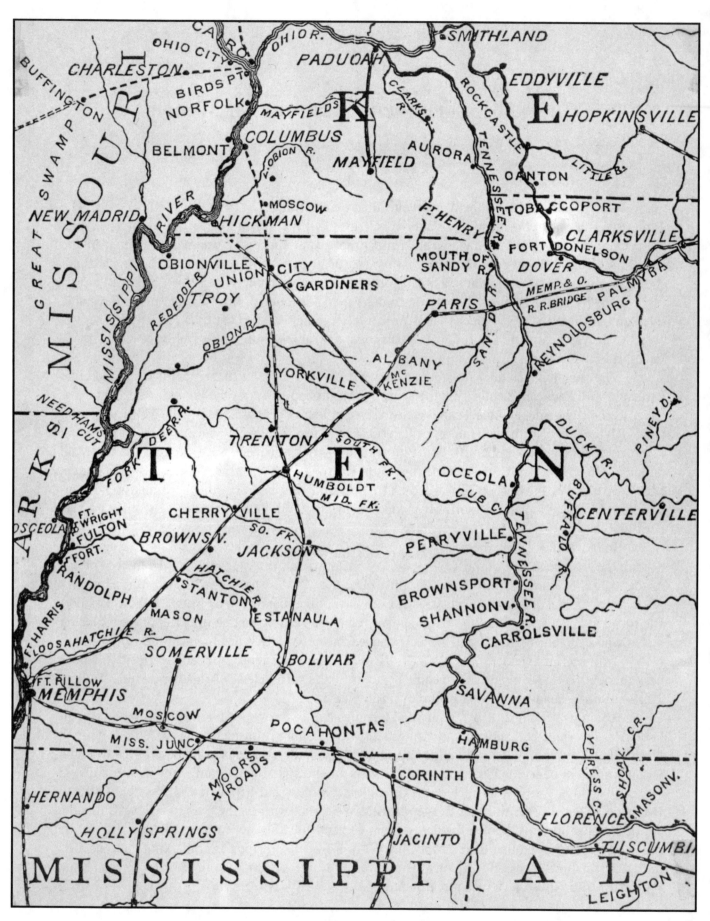

Map of Western Tennessee

THE TENNESSEE RIVER / EASTPORT, MISSISSIPPI

On November 25, the Battle of Chattanooga ended with an overwhelming defeat for Bragg. Next, Burnside was able to hold off Longstreet who retired after learning about Chattanooga. Now it was time for Grant to deal with the threat to Hurlbut from the south and he decided to consolidate most of his troops in Western Tennessee under General Smith at Columbus. He wired the commanding officer at Eastport on November 30, "You will evacuate Eastport and move all the forces at that place to Columbus, Kentucky reporting to Brig. Gen. A.J. Smith."[5] Hence, the 17th Veteran New York started north to relieve Burnside, returned to Eastport, and then on December 6, 1863, started north again.

Highlights

One major new experience for Westervelt dealt with guerrillas.

1. Guerrillas: With his trip to the West, Sergeant Westervelt entered territory occupied by guerrillas. The Confederate Congress passed an act on April 21, 1862, authorizing the organization of bands of partisan rangers to be given the same pay, rations, and quarters as other soldiers and to have the same protection, if captured.[6] These men were popularly known as rangers, but to their enemies they were known as guerrillas. Westervelt's first reference to them was to the Confederate leader John Hunt Morgan who was captured in Ohio on July 26, 1863, and was sent to prison in Columbus. His second reference is to the bands along the Tennessee River who tried to attack the troop transports. They would be a never-ending source of concern to Westervelt and his comrades until the end of the war.

Webster's Dictionary defines a guerrilla as "one who engages in irregular warfare, especially as a member of an independent unit carrying out harassment and sabotoge."[7] The guerrillas harassed Union troops as well as anyone suspected of being a Union sympathizer. As the war went on, the actions of the guerrillas became nastier, and the Union response was often equally nasty and violent.

Referring to guerrillas, "Rebel Cavalryman Thomas Rosser complained, 'They roam broadcast over the country, a band of thieves, stealing, pillaging, and plundering...an injury to the cause.' Lee stated flatly, 'I regard the whole system as an unmixed evil'."[8]

Woe unto the Union soldier who fell into their hands—at best, he could hope for parole; at worst, it was prison, torture, or death. The fear of guerrillas, particularly when he was alone in the field, is evident in Westervelt's later chapters.

We left here[*] on the 11th, and reached Paducah the 13th, and after stopping a few hours entered the Tennessee river. Two boats now joined us to act as convoy, to protect us from guerrillas, as they had a very unpleasant habit of concealing themselves on shore, and when a transport came within range would open on them with a battery, while the troops on board would be powerless to reply with their rifles, on account of the distance. On each side of the pilot house was a half circle of boiler iron to protect that worthy from sharpshooters. Usually a small detail was kept on the upper deck, so in case a shot was fired from the shore, we could give them a volley in return. As we were now running against the current our progress was slow. We kept a sharp lookout for the enemy. About noon we saw a small squad of cavalry on the bank, but they got away lively, showing no disposition to fight. Most of the way up the river the shores were low, and the land looked poor, and was covered with a small growth of timber. Sometimes, however, the shore rose high and rocky like the Hudson at West Point.

On the morning of the 15th we stopped for wood, and here we buried one of our regiment, who had died the preceding night. The next morning we arrived at Eastport; here we dismbarked[†] and went into camp near the shore.

We remained at Eastport about a week. It was the most desolate, deserted place we were ever in. There was not a house within sight, and no communication of any kind with the outside world. We received no mail, and could send none. The weather was cold and unpleasant, and each morning there was a heavy fog, all of which seemed to have a depressing influence on the spirits of the officers and men. I don't remember ever being in a place that we all looked forward so anxiously to the time of getting away. We changed our camp two or three times and each time it seemed worse than the last.

Finally on the morning of Nov. 25th, we received orders to pack up, and supposed we were to once more move our camp, instead of which we turned towards the shore and were soon once more on board the steam-boat Navigator. At noon we cast off and started down the river. About dark we stopped for wood, and while here two of our line officers went on shore to settle a little misunderstanding, not with pistols but according to the "Sullivan code of honor." In about fifteen minutes they returned—one with a black eye and the other with a cut on his lip—both apparently satisfied.

We were now running with the current, that is from five to six miles an hour, so it was no trouble to make good time. The next night, while passing some high bluffs, we were fired upon by guerrillas, but a shot from our gunboats put them to flight. About midnight we met a fleet of transports coming up the river when we turned about and joined them.

Just at daylight two men crossing the river in a small boat were run down by one of our gunboats. Their small boat was upset; one of them clung to the gunboat, while the other held fast to the small boat, that was bottom up and drifting down with the swift current, while he was screaming loudly for help. A small boat was quickly lowered from the gunboat, but by the time the crew were in it the man had drifted several hundred yards down stream. The crew now gave way with a

---

[*] Evansville, Indiana

[†] disembarked

will, that just drove the boat through the water, and in about a minute came up with the man and pulled him in without stopping their boat. It was well done, and witnessed by the fleet, who gave them three hearty cheers when they saw the man was rescued.

During the forenoon, as we were slowly sailing up the river, we were fired upon by guerrillas, who seemed inclined to stand and show fight, but a few shells from our gunboats made them skedaddle back from the shore. In the afternoon we passed another squad of them, but as they did not show fight we did not disturb them.

Saturday, Nov. 28th. — Called at five A.M. when we found our boat tied to the bank. The troops were then set to carrying a rail fence on board for fuel. About sunrise we started. We were then two hours behind the rest of the fleet, with but one gunboat for convoy yet we were not disturbed. We ran our best speed, the dry rails making good fuel, and plenty of steam. At two P.M. we passed the battlefield of Pittsburgh Landing, and a mile further we passed in sight of the memorable field of Shiloh, and at eight P.M.

reached Eastport, and tied to the bank, having been absent just four days.

Sunday, Nov. 29th. — About nine A.M. we landed from the steam-boat and marched back to our old camp. We remained here just one week; the weather was cold, and each morning the ground was covered with a white frost. We added a fireplace to our cabin, and tried to make ourselves comfortable. Our number had been increased by the arrival of several regiments, so the place did not appear so lonesome.

On the 3rd of December a steamer came up the river and brought our first mail since leaving Washington Oct. 31st. Our letters and papers gave us something to occupy our time for some days, and drove away the blues very effectually. Three days after we broke camp, and moved down to the shore and spent most of the day loading stores. About sundown we went on board the steamboat Mariner. Our company were put on the Hurricane deck. There was no shelter, but I found a large wooden saw-horse, over which I stretched my tent, that made far better quarters than being exposed to the weather.

Notes — Chapter 21

1. *O.R.*, Vol. XXXI, Part 3, p. 90.

2. Ibid., p. 101.

3. Ibid., p. 222.

4. Ibid., p. 251.

5. Ibid., p. 278.

6. Johnson, *Campfires and Battlefields* (New York, N.Y.: The Civil War Press, 1967, eighth printing), p. 316.

7. *Webster's Ninth New Collegiate Dictionary*, p. 541.

8. Ketchum and Catton, *The American Heritage Picture History of the Civil War* (New York, N.Y.: American Heritage Publishing Co., 1960), p. 531.

Chapter 22

A SCOUTING PARTY

Background

The Federal commander in Memphis, Major General Hurlbut expected a major attack from the Confederates in Mississippi. He had, at that time, 30,780 troops to hold the vast expanse of territory in the triangle.[1]

Instead of a major attack, there were minor ones along the Tennessee-Mississippi line designed to let Nathan Bedford Forrest (Picture on page 156) slip through the Federal cordon in order to go on a recruiting trip in Western Tennessee.

Forrest was given an independent command by President Jefferson Davis. On November 15, 1863, he arrived in Okolona, Mississippi to raise a fighting force.[2] His organization initially had 279 men and four guns to which Richardson's Brigade was added—a disappointing increase of only 240.[3] But this did not daunt Forrest for he considered Western Tennessee as his territory and all he had to do was go there and raise troops for his new organization. He was undoubtedly helped by a new order which Hurlbut issued on November 15, 1863.[4] In General Orders 157, promulgated on behalf of General Sherman, Federal officers were ordered to impress into the Federal army all able-bodied persons in West Tennessee and Northern Mississippi. This forced men to enter the war; many chose the South rather than the North (see highlight below).

Forrest slipped through the Federal lines on December 2 and started recruiting.[5] The Federals knew that West Tennessee was a nest for guerrillas and a source of recruits for the South. Thus, General Andrew Jackson Smith received orders from Hurlbut dated December 3, 1863, to "make up a strong flying column and clear all the country between the Hatchie and the Tennessee down as far as Jackson."[6] Forrest's new recruits "were scattered in the deep, confusing bottoms or in the heaviest part of upland forests in small detachments of twenty-five to thirty each."[7] While they had no arms for attack or defense, the terrain was theirs and they used it advantageously, to the frustration of the Yankees.

Major Martin, First Sergeant Westervelt and four companies went on a scout starting December 18. Martin and Westervelt went ahead of the rest and found traces of Confederates but had no success in catching them.

Westervelt's report of the scout from December 18-24, and another one on December 25, illustrate how difficult it was to capture guerrillas in their home territory. It also reflects the fear that brave men had of being trapped by guerrillas in their own domain.

Highlights

This chapter reflects the changes in the war in its last two years. Here, Westervelt experiences chasing the elusive Confederate General Nathan Bedford Forrest and enjoying, without fear of discipline, the fruits of foraging.

1. <u>General Nathan Bedford Forrest</u>: Forrest was a plantation owner and slave trader before the war. He was uneducated and untrained in the military arts. Without question, he was a brilliant

General Nathan Bedford Forrest

guerrilla leader, fearless, cunning, and ruthless. He could make the Yankees believe he had ten times the number he actually had. His greatest success was the defeat of Union General "Sooy" Smith at Bryce's Crossroads. His low point—in terms of following the accepted rules of war—was the Fort Pillow "Massacre." He was finally defeated at Tupelo by General Andrew Jackson Smith. After the war, he was the first leader of the Ku Klux Klan.[8]

2. General Orders 157: These orders read in part: "All persons residing under the protection of the United States and physically capable of military duty, are liable to perform the same in a country under martial law....all officers commanding district, division, and detached brigades of the corps, (the XVI) will immediately proceed to impress into the service of the United States such able-bodied persons liable to military duty as may be required to fill up existing regiments and batteries to their maximum, Nov. 15, 1863." As indicated above, this Order turned out to be a better recruiting device for the South than for the North. As a result, it helped Forrest swell his ranks before he returned to Mississippi and gave Smith and his troops more men to hunt down or chase.

3. Foraging: Of this scout, Westervelt writes, "We came up to a large farm house where we loaded our wagon with sheep and grain, a few chickens and geese...." Foraging (or pillaging) was legal now. It hadn't always been that way.

In 1861, William Tecumseh Sherman watched as his soldiers stole oats and corn for their horses, apples for themselves, and even fired houses. He said then, "No curse could be greater than an invasion by a volunteer army."[9] Under Army regulations, a soldier caught stealing chickens could be punished as severely as if he had gone absent without leave (AWOL).[10] During the Vicksburg Campaign, Sherman made his people give receipts for food taken and even made his men pay cash for provisions in one instance.[11] Then the change came and by the time of the Meridian Campaign he was saying that he would take vacant houses, provisions, forage, wagons, and livestock, since "it is clearly our duty and right to take them, otherwise they might be used against us."[12]

4. Protecting Bridges: At the end of this chapter, Westervelt alludes to their mission of protecting a bridge (presumably a railroad bridge) over the Obion River. The guerrilla typically attacked bridges, convoys of supplies, small garrisons, and troops on the move. Westervelt would spend the next several months protecting bridges and supplies in the face of continuing attacks from these partisan bodies.

We remained tied to the bank until next morning, when we ran down the river about twenty-five miles and stopped at Hamburgh* landing. A company of cavalry were now landed and sent across the country to Corinth, and we waited for their return. Soon rain came on, when our company was taken from the upper deck and sent on shore, where they found shelter under a shed. The rain continued all day and night. About daylight the next morning the cavalry returned, when our company were sent on board, and the fleet started down the river. The rain still continued and the weather was cold and disagreeable, while our quarters on the upper deck were not very pleasant. After becoming thoroughly wet, we were taken from the deck, and put into the hold, where it was dry and warm, but dark and crowded. The hold was from three to four feet deep, so we had to crawl in and out on all fours, but it was better than being exposed to the rain and wind on the upper deck.

On the morning of the 9th we reached Paducah. Here our ever-welcome mail awaited us, and having access to the officers' cabin, I spent a good part of the night answering letters. In the morning the steamboats commenced taking in coal, when, finding they would be delayed some time, I went on shore to see the town, that I found to be quite a thriving place, and well fortified. At three P.M. we started again with our boats turned down the Ohio river. About midnight we reached Cairo and stopped a short time, then ran on to Columbus, arriving there at daylight. There we remained until the 12th, when we landed in a drenching rain, loaded

---

* Hamburg Landing — see picture on following page.

on the cars and at dark we started.

The road ran through a level country, most of the way heavily wooded. All along the way we could see the picket fires, and once in a while a company snugly quartered in a block house, guarding a bridge or culvert. We envied them their comfortable dry quarters, as we were on open cars, exposed to the cold wind, and wet through with the beating rain.

At seven P.M. we reached Union City, where it was so dark we could not see to march to our camp, so we rolled ourselves in our blankets, under a freight shed, and slept soundly until morning. When on awaking at daylight, we were ordered to pack up, and although the rain still fell, we were marched away from the shed, and after going about a mile through the mud, were ordered to camp. Here, after some delay, we got our tent up, not very good, but so it would protect us from the rain. We occupied this camp five days it rained almost incessantly accompanied by thunder and lightning. We had to detail nearly our whole company to dig trenches, to draw the water off our camp, or it would have driven us out. The weather was cold and, taking it altogether, we were not favorably impressed with the weather at Union City, and began to wonder if the sun ever shown on that benighted country.

Friday, Dec. 18. — For the first time since our arrival at Union City the sun made its welcome appearance, when we dried our tents and blankets for the first time since our arrival. About noon orders came to march. Soon four companies of our regiment, under command of Maj. Martin, were on the road. The marching was rough and tiresome, but we stopped often to let our pioneers fix the bridges. At dark we had made about twelve miles, when we camped for the night.

Hamburg Landing

The next morning we started at nine A.M., and soon passed the small village of Jacksonville. Six miles further we camped at what is called the Obion bottom, a swamp through which flows the Obion river, that at certain seasons of the year covers the whole swamp. At this place a road is built across the swamp, or as the natives call it the "bottom," leading to the large bridge across the river. The road is raised about eight feet higher than the level of the swamp, that is here about a mile wide, with small bridges every few rods, to let the water flow through in time of freshet, and looked as though it represented an immense amount of work. At whose expense it was built I was unable to learn.

It was near noon when we camped and after dinner some twenty of us started out for a scout. We soon passed our outside pickets, when I was sent ahead with a small squad for an advance guard. We passed through some good farming land, with fine dwellings, and many tobacco houses filled with the weed. These tobacco houses are built of logs, and are about twenty-five feet square, and the height of a two-story dwelling. Spaces some six inches wide are left between the logs to allow free circulation of air. In these are hung the tobacco, tied in small bunches, one tier above another, from a few feet from the ground up to the eaves. As they had been unable to move the crop for the past two years, it was all stored in these buildings. Some of the large plantations would have as many as fifty of these houses, which at this time were all filled. Near one house was a deer park with eighteen deer, so tame they would come up and eat from our hands.

After marching some eight miles our advance came upon some rebel cavalry, but they being well mounted got away before we could bring them to. We soon came to a large farmhouse where we loaded our wagon with sheep and grain, and a few chickens and geese, and started to return. I was then ordered by our major to make a detour of about eight miles to the right, and meet him at a farmhouse, where we had seen the deer that afternoon in passing, as he intended to stop there for the night. I started off through the woods in the direction he gave, and was soon out of sight. By sunset I had reached the place I was ordered to go, and finding no signs of the enemy started to return. I soon realized the fact that it was getting dark and I was getting tired. Trudging on I soon reached a farmhouse, and under a shed found a fine looking mule, and near by was a saddle and bridle. Without stopping to ask if he had ever been ridden, I quickly put on the saddle and bridle and mounted. He proved to be as good a saddle animal as I ever mounted. I rode on lively for about a mile, when on coming to the edge of a woods heard footsteps coming towards me. Quickly drawing up to the roadside I listened attentively, and could hear voices, and the sound of horses' feet. A high fence prevented me from leaving the road, and if I returned the way I came, why I would be going away from our men, and then it was hard to tell whether it was our own troops or the enemy who were coming. Then another argument, that perhaps weighed stronger than any of the others, was this: If I ran away, when there was no danger, I would lay myself open to ridicule, that would never be forgotten, so I concluded to stay and meet whatever was coming. The steps came nearer, and I waited with my gun across the pommel of my saddle, trying to keep cool, with a determination to have one shot, and if the numbers were too great to trust to luck to escape.

A SCOUTING PARTY

On came the footsteps, when suddenly there emerged from the woods an old hayseed looking native, driving ahead of him a lean superannuated mule, while the noise I heard was him swearing at his mule, trying to make him move faster.

Laughing at myself for my unnecessary scare, I rode on and soon reached the farmhouse, where our company had one of the sheep already cooked, which with the addition of about a bushel of potatoes, made a supper to which we did ample justice, after which I curled myself up in front of the fireplace and slept soundly.

We continued in our camp near the Obion river until Dec. 24th. We were not allowed to become lonesome, as the enemy would occasionally make a dash at the bridge, evidently bent on destroying it, and it soon became evident that our mission here was to protect it until a forward movement of the

army could be made. These dashes were generally made at night, just as we were rolled up in our blankets and comfortably passing off to the land of dreams. First would come a few stray shots, then the long roll by our drummer, that would call us in line, and we would double quick to the bridge, arriving just in time to find the enemy gone.

On the night of the 25th, by way of variety, two of our companies were sent after some guerrillas, who were guilty of hanging some Union soldiers, who had fallen into their hands. They lived a few miles from our camp, and hearing they were at their homes, we were sent to capture them. We made a march of some twenty miles, and surrounded several of the houses, but found none of the male inhabitants home. Soon after midnight we reached an old farmer's house, and spent the remainder of the night killing, cooking, and eating his chickens and ducks.

Notes — Chapter 22

1. *O.R.*, Vol. XXI, Part 3, p. 564. Total XVI Corps strength was 65,610; but left wing, 12,439, was with Grant at Chattanooga, and 18,341 were in Arkansas; hence 30,780 were in the west Tennessee triangle.

2. Andrew Nelson Lytle, *Bedford Forrest and his Critter Company* (New York: Minton Balch & Co., 1931), pp. 243-244.

3. Ibid., p. 245.

4. *O.R.*, Vol. XXXI, Part 3, p. 160.

5. Lytle, *Bedford Forrest and his Critter Company*, p. 246.

6. *O.R.*, Vol. XXXI, Part 3, p. 323.

7. Lytle, *Bedford Forrest and His Critter Company*, p. 249.

8. John Allan Wyeth, *That Devil Forrest* (New York: Harper and Brothers, 1959), p. xi.

9. Lloyd Lewis, *Sherman—Fighting Prophet* (New York: Harcourt, Brace and Co., 1932), p. 171.

10. Ibid., p. 187.

11. Ibid., p. 298.

12. Ibid.

Chapter 23

CHASING NATHAN BEDFORD FORREST

Background

By December 24, General A.J. Smith had gotten his forces organized and reached the 17th Veteran New York at its advanced position which was Union City, Tennessee near the Obion River.

In the period from December 2-24, Forrest had reached Jackson and was vigorously recruiting. By December 6 he was able to report that he had arrived safely at Jackson, had already recruited 5,000 men, and if unmolested until January 1, would have 8,000 effective troops in the field.[1]

As indicated previously, General Hurlbut's Order 157 to conscript men in the area into the Union army was actually helping Forrest. The Order applied to all persons residing under the protection of the United States; i.e., all those where the Federals controlled the territory.[2] In the South, a conscription law had been passed by the Confederate Congress in 1862 and later broadened in 1864 so that all white men in the Southern States between the ages of 17 and 50 were "in the military service for the war."[3] The North had passed a conscription act in 1863.[4] Yet, here were able-bodied men in Western Tennessee who were in a Southern state controlled by Federals who had escaped both conscription acts. Sherman decided to put an end to this situation; hence, Hurlbut's Order.

To illustrate how Hurlbut's Order helped the South, Forrest reported that of a group of 130 men conscripted into the Federal forces, 100 had escaped and joined his ranks.[5] When the men in the area were forced to serve, most chose the South rather than the North.

Hurlbut started a plan to entrap Forrest as early as December 11.[6] By December 14, he knew that Forrest had about 1,100 men armed and 2,500 unarmed.[7] He ordered General Smith to move as soon as his force was organized and to go through Dresden, Paris, and Huntington to get to Jackson.[8] By December 16, Hurlbut was making specific plans to catch Forrest as he returned to Mississippi. He also wired Smith to protect Fort Pillow for he had "no doubt that unless soon attacked and crushed, Forrest will gather a formidable force and be of serious injury on the river..."[9] (The reference in this case is to the Mississippi.)

While Hurlbut was planning and acting, Forrest knew that the Federals were massing against him. On December 18, he contacted both General Joseph E. Johnston and Stephen D. Lee asking for help.[10] He got none. Lee's hands were tied until he talked to Johnston's replacement, General Polk.[11] By December 22, Forrest realized that he had to move south and asked for help in getting through the Federal lines.[12]

Thus, while A.J. Smith's column was moving against him, and Hurlbut's infantry and cavalry were forming a cordon around him, Forrest went south. He escaped Hurlbut's trap as evidenced by Hurlbut's report to Sherman on December 28, 1863: "Forrest, driven from Jackson, eluded Grierson's cavalry and crossed the railroad at LaGrange last night. This was owing to neglect of orders in not destroying the bridge over Wolf at LaFayette."[13]

Smith and his command, including the 17th Veteran New York had done their work well—others had failed. Smith would have to wait until the Battle of Tupelo on July 14, 1864, to meet Forrest and defeat him.

General Andrew Jackson Smith

CHASING NATHAN BEDFORD FORREST

He moved his troops back to Columbus and from there the 17th Veteran New York embarked to take part in Sherman's Meridian Expedition.

Highlights

Here, for the first time, Westervelt saw his division commander, A.J. Smith. He briefly describes the general and he also describes the cold weather of the winter of 1863-1864.

1. General Andrew Jackson Smith: Westervelt portrays Smith as "a fine-looking old gentleman" (see Picture on page 164). Smith graduated from West Point in 1838 and was forty-eight when Westervelt first saw him. He had served under Halleck, commanded one of Sherman's divisions at Chickasaw Bluffs in December 1862, and a division of the XIII Corps in the Vicksburg Campaign. He was considered to be "one of the most competent division and corps commanders in the service." He is credited with defeating Forrest at Tupelo, Mississippi on July 14, 1864.[14]

2. Weather in the Winter of 1863-1864: The weather in the months of December 1863 and January 1864 was really tough on the troops. Note the following from Westervelt's report:
    - the reference to frozen ground in Huntington, Tennessee
    - the frozen ground that was so slippery at Paris, Tennessee that the cavalrymen couldn't ride their horses
    - the fact that ten percent of the regiment were disabled due to the weather
    - the men had to be served commissary whiskey to overcome the effects of the cold and dampness

On the 24th the main body of the army arrived, commanded by Gen. Andrew Jackson Smith, a fine-looking old gentleman, who stood about six feet high, with long white hair reaching to his shoulders, and tough enough to be a worthy representative of his namesake.

On the 26th we passed through Dresden, a place of about two thousand inhabitants, many of whom turned out to see the Yankees pass. In two places they showed the Union flag, but I think most of them were of the rebel persuasion. On the 29th we camped near Huntington, and remained until Jan. 3d. The weather was very cold, the ground was frozen, and living in sheltered tents, with what few blankets we could carry on the march, made it difficult to sleep comfortably.

On the 3d we broke camp, and after marching a mile, reached Huntington, the county seat of Carrol County. About nine A.M. it began to snow, that continued all day. At two P.M. we went into camp in a swamp where the ground was frozen so hard that we could scarce drive a tent pin. We scraped away the snow, and put some small limbs under us to keep us from the wet, and then lay down and shivered through the night.

On the 6th, we passed through Paris, Kentucky* one of the finest cities of the state. We now found we were turning back by a roundabout course towards Union City. The ground was frozen hard, and so slippery that the cavalrymen could not ride their horses, so the infantry could get over the ground faster than they could.

I had no thermometer to tell the exact degree of cold, but our breath congealed,

forming huge icicles on our mustaches and eyebrows. The men would stand by the fire, and before they could feel the warmth their shoes would burn, so their toes would be exposed. These in turn would freeze, then swell up, turn black and burst open. Our ambulances were soon as full as the horses could draw on the slippery roads, so the men had to hobble along as best they could. Next our rations gave out, when we were put on roast corn diet, that to a man with poor teeth was slim feed.

On the 9th we reached Union City, and were quartered under an open shed, where for the first time, since the night of the 3d, we slept without snow under us. The next day we sent to the hospital those who were disabled by frost-bitten hands or feet, or sick from exposure. Nearly ten percent of our regiment were off duty; many of them never recovered. We could have taken part in a sharp engagement without a greater loss than we sustained on this raid.

We remained at Union City until the morning of Sunday, January 17th, when in a cold rain we were ordered to pack up for another move. At 7 A.M. we were in line, where we stood with our knapsacks on just two hours, then loaded on open cars, and ran to Columbus. Although the distance was but thirty miles we did not reach their† until dark, by which time we were thoroughly soaked. We were then quartered under an open shed.

In looking around I stumbled over an armful of hay that had been reserved for the Colonel's horse, which my tent-mate, C.S. Crist, and myself appropriated for our bed, and we were perfectly deaf when his hostler

---

* Tennessee not Kentucky

† there

came enquiring "whar dat hay am gone." We then spread our wet blankets and tents over us covering our heads and all. It was some time before we got warm, but when we did, we fell asleep and slept soundly until morning.

When we awoke we were covered with about three inches of snow, that had fallen during the night, and drifted under the shed. While we were badly chilled, with some difficulty we started a fire and made coffee.

The men were served with whiskey, but my tentmate and myself found more lasting warmth in a quart of hot coffee, and some vigorous exercise, than in all the whiskey in the commissary department. In the afternoon we went on board the steamer Perry, and took up our quarters on the main deck near the boilers, where it was warm and comfortable, and we spent most of the night thawing and drying our clothes and blankets.

Notes — Chapter 23

1. *O.R.*, Vol. XXXI, Part 3, p.789.

2. Ibid., pp. 160-161.

3. Guernsey and Alden, *Harper's Pictorial History of the Civil War*, p. 791.

4. Ibid., pp. 646-648.

5. *O.R.*, Vol. XXXI, Part 3, p. 789.

6. Ibid., p. 385.

7. Ibid., p. 412.

8. Ibid., p. 443.

9. Ibid., p. 428.

10. Ibid., pp. 844-846.

11. Ibid., p. 853.

12. Ibid., pp. 853, 854.

13. Ibid., p. 523.

14. Warner, *Generals in Blue*, pp. 454-455.

Chapter 24

SHERMAN'S MERIDIAN CAMPAIGN

Background

Sherman's Meridian Campaign occupied Westervelt's time from January 18, 1864, to March 14, 1864.

Few people know about this movement; Margie Riddle Bearss wrote about the Meridian Expedition under the title *Sherman's Forgotten Campaign*.[1] Orville James Victor, in his *History of the Southern Rebellion* published just after the close of the war, wrote, "The march of Sherman through central Mississippi to the Alabama state line was in execution of a masterly design, but little understood at the time, and one which did not receive the notice its importance merited."[2] Perhaps the most important aspect of the Meridian Campaign was that it is generally acknowledged to be the prelude to Sherman's March to the Sea.

Sherman had expressed a desire to carry out a campaign against Meridian as early as October 24, 1863.[3] His stated objectives were "to strike Meridian, and it may be Selma."[4] He further stated in a communication to General Nathaniel Banks that he planned "to strike a blow at Meridian and Demopolis. I think I can do it, and the destruction of the railroad east and west, north and south of Meridian, will close the door of rapid travel and conveyance of stores from Mississippi and the Confederacy east, and will make us less liable to the incursions of the enemy toward the Mississippi River."[5]

Grant stated the objectives of the campaign to be for Sherman "to move out to Meridian with his spare force [the cavalry going from Corinth] and destroy the roads east and north and south of there so effectually that the enemy will not attempt to rebuild them during the rebellion. He will then return unless the opportunity of going into Mobile appears perfectly plain."[6]

The expedition was a three-pronged affair. The main effort was led by Sherman personally and involved parts of three divisions of the XVI Corps under General Hurlbut and parts of three divisions of the XVII Corps under General McPherson, a total of about 22,000 men.[7] Cavalry under Major General W. Sooy Smith was to leave Memphis and follow the Mobile and the Ohio Railroad, destroying it, and join Sherman at Meridian. Smith had a cavalry force of about 6,600.[8] This was the second prong. The third prong was an expedition up the Yazoo River led by Colonel James Coates. Coates' effort was actually a feint for he had only 947 men.[9]

Westervelt and the 17th New York were assigned to the XVI Corps under Hurlbut, the Fourth Division (Brigadier General Veatch) and the Second Brigade (Colonel James H. Howe).[10]

Westervelt's Regiment went from Columbus, Kentucky down the Mississippi to Vicksburg and left Vicksburg on February 2, 1864, heading for Meridian. Orders were to be "lightly equipped— no tents or luggage save what is carried by officers, men, and horses." Wagons were reserved for food and ammunition.[11] The wagons were to go as far as Chunky River and await further orders.[12] The itinerary of the regiment was from Vicksburg to Jackson, through Brandon, Morton, Hillsborough, and Decatur to Meridian.[13]

Initially, the Confederates resisted the Federal advance at Joe Davis' plantation and kept up a constant skirmish for eighteen miles. This did not seriously delay the Federal movement to

Jackson.[14] After that, the resistance involved quick attacks upon the wagon train and the capture of any Yankee who strayed beyond the safety of his unit.

In this entire campaign, the 17th New York was significantly involved just once—when they protected the wagon train at Chunky Creek. They lost a total of 12; 1 killed, 1 died, 1 taken prisoner, and 9 missing.[15] The entire XVI Corps lost 143 and the expedition (XVI and XVII Corps) lost only 297.[16]

Sherman was successful in reaching Meridian where he destroyed depots, storehouses, offices, hospitals, hotels, and cantonments. Hurlbut's Corps destroyed, on the north and east, 60 miles of ties and iron, 1 locomotive and 8 bridges. McPherson's Corps on the south and east, destroyed 55 miles of railroad, 53 bridges, 6,075 feet of trestle, 19 locomotives, 28 steam cars, and 3 steam sawmills.[17]

Sherman waited near Canton for Sooy Smith until February 20, and then ordered his troops to return to Vicksburg. Smith was defeated by Forrest, with an inferior force, at Okolana and retreated to Memphis. That defeat ended the Meridian Campaign. It also ended Smith's career in the army.

Westervelt and the 17th New York returned to Vicksburg on March 4, 1864.[18] Their route took them through Decatur, Canton, and across the Big Black River to Vicksburg. From Vicksburg, they traveled up the Mississippi River by boat to Memphis.[19]

Highlights

1. Major General William Tecumseh Sherman: (See Picture on page 171) On February 7, 1864, Westervelt saw General Sherman for the first time and learned he was in charge of the expedition. Westervelt was delighted to be under Sherman's command then and later "on all his famous marches." Sherman was a favorite of his men; they called him "Uncle Billy." Westervelt took particular note of Sherman's "sharp piercing eye."

William Tecumseh Sherman graduated from West Point in 1840, ranking sixth in his class. He remained in the army until 1853 when he resigned his commission as captain and entered civilian life. He was a banker and lawyer, both unsuccessfully. He then became superintendent of the State Military Institute of Louisiana, resigning that post in 1861. He entered the service as colonel of the 13th U.S. Infantry of the Regular Army. Like Westervelt, he was in the First Battle of Bull Run.

His star fell in September 1861 when he became outraged at his volunteers. Later, his star rose again and he became famous for his capture of Atlanta, Savannah, and Johnston's army. After the war, he came commander in chief of the army. He was in great demand as a speaker, particularly by veteran groups. He thoroughly enjoyed that role.[20]

2. Sherman's Neckties: Westervelt describes how they destroyed a section of the railroad between Jackson and Brandon by burning the ties and twisting the rails while hot. The technique, particularly when the rails were bent around a tree, became known as making "Sherman's neckties."

General William T. Sherman

3. Foraging—its perils: On February 10, the troops of the Fourth Division were placed on half rations.[21] By March 1, the regiment was ordered to forage for subsistence; i.e., to live off the land. A member of Westervelt's Company brought in some meal which made everyone sick. Poison was suspected but later found not to be the cause. There was ample basis for concern, for troops in enemy territory were fair game. The Rebels, in their retreat from Vicksburg and in the same area in 1863, had dried up all the cisterns and contaminated all the streams and ponds so the water could not be used by the Federal invaders.[22] The Northerners did the same thing in Westminster, Maryland when Jeb Stuart was on his way to Gettysburg.

While foraging had its benefits, it also had its perils!

SHERMAN'S MERIDIAN CAMPAIGN

We remained tied to the bank at Columbia* for some days. The men were employed loading commissary stores and coal. There were quite a number of steamboats loading with troops and stores. What our destination was to be was a mystery, but we made ourselves as comfortable as possible, for a long trip. Finally, on the afternoon of the 22d, we cast off, and started down the Mississippi. As we were running with the current, it was no trouble to make good headway. The banks were mostly covered with snow, while the river contained a good bit of floating ice. We soon passed Island No. 10,† a low piece of land in the middle of the river, with some fortifications garrisoned with negro troops, who a few weeks later were destined to be massacred, after surrendering, by the troops under the rebel general Forrest.

On Saturday we reached Memphis. We did not land at the city, but crossed the river and tied to the bank. The next morning (Sunday) we marched on shore, had inspection and then formed square, and listened to the Articles of War, read by our Chaplain. This over, we again loaded on the boat, and crossed over the river to Memphis, where we commenced to take in wood and stores, that kept a detail busy the remainder of the day.

In the afternoon I was sent on shore to the office of the Chief of Transportation. This gave me a chance to see the city. At dark we again crossed the river and tied to the bank for the night.

The next day the paymaster arrived and commenced paying our regiment. At dark

we crossed the river to Memphis, and anchored. At twelve P.M. half the regiment were paid, when the signal gun to start was fired. The paymaster then packed up, and went on shore, leaving half the men unpaid. This caused great dissatisfaction, and at one time there was danger of mutiny, but at length the men were quieted and order restored and we ran down the Mississippi all night. In the morning we found the snow had all disappeared from the banks, and the ice from the river, and we could feel the weather getting warmer. The shores were lined with a thick growth of small willows. In many places the bank had slid into the stream, carrying with it large trees. The course of the river would gradually change, leaving the trees or snags near the middle of the stream, making navigation difficult. Besides, the river here was very crooked, and ran at all points of the compass. In looking at some of our fleet that were ahead, they looked as though they were coming towards us, while some in the rear would seem to be going away from us, and yet we were all drifting down the stream.

We ran steadily all night, heaving the lead continually. It seemed strange to hear them call out "three feet," "three feet scant," and yet there seemed enough water to run safely. At daylight on the 27th we reached a better part of the river and ran faster.

About noon we reached the small town of Providence, and a few miles further passed a Contraband camp, containing several thousand negroes, whose principal occupation seemed to be eating government rations. That fulfilled the idea of freedom with the most of them—that was a life of idleness, with plenty to eat.

About dark we reached Vicksburg, Miss., and after some delay tied to the bank

---

* Columbus

† The "massacre" was at Ft. Pillow, not Island No. 10.

173

for the night. The next morning we ran down the river about two miles, where we landed and camped near the bank. This was on Jan. 28th, and the fields were green, while the buds on the peach trees were beginning to burst open, and the leaves on many of the trees were quite large. The country had the appearance of the month of June in the north, while the weather was so warm many of the men were bathing.

On the next day, seeing no signs of a move, I got a pass and went to the city. On every side could be seen the marks of Grant's artillerymen. Not a house could be found that had not been perforated by shot or shell. In some places we would see holes in a bank, and on entering we would find large rooms, where whole families lived during the bombardment. After a stroll through the town we visited the fortifications on the heights, and found them fully as strong as represented, and well worthy of the name of the Gibraltar of America, and were it not for the presence of an invisible general in the rebel camp (General Starvation) they would have proved well nigh impregnable. After an hour spent in observations, we returned to town and took dinner at a hotel, being served with catfish steak, cut from a fifty pound fish, which we pro- nounced excellent eating. About dark we returned to camp.

We remained in our camp five days. That gave us our first Sunday in camp since leaving New York. We expected we would have divine service, but our chaplain was absent trading horses, and his record afterwards, while in the service, was such that it was evident he did not come with the regiment to advance its spiritual interest; his conduct made him so objectionable, that the officers fairly drove him from the regiment.

We lost sight of him for some months, when, taking up a New York paper one day, I read the following paragraph. "Rev. Albert F. Griffith, chaplain of the 17th New York Regt., who had charge of the mails at the hospitals at Nashville, was arrested for stealing money from letters the soldiers were sending home to their families. He was released on parole, pending examination, when he attempted to escape from the city. He was caught, brought back, and locked up." This was the last we ever heard from him, and we never had another chaplain. This was an office that with a few honorable exceptions was filled with the worst set of government frauds that ever wore a uniform. There were some who were good Christian men, who were an honor to their profession either in civil or military life, who gained the confidence of the officers and men, and no doubt did good, which will never be known until the last great day of accounting. But so many of them, who were incapable of making a living at home, managed to fasten themselves into the service, where their whole aim seemed to be to have an easy time, and draw their pay. Their conduct was so unchristianlike, and I may add, ungentlemanly, that they cast a stigma upon the office.

On Tuesday, Feb. 2d, orders came in the morning for the officers to send in all their extra baggage. At noon we packed up and at three P.M. we started, moving up along the river to Vicksburg. We passed through the city and took the road toward Jackson, the capital of the state. We soon passed some palmettoes, the first we had seen. The road was very rough, running over one continuous chain of hills, on each of which were fortifications. The next day we reached the Big Black River, which we crossed on a pontoon bridge.

On the 5th we were called at one A.M., and marched as soon as we could pack up. On reaching the road we were detailed as wagon guard. The woods we passed through were all on fire on both sides of the road, making it dangerous for our ammunition train to pass. The weather was very warm, which, added to the heat and smoke of the forest fires, made it almost intolerable.

On the 6th we camped near the small town of Clinton, which we found on our arrival mostly in ruins.

The next morning we were called at five and an hour after were on the road. The marching was good and we traveled fast. At nine A.M. we reached Jackson the capital of the state. The depot and most of the railroad buildings were destroyed, but the state house and the public buildings had not been disturbed. These were all fine structures, being built of marble and granite. We marched through the city, and halted on the Canton near the outside line of fortifications. While here, General W. T. Sherman and staff rode past, and we found he was in command of the expedition. It was the first time I had ever seen him and was struck with his sharp piercing eye. This was his first raid, and it was our good fortune to be with him on all his famous marches after.

We rested outside the fortification at Jackson until two P.M., when we started again, taking the road back through the city, past the state house, then turned to the left and crossed the Pearl river on a bridge of flat boats. We then left the road and started across the open country, and traveled until midnight, when our wagon train stuck in the mud, and we lay down beside them, and slept until daylight, when we got up and cooked the last of our rations for breakfast. We were then sent about a mile to destroy a section of railroad, which we did by tearing up the track, burning the ties and bending the rails while hot. About noon our work was done, and we started on our march.

At three P.M., we passed through the town of Brandon, a town of about ten thousand inhabitants, but entirely dead from the effects of the war. About midnight we went into camp, tired and hungry, but having no supper. I rolled myself in my blanket, and went to sleep.

In the morning we were called at four, when we drew rations and soon had our breakfast. At six we were on the road, traveling very fast. At three P.M. we came to a place where the advance had a skirmish the day before. The dead rebels were still unburied, while a little to one side were the remains of a women who was killed by a stray shot during the skirmish. At nine P.M., after a march of twenty-three miles, we camped, and could see the enemy's camp fires about two miles ahead.

We expected an engagement in the morning. This caused us to turn out early and get our breakfast out of the way. At seven we started, and on reaching the road were halted, and could hear the advance skirmishing with the enemy. We soon reached Hillsboro, where we found some of the enemy's dead by the road side, the effect of the morning's skirmish.

On the 12th we reached Decatur where we found some large tanneries and leather manufactories burning. Here we halted an hour, and while waiting I cooked some coffee on the ruins of one of the buildings. On leaving here we had to cross a long swamp. When about half our train was over, the enemy made a dash on the rear, killing one of the drivers and sixteen mules. We rallied as quick as we could to the spot, but the enemy being well mounted got away before we could get a shot at them. This put us on the alert, and raised quite an excitement, which soon passed over, and we moved on quietly until about ten P.M., when we went into camp.

The next day, the 13th, we were detailed to guard the train, while our troops pushed on to Meridian, where they expected to meet the enemy. We congratulated ourselves on the prospect of an easy time, and moved on slowly until the 14th, when we reached a place called Chunkey creek. Here the wagons were packed in the form of a circle, with the horses and mules inside the ring. Our battery was put in position and we made ourselves comfortable, as we expected to stay here several days. At three P.M. the enemy made a dash on our lines, that called us in order, but after a few shots they withdrew. An hour after they struck another part of our line, but finding us ready to receive them, quickly withdrew. This was kept up with a few variations all the time our troops were gone, and we did more real fighting than the main army. We were continually harrassed* night and day by the bands of guerrillas, who were determined to give us no rest, and if a man strayed a short distance from camp, he was sure to be picked up. Quite a number of prisoners were sent from the front for us to guard, which added to our duties, and we soon found that our expected easy time was not to be found guarding trains.

On Feb. 20th the troops returned from Meridian, and we being packed up and waiting besides the road, were ready to take our place in line. We were soon on the road. The next day we reached Decatur, where we halted, formed our line of battle, and loaded our pieces, evidently expecting to find the enemy. We halted about an hour and when we left, what few buildings remained on our outward trip, were in flames. We marched as fast as possible on our return making about seventeen miles a day. Most of the time we were train guard, which gave us a chance to have our knapsacks carried.

On the 26th we reached the town of Canton, a small place, but comprised of fine large houses, and said to be a very wealthy town. A few years ago, during the yellow fever scourge in the south, about one-half of the inhabitants of this place fell victims of that disease. We remained at Canton until March the 1st, employed destroying railroads and doing what damage we could. The fine houses in the town were respected. I believe not one of them was destroyed.

Rations were running short, and we were ordered to forage for our subsistence. One of our company brought into camp what he supposed was a bag of meal. All who ate of it were taken sick. At first we supposed it was poisoned, but on examination it proved to be a bag of ground beans, and the imperfect manner in which it was cooked was enough to upset the digestive apparatus of an ordinary ostrich.

While here we had a severe rain storm and put up our rubber blankets for shelter. This was the only time during the whole march we put up anything in the form of a tent. The weather was so warm we slept on the ground with no shelter but our blankets thrown over us, covering our heads and all, and experienced no inconvenience from the cold.

---

* harassed

On Thursday, March 1st, we broke camp at Canton, and in a pouring rain started on our march. The roads soon began to get muddy, which continually grew deeper. Soon after noon our wagon train got stuck in the mud, and we went into camp. The next morning we found the roads still muddy, but the day being warm and clear, the mud soon dried. A mile's march took us through the town of Livingston, a small but lively looking place of about one thousand inhabitants.

During the day we passed some fine plantations, with large dwellings and good negro quarters. The land was mostly cleared and under cultivation. On the 3d we crossed the Big Black river, and from there to Vicksburg we passed one line of fortifications after another, which grew stronger as we advanced, until about two P.M. of the 4th, when we camped about a mile outside of the city, on the top of a hill, where wood and water was scarce.

Here we remained until the morning of the 9th, when we were called some hours before daylight, and hurried into line, when we started towards the city. The morning was dark and the road we took was over rifle pits and trenches, which caused the usual amount of grumbling and swearing. At sunrise we reached the levee. Here we found about twenty steamboats loading with troops and stores to go on an expedition, that proved to be Bank's unfortunate trip up the Red river. Our regiment soon embarked on the transport, Sir Wm. Wallace, when we found we were not to go with the expedition, but started up the river. As we were running against a strong current we moved slowly.

There were several passengers on the boat; among others was cotton buyer from New Orleans, on his way to Memphis to purchase cotton, and as was usual with his class, he carried quite a fortune with him. To while away the time the captain and some of the passengers indulged in a game of poker. The weather being warm the door of the Captain's room was open, so we could see the game, and could see the broker losing and drinking heavily. The second night of our trip, he having lost the bottom dollar of his thousands, he sprang from the table, and out of the door, right past where I sat, and with a screech that sounded more like a animal than a human being, sprang overboard. The boat was stopped, and search was made, but he could not be found and we soon continued on our way.

On March 14th we arrived at Memphis and camped on the opposite side of the river. I spent one day in the city of Memphis, and saw all I wished to see of the place.

Notes — Chapter 24

1. Margie Riddle Bearss, *Sherman's Forgotten Campaign*, title page.

2. Victor, *The History of the Southern Rebellion*, Vol. IV, p. 351.

3. *O.R.*, Vol. XXXI, Part 1, pp. 720-721.

4. *O.R.*, Vol. XXXII, Part 2, p. 75.

5. Ibid., p. 114.

6. Ibid., p. 100.

7. *O.R.*, Vol. XXXII, Part 1, p. 172.

8. Ibid.

9. *O.R.,* Vol. XXXII, Part 1, p. 320.

10. Ibid., p. 169.

11. Ibid., p. 182.

12. Ibid., p. 186.

13. Ibid., p. 207.

14. Bowman and Irwin, *Sherman and His Campaigns* (New York: Scribner and Sons, 1865), p. 160.

15. *O.R.*, Vol. XXXII, Part 1, p. 204.

16. Ibid., pp. 191-193.

17. Bowman and Irwin, *Sherman and His Campaigns*, p. 161.

18. *O.R.*, Vol. XXXII, Part 1, pp. 207-208.

19. Ibid.

20. Warner, *Generals in Blue*, pp. 441-444.

21. *O.R.*, Vol. XXXII, Part 2, p. 363.

22. Margie Riddle Bearss, *Sherman's Forgotten Campaign*, p. 5.

Chapter 25

CHASING FORREST AGAIN

Background

The same day that Westervelt reached Memphis, March 14, 1864, Sherman received word that Grant had been given command of all the armies of the United States and he (Sherman) had been given command of the Military Division of the Mississippi,[1] i.e., all the armies between the Alleghenies and the Mississippi.[2] Between March 17 and March 24, he conferred with Grant. Out of that meeting came two objectives; Grant would go after Lee's army and Sherman would go after Joseph E. Johnston's army.[3]

Next, Sherman visited Athens, Decatur, Huntsville, and Larkin's Ferry in Alabama, and Chattanooga, Loudon, and Knoxville in Tennessee. He established the lines of communications and supply to be guarded and organized the troops for the next major campaign.[4] Plans were to have 100,000 men ready by April 25, at the same time sending 10,000 men under General A.J. Smith to participate in Bank's ill-fated Red River Campaign.[5] Had Westervelt's regiment stayed with Smith, he would have gone to Red River also.

Instead, General Veatch's Division, of which the 17th New York was a part, was ordered on March 15 to go from Memphis to Cairo, thence by the Tennessee River to Clifton or Carrollsville and then by land to report to General G.M. Dodge near Athens, Alabama.[6] This move was related to the forthcoming campaign.

The Fourth Division reached Cairo on March 21. While waiting there for water transportation to go up the Tennessee, word was received that Forrest was attacking Union City, Tennessee. General Veatch was absent, so General Brayman, who commanded the District of Cairo, "borrowed" four regiments to go and reinforce Union City. He had a force 2,000 strong which included the 17th New York. As Westervelt indicates, they got to within a few miles of the beleaguered city only to learn that the garrison, under Colonel Hawkins, had surrendered.[7]

Forrest attacked Paducah, Kentucky on March 25. Veatch sent one regiment to Paducah that same day and followed with the rest of the division on the twenty-sixth. The 17th New York was in this latter group and found that the garrison had successfully defended itself and Forrest had moved on, presumably to attack Columbus, Kentucky.[8]

On March 27, Sherman ordered General Veatch to go to Savannah, Tennessee and on to Purdy on the Hatchie River before Forrest returned to his base in Mississippi or Alabama.[9] Orders were issued by Veatch at Williams Landing for his division to march to Purdy and be prepared for battle. This was done on March 30.[10] On April 2, Sherman repeated his order to Veatch to go to Purdy and remain there. Veatch claimed he received information that Forrest was attempting to cross the Hatchie at some other point and therefore he returned to his transports on March 31.[11]

Westervelt reports that they came upon the rear of the enemy who were mounted and able to get away. As a result, they gave up the chase at Purdy. Forrest's version of the events was that 1,500 Yankees came up to Purdy and were driven back to their boats by one regiment.[12]

Sherman was displeased with Veatch's performance and wrote, "General Veatch should have remained at Purdy under his orders until recalled but now it is too late to remedy the error. I am willing to admit it was not intentional."[13] Actually, Forrest did not return to his base until after he had stormed Fort Pillow on April 12. His return route took him past Purdy.[14] Sherman was right.

Highlights

In this chapter, more than any other, Westervelt discusses the activities of the guerrillas and the intense hatred between those in the South who rebelled and those who remained loyal to the Union. These highlights are intended to help round out the picture with emphasis on the attitudes and actions of Forrest and his men.

1. How Forrest Intimidated Federal Garrisons: Forrest was an expert on intimidation. The first garrison to be attacked in Forrest's expedition into Tennessee and Western Kentucky was Union City. Colonel Hawkins was in charge of the fort. Four charges were made against the fort and all were repelled by the Federal defenders. Then, under a flag of truce, Forrest sent in a demand for unconditional surrender. He said, "If you comply with the demand, you are promised treatment due to prisoners of war, according to usages in civilized warfare. If you persist in defense, you must take the consequences."[15] Hawkins surrendered, over the objections of a large majority of his officers. This was the second time he had surrendered to Forrest.[16]

Paducah was attacked on March 25. The demand for surrender stated, "If you surrender, you shall be treated as prisoners of war; but if I have to storm your works, you may expect no quarter."[17] Colonel Hicks, commander at Paducah, refused the demand and successfully defended the fort.

At Columbus, on April 13, Brigadier General Buford called for the surrender of the Federal garrison. He sent a communique to the Federal commander, "Should you surrender, the negroes now in arms will be returned to their masters. Should I, however, be compelled to take the place, no quarter will be shown to the negro troops whatever; the white troops will be treated as prisoners of war."[18] Colonel Lawrence, in command at Columbus, refused the demand and Columbus was saved.

Forrest attacked Fort Pillow on April 12, 1864. He demanded unconditional surrender. In a written note, he said, "Should my demand be refused, I cannot be responsible for the fate of your command."[19]

Forrest used a variety of threats, from promises to treat those surrendered as prisoners of war, to promising such treatment for whites only, to saying he could not be responsible for the fate of Federals if they didn't surrender, to the ultimate one of "no quarter."

2. Forrest's and Northern Sympathizers, Federals from Kentucky and Tennessee, and Negro Troops: Forrest and his men referred to Northern Sympathizers as traitors[20] or tories. He wrote on April 20, 1864 (after Fort Pillow), "Large numbers of Tories have been killed and made away with, and the country is very near free of them." The "country" he was referring to was Western Tennessee, and he added, "Kentucky could be placed in the same condition had I had the time."[21] Union soldiers from Kentucky and Tennessee not only were traitors, they were derisively called "home-made Yankees."[22]

White men who fought with blacks were despised. One Confederate officer at Fort Pillow is quoted as saying, "Don't show the white men any more quarter than the negroes, because they are no better, and not so good, or they would not fight with the negroes."[23] If captured, negro soldiers were not entitled to be treated at prisoners of war; they were property.[24]

3. The Massacre at Fort Pillow: (See Picture page 182) The fight at Fort Pillow was looked upon by the North as a massacre of the Federal troops there.

Fort Pillow had 560 men when it was attacked by Forrest on April 12, 1864. In all, there were 350 colored troops, 200 white troops, and 10 white officers. The commanding officer of the fort, Major Booth, was killed early in the battle. His next in command was Major Bradford, a Tennessean. The North felt that the Confederates took advantage of a truce to gain a better assault position, and that most of the casualties occurred after the Federal troops surrendered—including the killing of Major Bradford.

On the first point, when questioned about the Rebels taking advantage of the truce, General Hurlbut, who was in charge of the district, said, "They always do that; it's a matter of habit with them."[25]

On the second point, The Committee on the Conduct of the War reported that "of the men, from 300 to 400 are known to have been killed at Ft. Pillow, of whom at least 300 were murdered in cold blood" after they had surrendered.[26] The report was widely circulated and accepted in the North. Forrest denied the accuracy and tenor of the report and Lieutenant General S.D. Lee, writing to Major General Washburn, said, "The version [of Fort Pillow] given by you and your government is untrue...."[27]

4. "No Quarter": "Quarter" in military sense, according to *Webster's Dictionary*, means "mercy granted to a surrendering foe."[28] "No quarter" means no mercy, take no prisoners, make sure there are no survivors.

As indicated above, Forrest took the position of "no quarter" for negro troops. Based on the Fort Pillow experience, negro troops believed they would be murdered if captured by Forrest and his men. To the alarm of Forrest, negro troops stationed in Memphis took an oath to show the Rebel troops "no quarter." The issue of "no quarter," also called "black flag," was extensively discussed in correspondence between Major General Washburn, Hurlbut's replacement, and Lieutenant General S.D. Lee of the Confederacy. Eventually, Secretary of War Seddon and President Jefferson Davis got involved.[29] The South had opened "Pandora's Box," and then the concern became one of how to close it.

The Massacre at Fort Pillow

CHASING FORREST AGAIN

On the 19th we again embarked on the steamboat Olive Branch, and continued on our way up the river. As we were going north we found the weather growing colder.

On the 20th we reached Cairo, where we landed, marched through the city, and after going about a mile, camped beside the railroad track, where we remained until the 24th, when we hastily embarked on the steamboat Navigator, and started down the river. Two hours sail brought us to Columbus, where we landed and hurried on board the cars, and started for Union City, Tenn., which place the rebel Gen. Forrest was marching to attack. Our train was drawn by an old wind-broken locomotive, and on reaching an up-grade, a few miles from Columbus, we came to a stand-still, when we got off, and walked up the grade. We then loaded on the cars and proceeded on our way. This delayed us so long that it spoiled the success of the expedition, for on reaching the state line, about five miles from Union City, we found the railroad bridge burned and heard that the garrison at Union city had surrendered to Forrest. We then ran back to Columbus, and at nine A.M. the next morning reached our old camp at Cairo.

After twenty-four hours rest at our camp at Cairo we, on Saturday, March 26th, at three A.M., packed up and marched through the city, and hastily embarked on the steamboat S.R. Pringle. Soon after daylight we started up the river in the company of quite a fleet of transports. Our boat was a shaky old thing, and although run at her best speed, was soon left far in the rear of the remainder of the fleet. At sunset we had inspection of arms and gave the men some fresh cartridges. We could see there was some work laid out for us, but what it was, or where it was to be, remained a mystery that was not solved until soon after dark, when we reached Paducah, Ky.

We found the town in a state of uproar and excitement, on account of an attack they had had that day from Forrest, who after taking Union City, had tried to capture Paducah, but finding it too well fortified and garrisoned, withdrew after suffering heavy loss, not only from our forts, but also from our gunboats in the river. The next morning I got ashore a short time and could see the effects of the fight on all sides. The enemy's dead were still unburied, while many of the houses were perforated with the shot and shell. We were all quite anxious to meet Forrest, as the week before the massacre of the colored troops had taken place at Island No. 10,[*] making the feeling very bitter against this noted rebel chief. He knowing thoroughly the country that he was campaigning through, gave him great advantage over us, and being well mounted he could choose his own fighting ground, or if it suited him any better could run away without giving battle. This made him seem ubiquitous, as we were continually hearing from him where he was not expected.

After a few hours at Paducah the fleet started again, and sailing around the city, entered the Tennesee[†] river. This being Sunday evening our chaplain was called upon to hold divine service in the cabin. He had now been with us about six months and this was his first sermon, and it proved to be his last, as he left us a few days afterward.

----

[*] The "massacre" took place at Ft. Pillow not Island No. 10 and occurred on April 12, 1864, not the week before (March 27, 1864).

[†] Tennessee

Tuesday, March 29th. — In the morning we got orders to get ready to land in light order, taking only our blankets, and two days rations in our haversacks, with sixty rounds of cartridges. We soon passed Savannah, and seven miles further stopped at Crump's landing, where we went on shore and marched back two miles from the river, and stopped for the night.

At six A.M. on the following day we started. Once more we were in pursuit of Forrest. The morning was cool, and we marched fast. At eight A.M. we passed the small town of Adamsville, and soon came up with the rear of the enemy, who leisurely rode about a mile ahead, and when a good opportunity offered would stop and exchange a few shots with our advance, then ride on. This little diverson* was kept up with slight variations until noon, when after traveling about fifteen miles we reached a place called Purdy station, when we gave up the chase and camped.

The next morning we were called early, but did not start until after dinner, when we began our march back to the river. At dark we were still five miles from the shore, when it began to rain and became so dark we could not see five paces in advance. Our course was through the woods, where we went stumbling over logs and fallen trees, and at ten P.M. reached the shore, finding the boats anchored in midstream. We learned that during our absence the pilot and three of the deck hands had gone on shore and had been taken prisoners. After some delay the boats came to the bank, and after throwing out a strong picket we went on board, and, although it rained all night, I was so tired that I rolled in my blanket, and lay on the upper deck, and slept soundly through it all until morning.

Friday, April 1st. — At daylight we found a commotion at the picket lines. Soon the pickets were driven in, and quickly followed by a company dressed mostly in Kentucky homespun, but as one of them carried a small Union flag we did not fire on them. Some of our troops landed as soon as possible and formed in line, but the enemy were careful to keep our of range. Soon the commander of this mounted company, a rough-looking old fellow of about sixty, came on board our boat, and asked for transportation for himself and company to some point further up the river. We soon had them all on our transports, and as we slowly ran up stream I learned from the old man the following story:

When the war broke out he was living with his wife and three sons, about fifty miles from where we met him. His sentiments were strongly in favor of the Union, and made him very obnoxious to some of his neighbors, and finally, when the guerrilla bands began to raid through the country, they marked him out for their persecution. For awhile he and his sons were able to take care of themselves, and more than one of the enemy fell before their ever ready rifles. Finally Forrest sent a company with orders to bring him in "dead or alive." He was warned of their approach and escaped to the woods, leaving his wife at home, thinking they would not disturb her. When the danger was over, he returned only to find his wife's dead body in the yard, while his house, outbuildings, and everything combustible were destroyed. From that time forth his life had but one object, his thoughts by day, his dreams by night, his very religion

---

* diversion

184

(if he had any) were all embodied in one single word—revenge! He gathered about him a score or more of just such spirits as himself, and woe unto the grayback who fell into their hands. He never hesitated to attack bodies of the enemy that numbered the same as his own or even more, but when they outnumbered him two or three to one, he had sense enough to get away. He never gave quarter, and never expected any. One of his sons had already been killed, and he expected to share the same fate. "But" said he, as his old steel grey eye lighted up with fire, "If I can only finish up that old ---- Gen. Forrest, my two boys and I will die contented."

That same afternoon we landed him about fifty miles up the river, and as he mounted his old sorrel mare, and prepared to jog away at the head of his company, he turned, and with a look that boded no good to those he was pursuing, as his hand tightened on his rifle, said: "Gentlemen, good bye; if we never meet again, I hope if you hear from me, it will be that I gave a good account of myself."

We never saw him again, but the following autumn, after the fall of Atlanta, we were pursuing Forrest through southern Tennessee and northern Alabama, and while at Athens I heard of his death, as follows: Like an avenging Nemesis he had continued to follow Forrest's troops, his numbers continually growing less, until his band numbered but ten. One of his sons was then taken sick with fever, and he left him with a friend in the mountains of Chickasaw, Georgia, to be nursed back to health, while he unwilling to lose any time, rode on at his vengeful work. Within a week his camp was surrounded, and although he and his little band made a good fight, the odds were too much against them, and every one of them was killed. His son, who was absent and sick, was the only one left.

These Union guerrilla bands formed the only feasible way of fighting the guerrillas of the South, and had the government paid more attention to arming bands of Union guerrillas the career of Moseby* of Virginia, Forrest of Miss., Rhody† of Alabama, and Quantril‡ of Missouri probably would have been shorter. There was no use sending our cavalry for them, much less our infantry, but independent companies of rough riders would fight them in their own way, and no doubt would have proved more effective than any regularly organized branch of the service.

---

* Mosby

† Roddey

‡ Quantrill

Notes — Chapter 25

1. Bowman and Irwin, *Sherman and His Campaigns*, p. 168.

2. Lewis, *Sherman—Fighting Prophet*, p. 344.

3. Bowman and Irwin, *Sherman and His Campaigns*, p. 168.

4. Ibid., p. 179.

5. Lewis, *Sherman — Fighting Prophet*, p. 350.

6. *O.R.*, Vol. XXXII, Part 1, p. 578.

7. Ibid., p. 503.

8. Ibid., p. 575.

9. Ibid., p. 578.

10. Ibid., p. 580.

11. Ibid., p. 576.

12. Ibid., p. 610.

13. Ibid., p. 577.

14. Wyeth, *That Devil Forrest*, Map, p. 302.

15. U.S. House of Representatives, 38th Congress, 1st Session Report No. 65, Report of the Committee on the Conduct of the War—Fort Pillow Massacre (Washington, D.C. Government Printing Office, 1864), p. 115.

16. Ibid., p. 68.

17. Ibid., p. 116.

18. Ibid., p. 118.

19. *O.R.*, Vol. XXXII, Part 1, p. 596.

20. Report of the Committee on The Conduct of the War—Fort Pillow Massacre, p. 102.

21. *O.R.*, Vol. XXXII, Part 1, p. 610.

22. Report of the Committee on The Conduct of the War—Fort Pillow Massacre, p. 85.

Notes — Chapter 25

23. Ibid., p. 46.

24. *O.R.*, Vol. XXXII, Part 1, p. 590.

25. Report of the Committee on the Conduct of the War—Fort Pillow Massacre, p. 66.

26. Ibid., p. 6.

27. *O.R.*, Vol. XXXII, Part 1, p. 600.

28. *Webster's New Collegiate Dictionary*, p.. 1190.

29. *O.R.*, Vol. XXXII, Part 1, pp. 586-607.

Chapter 26

IN GARRISON — AT DECATUR, ALABAMA

<u>Background</u>

After the attempt to catch Forrest in March, the 17th New York proceeded on to Athens, Alabama. The regiment, as a part of the 3rd Brigade of the Fourth Division of the XVI Corps (Colonel James H. Howe's Brigade) was assigned to Decatur, Alabama.

As of May 2, 1864, Howe's Brigade had 1,100 for duty; it was the largest brigade at Decatur at that time out of a total strength of 2,190 infantry and cavalry.[1]

The mission at Decatur concerned the Atlanta Campaign and is best described by Major General McPherson's instructions of May 1, 1864, to Brigadier General Stevenson, commanding at Decatur: "It is all important as a cover to our movement that Decatur should he held as long as possible....Occupying an advanced position on our flank, it is a constant menace to Northern Alabama and conveys the idea that we may at any time throw a body of troops from there down to the central position of the state. This compels the enemy to keep a force of cavalry in the vicinity of Decatur where they can really do us very little damage. Again, if Decatur should be abandoned, the enemy would undoubtedly hold it with a small force and throw quite a respectable force across the river into Florence and open communications with Forrest, thus endangering very seriously our line of communication and supplies.

"Impress upon all your railroad guards to hold their positions and defend bridges from their block-houses and stockades at all hazards; a surrender will entail disgrace."[2]

Almost from the day that the Federal forces took over Decatur, the Confederate General Roddey, one of Forrest's subordinates, was there. General Stevenson reported on May 6, 1864, "Roddey is still at my front. Every day and night tries to drive in my pickets, but as yet, without success."[3]

Stevenson constantly called for help and for scouts. Sherman said that if his superiors thought Stevenson to be "nervous and alarmed" he should be replaced by Gresham or Matthies.[4] This was done in May 12, 1864, with Matthies being assigned to command at Decatur.[5] Matthies' tenure was brief, for on May 28, Colonel Howe was commanding at Decatur.[6]

On May 26, Colonel Howe received orders from General Blair of the XVII Corps to capture or destroy Roddey's Command.[7] By sending out a small body of infantry to engage Roddey in the front, the trap would be sprung with Colonel Long and the cavalry attacking Roddey's forces in the flank and the rear. The infantry consisted of the 17th New York Veteran Volunteers, the 25th Indiana, the 32nd Wisconsin, and four pieces of artillery from the 2nd Illinois Light Artillery. (This is the action Westervelt reports in the first part of his chapter. No mention is made in available official records of the second action he recounts.)

Howe reported that he marched on the Courtland Road at 8:00 A.M. and soon encountered Colonel Pickett's Confederate regiment. The Rebels fell back and about 8 miles from Decatur were reinforced by all of Roddey's forces. The Federal infantry, now joined by Long's cavalry, pushed Roddey back until it was about 14 miles from Decatur. The Rebels, estimated to be 1,500 strong, made a stand and then fled in panic. Pursuit was continued as far as Courtland, where the Federals camped at night. The entire day involved 20 miles of marching and skirmishing. Howe's forces returned to Decatur on May 28.[8]

By June 6, Howe wanted to know when his command would be relieved.[9] Brigadier General R.S. Granger soon took command at Decatur in early June and upon his arrival found Howe ready to depart with his brigade, which he did on June 15, heading for Huntsville.

Before Howe's troops got very far, General McPherson ordered him to remain in Decatur. His communication, dated June 15, 1864, stated, "In consequence of the defeat of Sturgis by Forrest at Gumtown, Colonel Howe will remain at Decatur with his brigade until further orders even though Major General Thomas sends troops there."[10] (The Battle of Gumtown is better known as Brice's Crossroads.)

Thus, as Westervelt reports under his June 15 heading, Howe's Brigade returned to Decatur and remained there until August.

Highlights

1. General Roddey: (See Picture on page 190) The main enemy presence in front of Decatur was General Roddey's force. Philip Dale Roddey was a native Alabamian born at Moulton in Lawrence County in 1826. He had little or no formal education. Roddey worked as a tailor, served as sheriff of Lawrence County, and engaged in steamboating on the Tennessee River.

He organized a cavalry company in 1861 and served as its captain. He was commissioned colonel in December 1862 and recruited and organized the 4th Alabama Cavalry. He was promoted to brigadier general in August 1863. Most of his service was in Northern Alabama either under Forrest or Wheeler. He fought with Forrest in Forrest's last battle at Selma and escaped with Forrest by swimming the Alabama River under cover of darkness.

After the war, he engaged in business in New York. Roddey died in London in 1897 and is buried at Tuscaloosa, Alabama.[11]

2. Travel in the Civil War: Westervelt noted that from October 1863 to April 1864 (six months) his regiment had been in fourteen different states. Considering the fact that transportation was a) on foot, b) horseback, c) railroad, and d) by boat, this was a remarkable record.

3. Blockhouses: Fortifications to protect bridges and railroads were blockhouses. These structures are described in a report by the acting chief engineer, Department of the Cumberland, as follows:
>   Standard Blockhouse—Single thickness of logs covered with earth, water tanks inside.
>   Artillery Blockhouses—Double thickness of logs covered with earth, water tanks inside (in most cases).

While this report dealt with the Defenses of Chattanooga, it included Decatur railroads and it seems safe to assume that these were the same structures Westervelt and his comrades were engaged in building—procuring logs, running sawmills, and erecting the buildings needed.[12]

General P.D. Roddey

IN GARRISON — AT DECATUR, ALABAMA

On April 2d we passed Eastport, of which we had unpleasant memories, and a few miles further came to Chickasaw, where we landed, and after a march of a few miles camped at the village of Waterloo. The next day by an easy march we reached Grand Springs, and on the following day passed through a village called Cypress. We here found the remains of a cotton factory, the largest I ever saw in the south. No doubt in ante bellum days it had been quite a manufacturing place, but the different armies going through had completely destroyed it. Many of the women came out to see us pass, and seemed quite taken with our zouave uniforms, as we were the first they had ever seen. Some of them were quite good looking, but the majority of them chewed tobacco, or chewed snuff, or what was about as bad, ate clay, which seems to be a prevailing habit throughout the South. In fact chewing tobacco was so common among the women that often when out scouting I have ridden up to a house, and seeing one or more of them on the stoop, who in New York State would be called ladies, and if I stopped and asked them a question, before they could reply it would be necessary for them to crane their necks, to raise their heads above the railing of the stoop, when they would empty their pretty mouths of the contents of tobacco juice, with the force of a small hydraulic pump, and I would think nothing of asking one of them for a chew of tobacco. What would be thought of an Ulster County girl guilty of this habit? How proud the young men would be of their company, and how delightful it would be to kiss one of them. Yet, to turn the tables, how many young men whose systems are fairly saturated with tobacco juice, and whose breath reeks with the nicotine of poor cigars or worse cigarettes, expect the same young

ladies to kiss their tobacco stained lips!

But I am digressing. After passing through Cypress we traveled on slowly until five P.M., when we reached Florence, which is noted for its fine college and churches, as well as its princely dwellings. As we passed through the town our artillery turned to the right towards the Tennessee river while we went on about a mile and camped. Soon we heard the artillery at work giving the enemy a few shells across the river, but with what result we did not learn, as we quietly cooked our supper and soon turned in and slept under the soothing influence of the noise of the cannonading.

Tuesday, April 5th. — At daylight we were called and after a hasty breakfast were on the road. The morning was cool and the marching reasonably good. During the day we crossed three different streams on foot bridges, and as we had to cross in single file it took a good deal of time, and when once over we would take double quick two or three miles to close up our lines. By this means we made a day's march of about twenty miles. The 6th was a repetition of the 5th, crossing foot bridges and then a foot race to catch up. We passed through two worn out delapidated* looking villages, and over some high hills that seemed composed mostly of limestone, but the land in the valley appeared good and under a fair state of cultivation, though the houses were poor.

On the evening of the 7th we reached the Elk river, where the Nashville and Chattanooga R.R. crosses. Here was a large earthwork to guard the railroad bridge. We crossed just below the railroad on a pontoon

---

* dilapidated

191

bridge, and camped on the bank of a river. The next morning we were detailed as rear guard, which made us march slowly to let our wagon train get out of the way. In many places they were plowing for their spring crops of corn or cotton. Most of the work was done by negro women. Their plows were of the most primitive description, and were drawn by one animal—either a mule, ox, bull or cow. They were all driven with a bit, the plows just scratching over the top of the ground in a way that would disgust any northern farmer. The fields were very large. In one of them that contained about three hundred acres, I counted twenty-eight of these plows running from two to three inches deep in this light soil. We passed some fine large plantations that were worked by government agents. The agents would agree to employ the surplus contrabands to work the land under government protection, and give the government a share of the proceeds when the crops were gathered, but the result generally was that when the crop of cotton was gathered and sold, the agent would suddenly disappear, leaving the contrabands to whistle for their pay, and the government for its share. Some of these fellows made considerable money, with cotton at one dollar a pound, and able to raise from one to two thousand pounds to the acre, and all the help cost was their board, as their promises to pay were never realized. But this was only one of the many swindling games brought out by the war.

On the 9th of April, after a short march from Athens, we arrived at the Tennessee river, opposite Decatur, Ala. Here the Memphis & Charleston R.R. crossed the river. The railroad bridge had been destroyed, but the stone piers were still standing, and to these solid pieces of masonry our engineers had anchored the pontoon boats which formed the bridge. This proved a great convenience, as the current was so strong that it would have been very difficult to have made a permanent bridge without this firm anchorage, but with this help a bridge was made over which troops, teams and artillery crossed and recrossed all summer without a single accident. We now settled down to a steady camp for the first time since leaving New York, on the 21st of the preceding October. During this time we had been within the limits of fourteen different states, and had not occupied any one camp seven consecutive days. We could scarcely believe we were now to cease our wandering for a few weeks, but this proved to be the case. During the month of April we spent most of our time drilling, which had been neglected during our busy marches. This duty was varied with building fortifications and tearing down the buildings of the place, to get range for our guns.

When our work was done the town which contained some two thousand inhabitants before the war, had just three houses and a church left. Two of the houses were used for hospitals, one was a hotel, while the church was transformed into a theatre. The lumber from the torn-down houses was utilized by the troops in building cabins. Our regiment had been on the move so steadily that we seemed to take but little interest in fixing up our quarters, and the men seemed content to occupy their shelter tents and sleep on the ground.

On May 1st orders came to move, when most of the troops crossed the pontoon bridge and started for Chattanooga, to join Gen. Sherman, who was then starting on his Atlanta campaign.

We too had orders to pack up, and expected of course we were to go with them, instead of which we marched to the camp *deserted by the 43d Ohio, where we found A tents, raised on board foundations about six feet from the ground with banks, tables and every convenience ready for us to march in and take possession, which we cheerfully did.*

The next day the enemy, to find out the strength of the garrison left at Decatur, made an attack on our picket lines, and soon drove them in, and followed them up with a battery, sending a few shot into one of the fortifications, but our battery replied with so much spirit that they soon withdrew.

Our men were now set at work strengthening the forts and earthworks around the place, which made heavy details for fatigue or picket duty, and left but few men in camp. My duties as first sergeant were not very heavy. In the morning I would make my details and write up my reports, which would take perhaps an hour, when my work for the day would be over.

This continued through most of the month of May. The enemy, however, were quite troublesome. Two or three times a week they would make a dash on our picket lines, and drive them in. They proved to be a heavy guerilla force, under Gen. Rhody. *Finally, on the 26th of the month, we concluded to turn the tables, and instead of waiting for them to attack us, we marched out and attacked them. About noon we started in light order, accompanied by two guns of our battery. We were soon outside our picket lines and did not have to go much further to find the enemy, with whom we commenced a lively skirmish, that was kept up for an hour, with the loss of but one man on our side. Our battery now got in position, and a few shell made them fall*

back, but for some reason we did not follow them up, but turned to the right and soon reached the river, where the battery shelled some real or imaginary foe on the opposite bank, for about an hour. This over we started for camp, where we arrived at nine P.M., where we found orders to move at daylight the next morning. This kept us up most of the night drawing rations and getting ready for the move.

Friday, May 27th. — At six reveille sounded, when we hastened through our breakfast, packed two days' cooked rations in our haversacks, and rolled our blankets, as they were the only baggage we burdened ourselves with. We then inspected the cartridge-boxes and issued to each man enough to bring his complement up to sixty rounds. We were then ready for business. Our whole brigade, consisting of five regiments with a six gun battery, were on the expedition, and we expected a squadron of cavalry to accompany us, but as yet they had not put in their appearance.

At eight A.M. we started, taking the Courtland road. A few miles brought us to the place where we engaged the enemy yesterday, and here we found them waiting for us. We did not halt but marched right up to where they were stationed, when they began to fall back, and we to follow. We then commenced a running fight, that was kept up for the next ten miles. Our cavalry then joined us and took the advance. Soon they ran into one of the enemy's batteries. That stopped them, and they waited for us to come up. Our battery soon was in position, and while our guns were sending over a few volleys we were ordered to get ready to charge. Our regiment was to take the advance.

---

* Roddey

IN GARRISON — AT DECATUR, ALABAMA

Just as Col. Grower was about to order us forword* we looked up and saw the enemy's battery had limbered up, and were on the retreat. We followed after, still skirmishing. The enemy would fall back on our approach, until they came to a turn in the road, or a piece of woods, or the brow of a hill, or any place that offered a vantage ground. Here they would wait until we came within gunshot, then give us a volley and retreat, but with all this advantage in their favor our loss was but small, and from the dead they left behind them, by the roadside, we know their loss was greater than ours.

We soon learned their little game, and were on the lookout for them at every turn, or where we could not see a good distance in advance, and at the first puff of smoke from one of their guns we would pour in a volley. Twice we chanced to catch sight of them before they fired and got in the first volley. After that, whenever we came to a place that looked as though it might conceal a squad of them, we would fire at it, whether we saw anything or not. Once, after one of these random vollies, on coming to the place, we found one of their dead by the roadside with the rank of major on his coat collar.

We continued this running fight through the village of Hillsboro, and on through Courtland, and several miles further. At nine P.M., after traveling about twenty miles, we camped beside a fine stream about half way between Courtland and Leighton. Here, after a cool bath in the stream, we rolled in our blankets, and enjoyed a good night's sleep, and the next day leisurely returned to Decatur, flattering ourselves that we had taught the enemy a lesson that they would not soon forget, and would not be apt to trouble us very soon again. Judge of our chagrin, when four days after, a party of our men went outside our lines a few miles, and found the enemy in their old position, as belligerent as ever, in fact so full of fight that our men were run back to camp.

On June 1st I was taken sick with a billious fever that was carrying off many of our men. Our hospital accommodations were very poor, so I got permission to remain in our tent. Sergeant Crist, my tentmate, took the best of care of me, but it was over a week before the fever was broken. The weather was extremely hot, the thermometer frequently reaching 110 in the shade, the sun beating down upon our tents, making the heat almost intolerable, while the enemy in our front, ever active, were continually skirmishing with our pickets, and threatening to attack us in force—while there I lay, almost helpless in our tent—all of which did not tend to quiet the nerves of a sick man. But, thanks to the careful nursing of my chum, backed up with a reasonably good constitution, I finally got out all right. This sickness lasted about two weeks, and was the longest I was off duty, at one time, during my four years' service.

Wednesday, Jan.† 15th. — About daylight orders came to move, when we packed up and at nine A.M. we crossed the pontoon bridge and soon turned to the right towards Huntsville. Five miles brought us to Mooresville, which contained more good looking girls than any place of its size I ever was through—that is, in the South.

About noon we halted for an hour, and seeing a farm house near by I started to see what were the prospects for a good dinner. At

---

* forward

† June

the door I was met by a vinegar faced old maid, who informed me in language too plain to be mistaken that she never had, or never would be guilty of feeding one of "Lincoln's yankees." Not at all abashed by this reception, I pushed past her into the room and sat down, and commenced talking to her. If ever I dealt out pure, unadulterated taffy to any female in my life, I did to her. Soon the angular lines of her countenance began to assume a more pleasing expression; even the corkscrew curls that adorned the sides of her homely physiognomy shook, as with half suppressed laughter at one of my stale jokes (new perhaps to her), she exclaimed, "Well, you are the funniest yankee I ever see." I then delicately broached the subject nearest my heart (or stomach)—dinner, when she bustled around, and with the help of a couple of old negro women, set out a very fair dinner, and while praising her excellent cooking, good taste, intelligence, refinement, etc., I proceeded to do ample justice to her table, and when through she unbent her dignity sufficiently to bid me good bye, and say, "if you should ever come this way again, I should be pleased to have you call."

At two P.M. our column again started, and after a march of some fifteen miles we camped for the night at a place called Beaver Dam. The next morning we were called in line at three A.M. and started. From the road we took it was evident we were returning to Decatur. We marched quite fast, and by seven A.M. we reached Mooresville. Soon after we took an hour for breakfast, and about noon crossed the Tennessee to Decatur. We expected to go right back to our old quarters, but found that during our absence the 18th Michigan had arrived from Nashville and taken possession, so we were marched to some shanties outside the fortifications, which, after a few days spent fixing up, became very comfortable quarters.

Our men still kept at work strengthening the fortifications. The enemy at our front was very active, and from the preparations we saw in progress it was evident that an effort was to be made to get rid of them.

On Sunday, June 26, we started out in the afternoon, and by going some eight miles we found the enemy, and after skirmishing for an hour or two they withdrew, and about midnight we returned to camp.

The day following we rested and got ready for another excursion, as the boys now began to term these trips. On Tuesday we were called at four, and at six A.M. we fell in, with two days' rations and sixty rounds of cartridges, leaving all our baggage behind us. In fact the weather was so extremely hot that, except for stormy weather, blankets and tents were superfluous. We were soon on the road, and as usual found the enemy occupying their position, ready to fight and run.

We skirmished with them for a few miles, then halted some hours, when we started to return, but instead of marching back to Decatur, when we reached a convenient place we turned into the woods, where we were concealed the rest of the day, and a good part of the night. After midnight we were called up, and without the sound of a drum, or any other unnecessary noise, we moved through the woods, taking a circuitous route. After a few miles march we again halted, while the troops were put in their proper position for an advance. All the orders were given in a low tone of voice, and it was evident that there was to be a surprise party somewhere.

IN GARRISON — AT DECATUR, ALABAMA

About three A.M. all the arrangements were complete, when we were ordered to advance at a brisk walk. We soon reached the enemy's pickets, who fired on us and quickly retreated. We followed them at double quick, reaching their camps but a few rods behind them. The surprise was complete. Day was just breaking, and it was amusing to see the enemy spring from their tents, and make for the adjoining woods, some of them with but a single garment, and that fluttering in the morning breeze, as they, bent on making the biggest time on record, ran for the woods, and we pouring shot after shot at them to accelerate their progress. Not a gun was fired in return. In fact about all their guns were left behind them, as well as their tents, camp and garrison equippage. Even their wagons and teams were left just as they were packed the night before, as they in their wild skedaddle did not stop for anything.

After witnessing the enemy's retreat from their camp near Monton,* Ala., we loaded the twelve wagons they so kindly left us, which proved to be the same wagons Forrest had captured at Union City, Tenn., on the 24th of Mar. previous, when we made our unsuccessful effort to re-inforce the garrison. But these wagons would not carry half the spoils, so we made a bonfire of the rest, then with our prisoners, some fifty in number, started to return. The day was extremely hot, and we marched slowly, stopping several hours at midday in the cool shade of a wood, so we did not reach Decatur until dark. Our expedition was a success, Gen. Rhody† never

troubled us after. In fact, our camp at Decatur was left very quiet during the remainder of the summer.

About the 1st of July a company of strolling players came to Decatur, and commenced turning the only church left standing into a theatre. We celebrated the 4th by a salute of one hundred guns at sunrise, and again at noon, from fort No. 1. At night the theatre opened, and night after night, during the following month, it was crowded. The plays were about as good as school children would produce, but the men would crowd the building at 50 cts. and $1.00 a ticket, and applaud them to the echo.

During the month of July we resumed our drilling, which had been laid aside while working on the fortifications. The Tennessee gave us an excellent place for bathing, as well as a good place to fish. The varieties of fish were catfish and buffaloes, which would often reach as high as thirty or forty pounds weight. The first named were good, but the buffaloes after growing above five pounds were dry and tasteless. Small ones were good. Another thing added to our bill of fare. The natives were allowed to come to our picket lines and trade their produce for commissary stores. We soon learned that a pound of salt would buy just as much as a pound of sugar or coffee, so my chum, Sergeant Crist, who was sharp for a deal, would take ten one pound packages of salt to the picket lines, and return with enough butter, eggs and vegetables to last us several days. Snuff was the only thing that would tempt them to part with their gold or silver money, but that was difficult even for us to get, except through our sutlers.

---

* Moulton

† Roddey

IN GARRISON — AT DECATUR, ALABAMA

Our duties here were not onerous. Our Adjt., G.A.C. Bartlett, was willing to instruct the 1st sergeants in any part of their duties they did not understand, but after he had once instructed them he exacted strict obedience, and woe unto the sergeant who did not come up to his standard of perfection. However, in justice to myself as well as to him, I will say he never reprimanded me.

Notes — Chapter 26

1. *O.R.*, Vol. XXXVIII, Part 4, p. 6.

2. Ibid., pp. 9, 10.

3. Ibid., p. 50.

4. Ibid., p. 142.

5. Ibid., p. 157.

6. Ibid., p. 341.

7. *O.R.*, Vol. XXXVIII, Part 3, p. 528.

8. Ibid., pp. 527, 528.

9. *O.R.*, Vol. XXXVIII, Part 4, p. 427.

10. Ibid., p. 489.

11. Warner, *Generals in Grey* (Baton Rouge, Louisiana: Louisiana State University Press, 1959), p. 262.

12. *O.R.,* Vol. XXXVIII, Part 4, pp. 639-640.

Chapter 27

AT THE FRONT — ATLANTA

Background

Sherman started his Atlanta Campaign on May 6, 1864. After a series of flanking movements around Joseph E. Johnston's army and a serious setback at Kenesaw Mountain on June 27, he reached the outskirts of Atlanta on July 17.[1] The siege of Atlanta began almost immediately.

On August 2, 1864, Sherman contacted General Granger at Decatur. He said, "If that brigade of the Sixteenth Corps commanded by Colonel Howe can possibly be spared, I want it sent to the front by cars. Our losses have been heavy and we want that brigade more than you possibly do."[2] Sherman repeated his request on August 5, saying, "Keep the battery and send only the infantry of Colonel Howe's brigade."[3] By August 6, Granger reported that the brigade had gone.[4]

Thus Howe's brigade went to Atlanta and rejoined the XVI Corps, Fourth Division, Third Brigade. General Fuller, who commanded the Fourth Division at that time, reported that the Third Brigade (Howe's) rejoined the division on August 8 and "took its place in the front line, bearing cheerfully their part in the toils and dangers of the campaign."[5]

Westervelt reports in great detail what it was like to serve on the front line at Atlanta. Union reports for that period speak of the work of Confederate sharpshooters and artillery. During its brief period with the XVI Corps on the front line (August 8-20), the 17th New York Veteran Volunteers lost 9 men—1 killed and 8 wounded.[6]

Then, on August 21, 1864, the 17th New York Veteran Volunteer Regiment was transferred from the Army of the Tennessee (McPherson) to the Army of the Cumberland (Thomas).[7] The regiment became a part of the XIV Corps (Major General Jefferson C. Davis), the Second Division (Brigadier General James D. Morgan).[8]

The fighting at the front continued at this new location for Westervelt and here he escaped from some harrowing experiences with sharpshooters. The total losses for the 17th New York Veteran Volunteer Regiment in the investment of Atlanta from August 8 to September 1 were 2 killed, 3 died, and 12 wounded—a total of 17.

At the end of this period, the regiment moved south again, heading for the fateful Battle of Jonesboro.

Highlights

1. Galling Fire: General Frank Blair of the XVII Corps reported on Atlanta saying, "The Command was occupied for 28 days in making approaches, digging rifle pits, and erecting batteries, being subjected day and night to a galling fire of artillery and musketry."[9] This corps commander's report, and others, reinforces Westervelt's comment about the nature of the fight before Atlanta fell.

2. General Jefferson C. Davis: Westervelt's new corps commander (of the XIV Corps) was one of the most colorful figures in the army. Jefferson C. Davis was born in Indiana in 1828; his first military service was in the Mexican War. In 1848, he was commissioned a 2nd lieutenant in the Regular Army and rose to captain by 1861. He was at Fort Sumter and later made colonel of the

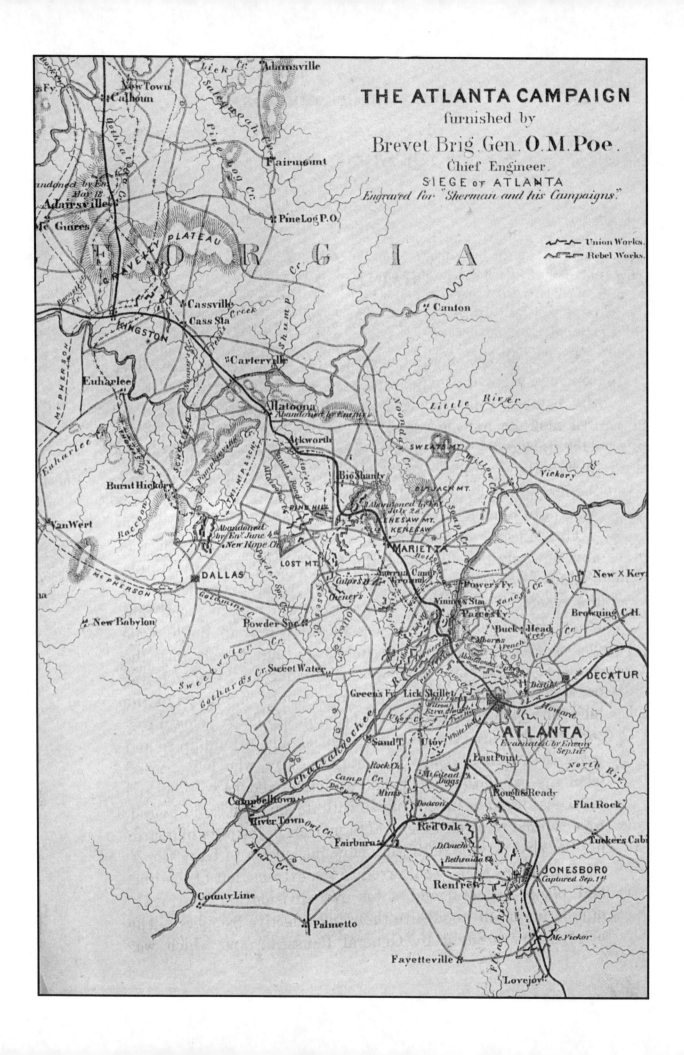

THE ATLANTA CAMPAIGN
furnished by
Brevet Brig. Gen. O. M. Poe.
Chief Engineer.
SIEGE of ATLANTA
Engraved for "Sherman and his Campaigns."

22nd Indiana. On September 29, 1862, he was in a quarrel with his ex-commanding officer, General William Nelson, and shot him to death in Louisville, Kentucky. No action was taken against Davis. He then had a long record of success with the army and led the XIV Corps at Atlanta, in the March to the Sea, and in the Carolinas Campaign. While he served as a major general, he was breveted only and never given full rank.[10] Davis is described as being "half-admired and half-feared"; he was a favorite of Sherman's and was reputedly the most talented swearer in the Union army.[11]

AT THE FRONT — ATLANTA

On Aug. 4th orders came to move. Of course our destination was unknown to those in the ranks, and many of us thought it was merely another excursion in the country, that would last a day or two, when, after a little skirmish, we would return to our comfortable quarters. But when it was supplemented with the order to "send all who were not well and strong to the hospital" we knew it meant to go to the front. We packed up our personal effects, but did not start, as the cars that were to transport us failed to arrive. The next morning I sent the sick of our company to the hospital. Among others was my tentmate, Sergt. Crist, who had been sick for some time. I felt bad to see him go, because sending a man to the hospital seemed that bourne from which no soldier ever returned. But he had kept up from day to day, and from week to week, hoping to get better. While in camp I could favor him some about his duties, but when starting on a march I knew he had not strength to keep up, so unwillingly he started for Nashville, while we loaded on the cars, and at 4 P.M. started and ran to Huntsville, where we were delayed a short time, then started again and in the morning found ourselves at Stephenson. Here we joined the main line of railroad, that runs from Nashville to Atlanta. We stopped here a short time, when we again started and ran slowly all day and night, and on Sunday, Aug. 7th, we unloaded from the cars within three miles of the city of Atlanta, and joined Sherman's Army, who were then drawing their lines closer and closer around that doomed city. Here we put up our tents for the first time since May, and as we rolled ourselves in our blankets at night we dropped asleep, to the dull booming of cannon at different parts of our lines, that with an occasional sharp rattle of musketry, seemed a foretaste of what was in store for us.

Monday, Aug. 8th. — We woke in the morning to the music of cannonading and musketry. After hurrying through my breakfast and reports, I went a few miles to the headquarters of the 150th N.Y. This being a regiment from Dutchess Co., I found many of my old friends and school-mates from Po'keepsie.

About noon I returned, and soon after we packed up and moved to our position in line, when we found we were assigned to a division of the 16th corps. It rained very hard in the afternoon, and before our tents were up we were thoroughly soaked. This did not stop the firing at different parts of our line; in fact it never stopped night or day while we were around the city. In the afternoon one of our regiment, by the accidental discharge of his piece shot away part of one of his hands, so his days of soldiering were over.

We were occupying the rear line of battle, but near enough for an occasional stray shot to come into our camp. In front of us was another line of battle, behind breastworks that were continually strengthened. In front of these were our line of pickets or skirmishers, occupying some hastily dug pits for shelter, as the enemy's sharpshooters were ready to pick off any who raised their heads above the ground.

The next morning we were called at three A.M., and sent to the skirmish line, and ordered to build a line of breastworks, so that our line of battle could be advanced and support the skirmishers, while they too made an advance nearer the enemy's works. As soon as it was light enough the enemy caught sight of us, and throwing out a line of sharpshooters proceeded to make it decidedly warm for us.

Our captain was at the rear superintending the cutting of trees into logs to be used in building the works, and we having no lieutenants, it left me in charge of the working party at the front. I soon found a convenient tree for shelter, behind which I could stand and oversee the work as it progressed without unnessary[*] exposure. Once I stepped from behind the tree into the trench, and after marking out where the line should run, stepped back behind the tree. Private Jordan stepped right into the tracks that I had vacated, and before he could strike a blow received a sharp-shooter's bullet just above the left temple, making a wound from which the brain protruded. I sent him to the rear to the surgeon, and, strange as it may seem, he lived nearly three days even after losing a part of his brain, and with the bullet in his head. The next to catch it was a German boy named White, who was struck in the lower part of the abdomen, giving him a severe and painful wound from which he never recovered. Several others of our regiment were wounded before the trench was deep enough, and the logs high enough to shelter them. Finally they got range of the tree behind which I stood, which was so small it was necessary to stand straight so as not to expose myself either front or rear. At one time I leaned forward while giving an order and as I quickly withdrew my head, a bullet cut the bark not two inches in front of my nose, and as I had objections to having my nose "blowed" in such a summary manner, I was careful to keep out of sight the remainder of our tour of duty.

About noon we were relieved, and returned to our camp and rested until the next noon, when we packed up and moved forward and occupied the next line of works, where the enemy shelled us most of the night, making many of the men leave their tents and sleep behind breastworks that sheltered them from the enemy's firing. About midnight part of our regiment were sent out to help advance our lines; the rest of us were formed in line so that if our men failed in their efforts to advance, and were driven back, we could check the enemy. Our services were not needed, as our men advanced and held their ground, but the enemy shelled them and us all day. At dark their firing ceased and we slept soundly until about midnight, when the enemy charged our line and endeavered to recapture the ground our men had taken in the morning. This called us in line, where we remained until the enemy retired, when we lay down in the trenches and slept until morning.

Friday, Aug. 12th. — Scarce a shot was fired along the lines in front of us until near noon. Then the musketry commenced, followed by artillery. Soon the cannon shot began to come over the breastworks into our camp. One of them, a solid twelve pounder, came over and passed through one of the tents of an adjoining company, then struck the ground in our company street, and with a rebound passed through a tent striking a cartridge box, the pieces of which flew in all directions, knocking out the eye of one of our company, and giving another a bad scalp wound. The next tent it struck was occupied by a private named Hill, who lay on his back sleeping soundly. The shot struck him just back of his ears and carried away the whole back of his head. I was standing within about twelve feet of him, and happened to be looking right at him the moment he was struck, and

---

[*] unnecessary

don't think he moved the slightest muscle. I dropped my frying pan, that contained the dinner I was about to cook, and stepped by his side. There he lay, with his hands crossed above his breast, his eyes closed, his features unmarred—as calm as they were a moment before while he was peacefully sleeping. But, on raising him from his blanket, we found the whole back of his head and his entire brain carried away. We rolled him in his blanket, and as the sun went down that night we laid him in his grave at the foot of a large pine, which, as the southern breezes blow, will sing his requiem long after those who performed those last sad offices are crumbling in the dust.

Sunday, Aug. 14th. — At three A.M. we were called, and quietly moved out to the front to relieve our skirmishers, as it could not be done in daylight without risk of considerable loss. We took posession* of the skirmish pits, and remained quiet until daylight, but just as soon as it was light, the fun commenced, as the enemy opened on us, and just as soon as a man's head appeared above ground, they would fire at it. At first we had orders not to return their fire unless they advanced. This was too much one sided, and after taking their fire for an hour or two, with our backs aching from the cramped position of keeping our heads below ground, I called to Capt. Fisher, of company D, who was near me, "Say, Captain, don't you think this is getting monotonous?" "Well, rather." "I wish they would advance, or do something to give us an excuse to fire" said I. "Let's fire anyhow, for fear they advance and we won't see them." And suiting the action to the word I started my squad firing. Capt. Fisher, only

---

* possession

too glad to take it up, set his men firing too, and in a few minutes our whole battalion were at it, loading and firing as fast as possible.

Soon our ammunition grew scarce, when we sent men for a fresh supply who brought up one or two boxes of one thousand rounds to each company. These were placed in the most convenient place to use, and the firing continued.

Soon the line of battle in the rear of us, thinking we were heavily engaged commenced firing too, and instead of shooting over our heads, would fire right into our pits, when Maj. Martin ordered me to go back, and have the firing stopped. It was no pleasant task, for as soon as I was out of our skirmish pit, I was exposed to the fire, not only of the enemy, but also of our own men in our rear. I made as good time as possible, and while delivering the message to the officer in command of the line of battle, a sharpshooter caught sight of me, and as I turned made four bullet holes through the shoulder of my zouave jacket. It is needless to say I tarried no longer than necessary, but hurried back, and was glad to get into the rifle pits, where I could sit down and rest.

During the night the enemy kept up a continual firing, that we did our best to answer. During the twenty-four hours we were on duty, our company fired fifteen hundred rounds of cartridges. Our only casualities were two men slightly wounded. The next morning just before daylight we were relieved, and went back to the rear line of battle, where we enjoyed twenty-four hours' uninterrupted rest.

Tuesday, Aug. 16. — In the morning all the officers' baggage was sent to the rear, under guard of some of our men who were unable to do heavy duty, and it began to look as though there was some sharp work waiting for us somewhere. In the afternoon we broke camp and moved out to the front and were placed in position to support one of our batteries. Here we soon found it necessary to keep our heads below ground, as the firing was kept up lively all day and night.

We remained until the afternoon of the 20th, and were continually under fire. No part of our position was safe. Our major had put up a temporary shelter in the safest point he could find, and one morning invited our colonel to breakfast, telling him as an inducement that he could offer him some butter, which was almost an unknown article in the army at that time. Just as they seated themselves at the table, a ten pound shot came through the roof of their quarters, and cut off one corner of the table. Major Martin did what any ordinary man would do under the circumstances—he turned a back somersault off his camp stool and hugged the ground close, thinking it was a shell and would likely explode. Not so with Col. Grower. He coolly laid down his knife and fork, folded his hands, and leaning back on his stool, with an air of offended dignity remarked, "Major Martin, that is a great way to treat a man when invited to breakfast."

It rained most of the time we were here, and filled our trenches half full of water, and sometimes it was a choice whether we would take a bath or a bullet, as it was almost certain death to leave the trenches. After one of our men was killed and one wounded we concluded to stick to the trenches, so placing some poles across, above high water mark, we roosted on them until the storm ceased.

Saturday, Aug. 20th. The sun came out bright and warm, and soon dried our clothes and blankets, while the enemy kept very quiet in front of us. In the afternoon we

were relieved and moved back to the rear, where we enjoyed the pleasure of walking around without feeling that we were making a target of ourselves for some sharpshooter. At night we put up our tents and had the first undisturbed night's rest we had enjoyed in over a week.

The next morning we were called at four, and after a hurried breakfast packed up and started, taking the road towards the right of our line. We soon found we were transferred from the 16th to the 14th Corps, and marched on lively, as the morning was cool and pleasant. While passing the lines of the 15th Corps, the enemy opened on us with one of their batteries, that made us make some lively movements to get under cover of the breastworks. One of their shots, a solid six-pounder, struck the ground just in front of our line, and in bounding through the air, struck the knapsack on the back of one of our men, cutting it off of him without hurting the man.

On leaving, we moved further to the rear, taking a roundabout course, over hills and through gullies, that abound on all sides of Atlanta. About nine A.M. we reached the headquarters of the 14th Corps, and after a short delay moved to our place in line. We found we were assigned to the first Brigade, 2d Division, 14th Corps. We soon put up our tents, and found the bullets were flying as thick here as where we came from. Our regiment escaped any casualities, but in a camp adjoining ours on the left, one was killed, and several wounded by these stray shots. The next day the right wing of our regiment went on picket, and while they were taking their place in line, the enemy opened on them, but without loss on our side.

Night and day, while we were on this line, we could hear the whistle of bullets, as they passed over our heads, or hear the sharp "ping" as they struck in and around our camp. Frequently a tent would be perforated, but not one of our men was hurt.

About the 25th it became evident there were preparations making for an important move of some kind, but whether it was to be an assault on the works around the city, or we were to raise the siege and retreat, was a mystery that we knew would be solved in a few days to those who lived to see it.

Friday, Aug. 26th. — All remained very quiet along our lines; scarce a gun was fired. In the afternoon we packed up everything but our tents, which were left standing until after dark. A visit to our batteries showed they had wrapped the wheels of the guns and caisons[*] with empty feed bags, which looked as though we meant to retire without noise.

At sunset we had inspection of arms and issued sixty rounds of cartridges to each man. We then quietly took down our tents, and formed in line behind our breast-works, where we stacked arms, and lay down behind the stacks and slept quietly until two P.M.,[†] when we were awakened, and moved off very quietly. We soon left our works and moved on, until six A.M., when we formed in line of battle, on the top of a high hill, to cover our wagon train while passing.

An hour after we moved on a short distance and threw up some breastworks, where our company were left on picket. Soon the enemy advanced, and we exchanged a few shots, when they withdrew. Not long after a line of battle advanced from the woods into an open field about half a mile distant, with a line of skirmishers a few paces in front of them. The skirmishers gave us a few shots, but we, acting under orders, did not reply, but each man in his place was ready to do his best, if they came within fifty yards. After standing in line about an hour they withdrew, and we had a very quiet tour of duty, but 'tis needless to say we were continually on the alert during the night, and there was no sleeping on post, for we knew the enemy were near, and could advance upon us at any moment, and we did not mean to be caught napping.

At daylight we were relieved, and after some four miles run through the woods caught up with our regiment, who had marched two hours before. About noon we came up with some small parties of the enemy, and for a few miles skirmished as we went. At four P.M., after a march of about twelve miles, we reached the Atlanta & Montgomery R.R., where we formed in line of battle, and then lay down behind our stacks of guns and enjoyed a good night's sleep, as we had slept but little the two nights previous.

The next three days we advanced very slowly, and each night threw up a strong line of breastworks. From the manner in which the army was moved, it was evident we were skirmishing for a position, to fight a decisive battle. Still this did not interfere with carrying out the small details of army duties.

On the 31st, during a halt of a few hours, we made out our muster rolls, when Col. Grower called the regiment in line, and mustered the men, just as though we were miles away from any enemy. This was the last muster Col. Grower ever made, and scores of our regiment who that day answered "here" were destined to be "mustered out" by that grim officer, Death, within the next two days.

---

[*] caissons

[†] presumably A.M.

But in a blissful ignorance of the future, we cooked our suppers, and made ourselves comfortable, and as we stretched ourselves before the fires in the cool evening, and enjoyed our evening smoke, the jokes went round, songs were sung, and stories told, and at an early hour the men rolled themselves in their blankets, and many of them were soon taking their last sleep on earth, and perhaps dreaming of loved ones in their distant northern homes, whom they were never to meet again. How fortunate for us all that our future is hid by a vail we are not allowed to lift, but it is unfolded to us only as fast as we are required to perform our part.*

---

* veil

Notes — Chapter 27

1. *O.R.*, Vol. XXXVIII, Part 1, pp. 61-71.

2. *O.R.*, Vol. XXXVIII, Part 4, pp. 332-333.

3. Ibid., p. 377.

4. Ibid., pp. 396-397.

5. *O.R.*, Vol. XXXVIII, Part 3, p. 487.

6. Ibid., p. 374.

7. Ibid., p. 487.

8. *O.R.*, Vol. XXXVIII, Part 5, p. 389.

9. Johnson and Buel, *Battles and Leaders*, Vol. IV, p. 321.

10. Warner, *Generals in Blue*, pp. 115-116.

11. Lewis, *Sherman—Fighting Prophet*, pp. 348-349.

Chapter 28

JONESBORO AND THE FALL OF ATLANTA

Background

On July 17, 1864, the Confederates relieved the wily General Joseph E. Johnston of command and replaced him with the audacious John Bell Hood. His attack on July 22 in which the Union General James McPherson was killed marked the turning of events in the Battle of Atlanta.

Sherman knew that Hood was totally dependent upon two railroads for supplies and ammunition. One was from Montgomery, Alabama through Opelika to Atlanta. The other was from Macon, through Lovejoy and Jonesboro to Atlanta. If Sherman could destroy or control those railroads, Hood would have to fight or abandon Atlanta.

General Rousseau, commanding the District of Tennessee, asked permission to destroy the road from Montgomery. He left Decatur, Alabama on July 10 and broke up the railroad and joined Sherman at Marietta, Georgia on July 22.[1]

To get to the Macon road, Sherman decided that cavalry couldn't do the job and that he would "have to move the whole army."[2] He withdrew most of his army, except for the XX Corps under Slocum, and attacked the railroad below Atlanta, with Jonesboro (Jonesborough) as the focal point. Sherman summarized the decisive Battle of Jonesboro on September 1, 1864, by saying, "About 4 p.m., General Davis was all ready and assailed the enemy's lines across open fields, carrying them handsomely and taking as prisoners the greater part of Govan's brigade, including its commander, with two 4-gun batteries."[3] That night, the enemy retreated south and at the same time, Atlanta was abandoned.

The actions of the 17th New York in the fight are described by General Morgan who commanded the division at Jonesboro:

The Seventeenth New York had been directed to form on the left of the first line, but owing to the difficulty of crossing the swamp did not succeed in getting into position, but its right had commenced forming on the left of the Tenth Michigan at the commencement of the movement....The second line was now parallel with the first line....

The second line, following the first's, bent away to the angle, swerving to the left, and two regiments, the Seventeenth New York and Tenth Michigan, uncovered the first line and covered that of Colonel Estes' brigade. Upon entering the woods, under cover of which the enemy had intrenched, they were subjected to a merciless fire under which they were staggered for a moment....The Seventeenth New York under the heavy fire they were subjected to, fell back for a short distance, but reformed under fire and again marched and carried the works—no better test of brave and good soldiers than this reforming under fire. The Seventeeth New York are entitled to all praise. Its brave Colonel (Grower) fell mortally wounded at the head of his regiment. In the short time he had been with the Command, he had endeared himself to all by his soldierly bearing. The Tenth Michigan and Seventeeth New York lost heavily as the casualty reports will show.[4]

Confederate Prisoners at Jonesboro

JONESBORO AND THE FALL OF ATLANTA

The surrender of Govan's Brigade was the key point in the Federal success at Jonesboro. In turn, the loss of Jonesboro meant the loss of Atlanta for the South.

With the death of Colonel Grower, the command of the 17th New York devolved to Major Joel O. Martin. He reported the regiment's losses at Jonesboro as "four commissioned officers wounded, 23 enlisted men killed, and 70 wounded." Two of the officers, Colonel Grower and Captain Canty, were mortally wounded.[5]

In this chapter, Westervelt vividly describes the action at Jonesboro. He then speaks of returning to Atlanta and reminisces about his fallen comrades and about three "skulkers" in his company.

Highlights

1. Colonel Grower: Colonel William T. Grower was a major in the 17th Infantry during his first two years of service. He was commissioned colonel at Albany, New York on June 3, 1863, and was authorized to reorganize the 17th New York Volunteers which then became the 17th New York Veteran Volunteer Regiment.

Westervelt respected him as indicated by his admiration for his coolness in chapter 27. Grower was lauded by others, too. General Morgan referred to Grower in his report of Atlanta as "a brave and accomplished officer."[6] General Baird reported of Grower at Jonesboro, "Grower was in Morgan's left brigade, and Col. Estes appealed for help. The fire of the enemy position at the point was most destructive, yet the gallant Colonel (Grower) carried his regiment into position with a heroic bravery challenging the highest admiration and was himself almost the first to fall."[7]

2. Confederate Losses at Jonesboro: It is difficult to get a precise figure in Confederate losses in battle in the Civil War. Jonesboro is no exception. (See illustration page 210)

Brigadier General Mark Lowery, CSA, who commanded Cleburne's Division at Jonesboro reported that "Brigadier-General Govan, about 600 of his officers and men, and 8 pieces of artillery fell into the enemy's hands." His division's total losses, including Govan's, were 83 killed, 344 wounded, and 659 missing—a total of 1,086.[8]

General Jacob Cox, writing in 1882, said of Jonesboro, "Over three hundred of the enemy's dead were left in the field, eight hundred and sixty-five were surrendered with General Govan, and on the following day nearly a thousand, involving wounded left in hospitals by Hardee, were added to the list of captured."[9]

Pollard, writing in *The Lost Cause*, places the Confederate losses at Jonesboro at "more than two thousand."[10]

Westervelt claims they captured "about a thousand."

Thursday, Sept. 1st. — At three A.M. we were called in line and kept on the alert until daylight. Then, after a hearty breakfast (that proved the last meal to many) we started on our march. It was evident we were drawing up close to the enemy, and that an engagement could not be much longer postponed. Some prisoners captured reported that Gens. Hardee and Clayborn* were but a few miles from us, at a small place called Jonesboro, running south from Atlanta. As that was the only road left for Gen. Hood's force at Atlanta to transport their stores, we knew that a desperate effort would be made to hold the line, as its loss would render Atlanta untenable.

During the forenoon we were ordered to inspect the arms and ammunition of the men, to keep them well closed up and everything in readiness for work. About noon we halted, and while our lines of battle were deploying to the right the enemy opened on us with a light battery in our immediate front. Three of our batteries were thrown forward and made short work of silencing the enemy's guns. In fact their shooting was so wild, and their gunnery so poor, that our regiment, while supporting our batteries, paid but little attention to them. Some of our men, tired with the morning's march, went to sleep. Others to pass away the time read books or papers they had picked up on the march. Occasionally a shot or fragment of shell would come over uncomfortably close, but, as Capt. Fisher expressed it, we "let them go on and amuse themselves; it will keep them out of other mischief."

Soon our lines on the right were established, forming two sides of our square,

when we moved off to the left to form the third side and strike them in flank. After passing through several swamps, and fording some small streams, we found ourselves separated from our brigade, when one of Gen. Thomas' aids rode up and ordered us to move forward and fill a break in our lines, where a brigade of regulars had been driven back. It made no difference to Col. Grower whether he was ordered to do the fighting for a brigade or corps. He was willing to try it, and take the lead in the fight himself. We soon came to some foot bridges, obliging our colonel to dismount, which he was unwilling to do, as he was suffering from a wound received the year before at the second battle of Bull Run, making walking very painful to him, but with the help of a cane he kept up with the regiment.

We soon reached an open field, where the regulars were hugging close to the ground. We passed over them, across the field, and on reaching a wood beyond we spread out to cover as much as possible of the break in our lines. As we entered the woods we were within about thirty yards of some hastily constructed works of the enemy's, when they opened on us with the sharpest fire I ever experienced. Their bullets seemed fairly to come by double handfuls, and at short range with terribly fatal effects. We held our ground, however, trying to give them as good as they sent, until Col. Grower fell, mortally wounded, when the command devolved upon Maj. Martin, and seeing a likelihood of our small regiment being annihilated, ordered us to about face and march out of the woods, when a break occurred that threatened to become a rout, when our color sergeant halted, and planted the colors, around which our men instantly

---

* Cleburne

rallied, when with a cheer we once more went for the woods.

This time we did not stop to exchange shots, but with a zouave yell, that would have done credit to a band of Comanche Indians, we went for their works, right up to them, on to them, over them. Our color bearer was the first to mount them, with Capt. Horner of H company close behind, and Capt. W.E. Fisher, with the vizor of his cap turned up like a member of the Irish militia, making a good third. Over the works we went, "pell mell," or as Fisher expressed it, "the devil take the last one." We were by this time just getting fighting mad, and went for them so sharp we drove them away from their works, and as we started to follow them we saw the woods full of the enemy, outnumbering us three to one, but what surprised us was, as they came towards us, they were calling out, "Don't shoot! Don't shoot! we surrender." So great was their number that we had to extend our lines to surround them until the regulars came up and took them in charge. This was afterwards explained by the fact that the right of our line had swung around nearly surrounding them, when after a sharp fight they had been driven back in disorder, and on their retreat had run into us, when, thinking they were entirely surrounded, were anxious to surrender before we opened fire on them.

About one thousand of the enemy were gathered in at this place by our regiment, who at this hour could not have numbered more than three hundred men. This gave us possession of the railroad, and closed the fighting for the day, when we cared for the wounded as well as we could, and turned and strengthened the line of rebel works, to aid us in case they tried to recapture them, and about midnight lay down to try to catch a few hours' rest, expecting the fight to be renewed

at daylight. During the night we heard some loud explosions in the direction of Atlanta, some fifteen miles distant, that afterward proved to be the enemy under Gen. Hood, who, hearing of our success, that cut their last remaining line of railroad, were blowing up their ammu-nition and destroying their cars preparatory to retreating from the city.

Tuesday, Sept. 2d. — After the stirring events of yesterday we were so nervous that although worn out by fatigue we slept lightly, and were awake at daylight, when, finding the enemy had retreated from our front, we sent out a detail to bury the dead. Our regiment had suffered heavily. We were but a small regiment when we entered the fight—not over five hundred—and although it lasted less than a half hour we lost in killed and wounded just one hundred and seven,[*] and the majority of the wounded either died from their wounds, or were disabled from farther service. Col. Grower died on the evening of the second. His remains were embalmed and sent to N.Y. city, where they were received by the 7th Regt., N.Y., and after lying in state at the City Hall were buried in Greenwood. On the 6th we took up our line of march toward Atlanta, arriving there the next day, when we were given to understand that we would have several weeks' rest before starting on another campaign, so we fixed up our quarters and put things in order for comfortable housekeeping, while many of the officers went home to help boom the presidential campaign that was then just fairly under way. As we settled down to the quiet of camp life we began to miss our comrades who were killed or wounded Sept 1st. Of course it was not the cowards

---

[*] Westervelt's figures for the loss are high, see Background on page 211.

213

who were gone, but the good, hearty, brave, rollicking fellows, who were always up in their duties, and always ready for a "lark" if it promised fun or fighting, who would stick to a comrade through thick or thin. These were the men always found at the fore front of the battle and the men whom we missed, and many a silent tear was dropped to their memory.

There was another class diametrically opposite to these; they were known as "skulkers", a class of cowards whom no power could ever get into a fight. Watch them as we would, they always found some means of getting out of range of the bullets, and when the fight was over would walk into camp with a well formed excuse for their absence. It was often amusing to hear them draw on their imagination for some reason for not being present during the fight. One of them told of being taken a prisoner, and after some hair-breadth adventures had escaped from the enemy and got back to our lines. Another had been overcome with heat and unable to keep up.

But the most amusing of all the flimsy excuses was from one of our company who had joined us some days after our arrival at Atlanta. He came into camp led by one who, noted for his quarrelsome disposition and fighting qualities while in camp, was never known to stay where there was any danger of his precious skin being perforated with a bullet. The excuse offered by this precious pair was that one of them was sunddenly* struck with "moon-blindness" so he could not see to keep up, and the other had to lead him off or he would certainly run right into the enemy's lines.

---

* suddenly

I found we had three of this class in our company, and on their arrival they were called in front of the company and ordered to tell their story, which was greeted with shouts of derision, when I, as 1st sergeant, notified them that their conduct had forfeited their rights as soldiers, and they could not take rank as such until by some special act of bravery they proved themselves worthy of being members of our company; that until then they would be required, as far as in their power, to do all the fatigue duty of our whole company. And this was carefully carried out. All through Sherman's marches, if after a long day's march a detail was called for, to build corduroy road, shovel dirt, or anything else that is distasteful to a soldier—especially a tired one—these men were the first ones called, greatly to the satisfaction of the other members, as it made their duties corresondingly lighter. This was kept up until the following March, before we were called into another regular engagement, at which time I found myself in command of the company, when, just as we were entering the fight of Averysboro, I called the three men and our sergeants out and gave the sergeants orders that when the fight commenced the only duty they should do was to watch these three, and the first move they made to run away should shoot them down. This the sergeants agreed to do, but in spite of their vigilance two of them, Mr. Moonblind and his mate, got away again. The other one stayed and faced the music. During the sharpest part of the fighting I chanced to look towards him and saw his face was pale and his nervousness had produced a severe fit of vomiting, yet his features showed a determination to stay, and stay he did. After that there was no braver man in our regiment.

214

Notes — Chapter 28

1. *O.R.*, Vol. XXXVIII, Part 1, pp. 70-71.

2. Ibid., pp. 79-80.

3. Ibid., p. 82.

4. Ibid., pp. 644-645.

5. Ibid., pp. 676-678.

6. Ibid., p. 642.

7. Ibid., p. 752.

8. *O.R.*, Vol. XXXVIII, Part 3, pp. 726-733.

9. Cox, *Atlanta—Campaigns of the Civil War* (New York: Scribner and Sons, 1882), p. 207.

10. Pollard, *The Lost Cause*, p. 580.

Chapter 29

FORREST'S RAID INTO NORTHERN ALABAMA AND TENNESSEE

Background

After Hood evacuated Atlanta, Sherman gathered his army in the vicinity of Atlanta.[1] Hood went south to Lovejoy's Station on the Atlanta-Macon Railroad; later he moved westward to a place near Palmetto Station.[2]

The XIV Corps moved from Jonesboro on September 7, and went into camp at White Hall (southwest of Atlanta) on September 9. The officers were resupplying the troops for another campaign; the troops were anticipating a well-deserved rest. For Morgan's Division, and the 17th New York Veteran Regiment, this did not last long.

The rest was cut short because on September 25, Forrest captured the garrison at Athens, Alabama. He further threatened the railroad from Decatur, Alabama to Nashville, Tennessee at several points.[3] Part of his force, under Brigadier General Buford, threatened Huntsville, Alabama on September 30 and Athens, on October 1, 1864. These thrusts were unsuccessful and he left the area just as Morgan's Division arrived.[4]

The division had received orders on September 28 to go after Forrest. The First Brigade, under Colonel Robert F. Smith, including the 17th New York, left White Hall that evening and reached Chattanooga by rail on the thirtieth.[5] General George H. Thomas, second in command to Sherman, and Brigadier General James D. Morgan, division commander, followed immediately.[6]

The division left Chattanooga, traveling through Stevenson, Alabama, and Huntsville, Alabama, and arrived in Athens on October 3. They had to march the last two miles for Forrest had destroyed the track for that distance.[7]

Sherman gave Thomas the responsibility of pursuing Forrest. In addition to Morgan's Division of the XIV Corps, Thomas had General Rosseau's 4,000 cavalry and mounted infantry, General Steedman's 5,000 infantry from Chattanooga, and Washburn's 3,000 cavalry from Memphis. Forrest was estimated to have had a cavalry force of 7,000.[8] His biographer, John Wyeth, contends that he had started the raid with but 4,500.[9]

Knowing that all these Federals were on his trail, Forrest escaped back to Cherokee, Alabama (his point of departure) on October 6 crossing the Tennessee River on October 5, and leaving a rear guard of 1,000 to slow the Federal pursuit. This unit had a narrow escape, but did reach the south side of the Tennessee on October 13.[10] Lieutenant Colonel Joel Martin, commanding the 17th New York, says laconically in his report, "...had a little skirmish with Forrest October 6th...."[11]

While Thomas and his group were busy chasing Forrest, Hood attacked Sherman's supply line from Chattanooga to Atlanta—Allatoona on October 5, Resaca on October 12, and Dalton on October 13. All these efforts were unsuccessful and Hood then took his army to middle Tennessee.[12]

Westervelt missed most of the excitement in this expedition, having been taken ill on October 3 at Athens, and advised by the regiment's surgeon to remain in Athens with him.

As a result, his commentary in this chapter covers his trip to Athens and the return and his forays against the local sheep folds, pig yards, and poultry houses. He also takes time to castigate both the Sanitary Commission and the Christian Commission.

Hospital Scene

FORREST'S RAID INTO NORTHERN ALABAMA AND TENNESSEE

Highlights

     1. The United States Sanitary Commission: In 1861, the Women's American Association of Relief was organized in New York City. This group united with the advisory committee of the Board of Physicians and Surgeons of New York and the New York Medical Association for the purpose of sending supplies to the army. The group advocated a "Commission of Inquiry and Advise in respect to the Sanitary Interests of the United States Forces." The Commission was established and became known as the United States Sanitary Commission.[13]

     The first actions were advisory but some became executive. They inspected food, diet, clothing, camp grounds, among other things, from a sanitary point of view. Later, they provided food, delicacies, and drink for invalid soldiers and ambulances for the wounded. Westervelt's complaint was that the delicacies were, in his view, consumed by the hospital staff and never reached the invalids for whom they were intended.

     Most of the activities that the Sanitary Commission carried out in the Civil War have been integrated into the functions of the Medical Corps of the Army.

     2. The Christian Commission: The Christian Commission was organized by the Young Men's Christian Association (YMCA) of New York in September 1861. It started by distributing bibles, tracts, and hymn-books to soldiers. It also held prayer meetings and visited men in camps and hospitals.

     Later in the war, the Commission distributed food, delicacies, hospital stores, stationery, and clothing to the soldiers.[14]

     It was this later activity that Westervelt criticized. He felt that the Commission staff misused the funds the public gave it for the soldiers' benefit.

     3. Confederate Pilfering of Southerners: Westervelt relates in this chapter how Forrest's men robbed the citizens of Huntsville, Alabama.

     Wheeler's cavalrymen were considered by many Southerners to be worse plunderers than Sherman's troops.[15] A soldier in a Texas Brigade said his was the best fighting unit "in the army and a set of thieves otherwise."[16] In many instances, the turmoil in the South was unbelievable. First Yankee foragers or Confederate cavalry would raid a planter's or farmer's stores; in the end, the victim's neighbors, local tramps, and deserters would complete the devastation.[17] A Southerner anywhere near troops of either side was fair game for plunder near the end of the war.

FORREST'S RAID INTO NORTHERN ALABAMA AND TENNESSEE

Our period of rest at Atlanta proved of short duration. In a few weeks a portion of Hood's army moved around to our rear, and threatened our line of communications, or, as a soldier would express it, our cracker line. Gen. Forrest became uncomfortably active along the same line; in fact his mission in the army seemed particularly directed toward destroying all of our peace and quietness.

Towards the close of the month orders came to prepare for a move. On the night of the 28th we loaded on the cars and started back on the road we came when journeying to Atlanta. We ran slowly with many halts, until the night of Oct. 1st when we reached Huntsville, and found the place in a state of excitement, as Forest had been there. In fact the last of his troopers disappeared over one of the adjoining hills just as our train rolled into the town.

Having a slight acquaintance with one of the hotel keepers, I determined to try if his friendship was sufficiently strong to insure me a supper. Fortunately I found it was, and while enjoying my first meal at a table for some months, Mr. Easley, the proprietor, related the experience of the day: how Forrest had appeared before the town in the morning, and not daring to enter the place, as it was commanded by a strong earthwork, on an adjoining eminence, had sent word into the place that he intended to shell it, and would give all who desired an hour to move out. Many took advantage of his humane offer, and packing their most valuable effects moved out of town to what was considered a safe place, when Forrest's men came upon them and robbed them of everything portable, when they returned to town, feeling that they had been "shelled" worse than if they had remained at home, as not a gun was fired into the town.

A few miles from here we found the enemy had torn up some of the R.R. track, and we were delayed about twenty-four hours while the engineers repaired it. We then ran on to within a few miles of Athens, where we found a bridge destroyed, and marched into the town and camped. During the night I was taken with cramps and in the morning sent to the hospital, while our regiment moved off toward the Elk River. In two days' time I was as well as ever and wanted to start off alone and join my regiment, but, as the country was full of traveling bands of guerrillas, the surgeon advised me not to try it. But I organized a band of reckless "devil may care" fellows and we made daily excursions into the country, where we carried on a war of extermination, not on the enemy, but on the sheepfolds, pig yards and poultry houses. The surgeon in charge knew these marauding expeditions were forbidden, but when his cook placed upon his table a pair of chickens, a roast of pork or a leg of lamb, he seemed perfectly oblivious as to where they came from and with a "smile that was childlike and bland" would partake of these succulent viands, following explicitly the commands of St. Paul—"eat whatever is set before you, and ask no questions for conscience sake." While we in turn were very careful to see that his larder was well supplied.

Still this was a very unsatisfactory sort of a life, and I was extremely homesick to be back with our company. One thing served to mitigate my loneliness: our mail arrived and brought me quite a number of letters, and after reading over those from "the girls left behind" I picked up one from an acquaintance of years before, who was at that time a married lady living in Po'keepsie, who showed she had the good and welfare of the soldier at heart, as the letter was filled with good, sound sisterly advice, and was an agreeable change from many received by soldiers from their girl friends in the North.

One more abuse of Northern generosity and Christianity was brought to my notice during my short sojourn in the hospital, and that was the Sanitary Commission. While the people of the North were pouring out their wealth to support this work, but few of them ever looked after the money they gave, to see how it was used. Tons after tons of wines, liquors, canned meats, fruits and jellies, and every delicacy calculated to tempt the apetite* of the feverish patient, were sent to the hospitals. But, what was done with them when they arrived? How large a percentage does the average reader suppose ever reached the bedside of the sick? One percent, would be a very liberal estimate. First, the table of surgeon-in-chief and the assistant surgeons had to be supplied. Then their cooks, waiters and attendants would have the best—and their name was legion, being made up of those who would do any menial service rather than return to their company after they were well enough for duty. Then came the hospital and dispensary stewards, ward attendants, waiters and other hangers on. And what do you suppose was left for the sick and wounded, after these cormorants were filled with the best of these delicacies?

A twin brother to this was the Christian Commission, which swallowed up hundreds of thousands of dollars of Northern wealth, ninety-nine percent of which went to support a lot of hypocritical frauds, who were a disgrace to Christian religion or anything else connected with Christian civilization. At

one time they pretended to supply soldiers with stationery, and sent a lot of it to our regiment. It was the poorest quality of writing paper manufactured, so soft it could not be written upon with ink, and about as thin as the love of the average Christian Commission agent for the soldier. Then, as an open insult to the ones they pretended to serve, was the printing across the paper and envelopes in glaring red letters of these words: "A free gift from the U.S. Christian Commission." So that every soldier who sent one of the flimsy sheets through the mails, and every one receiving one, had to proclaim that the sender was in such an impecunious condition as to be an object of charity. This may sound like drawing it strong, but the truth of these statements will, I know, receive the endorsement of every soldier who served his time at the front and had an opportunity of knowing.

Wednesday, Oct 12. — About nine A.M. the head of the column of our Division marched into the town, when I gladly finished the only hospital service I ever performed, and was soon with our company again. The following day we loaded on the cars, and on the 14th arrived at Chattanooga. Here we camped four days, and while here were joined by a squad who had been absent in the hospital. Among others was my old chum and tentmate, Sergt. Crist, who had been at Nashville since Aug. 5, and now returned with health re-stored and ready for duty.

On leaving Chattanooga we took up our line of march toward Atlanta, passing over part of the ground Sherman's army had fought over when advancing toward that doomed city. The 22d found us at Gainsville, where we remained a week. Most of our troops moved on to Rome, leaving our one Brigade to watch the doings of a portion of

---

* appetite

the Rebel army who were operating near us.

By some mistake there were no rations left for us, except some live beef and some graham flour that had been captured somewhere, but no salt. For several days we lived on this beef and flour unsalted, and for the first time in our lives we learned the value of this cheap commercial article. Very few of the men were provident enough to have any of it in their haversacks, and those few would not part with what little they had at any price. I had two gold dollars in my pocket that I had carried for months, and was holding them against an emergency. After eating this tasteless food for two days I concluded the emergency had arrived, so finding a man with a little of this precious article on hand, I offered him one of the dollars for two spoonfuls of salt, which to my surprise was refused. Even when I doubled my offer I was informed that money was of no value when com-pared to salt. Finally, a short distance from camp I found in a farmhouse an old pork barrel, that to all appearance had been empty some years, in the bottom of which, mixed with accumulated dust and cobwebs, was about a handful of rock salt. This was a perfect windfall to our mess, as by dissolving and straining we managed to take out the worst of the dirt, and not being over fastidious as to some of the smaller particles of dust, we pronounced it the best salt we ever tasted.

On Oct. 28th we bid good bye to this place, which the boys called "Camp Freshet", and the next day arrived at Rome, and stopped a few days, when we moved on to Kingston, and while here (on Nov. 3) the pay-master put in his appearance, and distributed two months' pay to the men.

On Nov. 8, the day Pres. Lincoln was re-elected, we broke camp and passed through the ruins of Cassville, and near night camped near Cartersville, where we received our last mail until we arrived at Savannah, the latter part of December. On the 13th we again broke camp, and after marching a few miles we crossed the Ettawa* river and burned the bridge behind us. We then tore up several miles of R.R. track, burning the ties and twisting the rails. This was the first break in our line and cut off all communication of Sherman's army with the North, and caused a considerable speculation among us in the ranks as to what the move was to be. The next two days we made long marches, and by way of variety would stop occasionally and tear up a few miles of R.R. track.

On the night of the 15th we reached Atlanta, and found most of the troops had left the city. We camped about a mile from the centre of the city, on an elevation that gave us a fine view. During the night Atlanta was burned, and from our camp it was one of the grandest sights I ever witnessed. Flames rolled from house to house, and from block to block, like waves of the sea, and lighted our camp so we could easily read the finest print any where about it. The clothing intended for our regiment had been left in the city, and by some mismanagement part of it was in one of the burning buildings, and although Quartermaster Corry made every effort to save it, the bulk of it was destroyed. That was a serious loss just at that time, when we had severed our communications, and knew not where the next would come from, and were sadly in want of refitting.

---

* Etowah

Notes — Chapter 29

1. *O.R.*, Vol. XXXIX, Part 1, p. 580.

2. Ibid., p. 581.

3. Wyeth, *That Devil Forrest*, pp. 427-432.

4. Guernsey and Alden, *Harper's Pictorial History of the Civil War*, p. 671.

5. *O.R.*, Vol. XXXIX, Part 1, p. 620.

6. Ibid., p. 633.

7. Ibid.

8. Guernsey and Alden, *Harper's Pictorial History of the Civil War*, p. 671.

9. Wyeth, *That Devil Forrest*, p. 427.

10. Ibid., pp. 445-447.

11. *O.R.*, Vol. XXXIX, Part 1, p. 640.

12. Ibid., p. 582.

13. Guernsey and Alden, *Harper's Pictorial History of the Civil War*, p. 792.

14. Benson J. Lossing, *Mathew Brady's Illustrated History of the Civil War* (The Fairfax Press), p. 438. Originally published as *A History of the Civil War* (The War Memorial Association, 1912).

15. Glathaar, *The March to the Sea and Beyond* (New York: University Press, 1986), p. 151.

16. Ibid., p. 152.

17. Carter, *The Siege of Atlanta* (New York: Ballantine Books, 1973), p. 381.

Chapter 30

THE MARCH TO THE SEA

Background

While Sherman was at Atlanta and pursuing Hood, he was also trying to determine his next steps. He reasoned that the correct action was to march to Savannah, and he wrote:

> Until we can repopulate Georgia, it is useless to occupy it; but the utter destruction of its roads, houses, and people will cripple their military resources. By attempting to hold the roads we will lose a thousand men monthly, and will gain no result. I can make the march and make Georgia howl.[1]

Grant approved Sherman's plan on October 12 and advised Sherman to "clean the country" of railroads, livestock, amd negroes, arming and organizing the latter.[2]

Sherman sent the IV Corps under Stanley and the XXIII Corps under Schofield to Thomas and left it up to Thomas to take care of Hood and Forrest. Hood rashly attacked Schofield at Franklin, Tennessee on November 30, and suffered terrible losses. Thomas attacked Hood at Nashville on December 15, defeated him and pursued him until his Army of the Tennessee was so decimated that it was no longer an organized force.[3] Forrest, who had fought with Hood at Franklin and in the retreat after Nashville, was finally tracked down by Wilson and his cavalry and Forrest's forces were severely defeated at Selma, Alabama on April 2, 1865.[4]

There were many critics of Sherman's venture. *The London Times* doubted that it would succeed. *The British and Army Navy Gazette* said, "He had done either one of the most brilliant or one of the most foolish things ever performed by a military leader." *The London Herald* was of the same opinion.[5]

A Richmond minister said, "God has put a hook in Sherman's nose and is leading him to destruction."[6]

Lincoln compared Sherman to a burrowing animal and said that he knew what hole he went in but didn't know which one he'd come out. Lincoln was confident, but apprehensive.[7]

For his March to the Sea, Sherman had four corps which he organized in two wings—the Left Wing under Slocum had the XIV Corps under Davis and the XX Corps under Williams; the Right Wing under Howard had the XV Corps under Osterhaus and the XVII Corps under Blair. The cavalry was under Kilpatrick; Sherman's total force on November 30, 1864, totalled 62,204.[8]

On November 15, after Sherman burned Atlanta, he headed toward Savannah.[9] The Left Wing moved to threaten Augusta, then south to Milledgeville (the capital) and then on to Savannah. The Right Wing moved southeast to threaten Macon and then to Gordon, below Milledgeville, from there it paralleled the Left Wing to Savannah.[10]

In contrast to the concerns about "the Lost Army" (all communications with Grant and Lincoln were cut off from November 15 to December 22), the march was more like a pleasant hike.[11] The men lived off the land; food was plentiful. Lieutenant Colonel Martin's report for the 17th New York Veteran Volunteers said that from November 16 until December 12, "...my command received from the Government but four day's rations of bread and meal and about half rations of sugar and

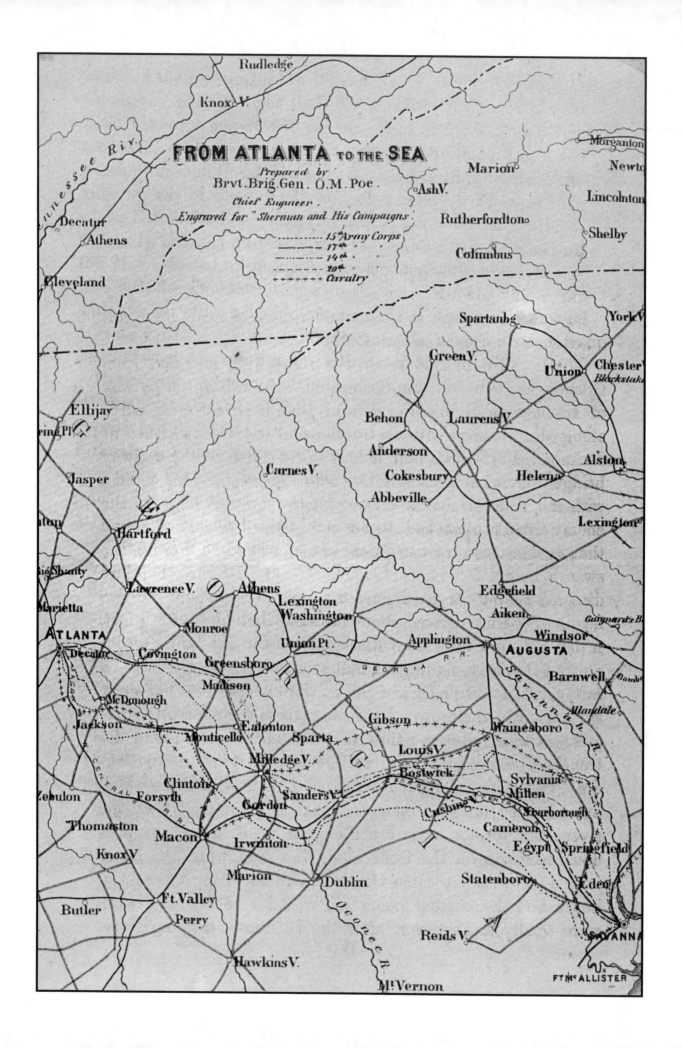

FROM ATLANTA TO THE SEA

Prepared by
Brvt. Brig. Gen. O. M. Poe.
Chief Engineer.
Engraved for "Sherman and His Campaigns".

------------- 15th Army Corps
— ·· — ·· — 17th ·
— — — 14th ·
------------- 20th ·
+ + + + + + Cavalry

coffee. The rest of the food which the men had was picked up by foraging parties along the line of march..."[12] General Morgan reported "...the men always having an abundant supply [of food] furnished by forage details."[13]

There were three dangers the army faced during the "March," (1) resistance by Wheeler's cavalry en route and by Hardee at Savannah; (2) attacks on foragers by Confederate cavalry and guerrillas; and (3) efforts of the Confederates to capture Yankees who foraged and strayed from the main body of the army.

Resistance

Wheeler made several attempts to attack and harass the Union advance. At Sandersville, on November 26, the 17th New York, was called upon to repel Confederate cavalry. On December 8, a rebel gunboat shelled Westervelt's Brigade as it crossed Ebenezer Creek. And Rebel artillery shelled the brigade when it was in front of Savannah. A man of the 17th New York was hit by an artillery shell at Savannah. The shell tore off one of his legs and he died the next day. Another man of the regiment was slightly wounded by the same shell.[14]

Attacks on Foragers

Westervelt recounts how, on November 22, he tried foraging. A squadron of Rebel cavalry appeared, outnumbering the six in the foraging party, and started shooting. Westervelt and his companions beat a hasty retreat. He never went forgaing again on the March to the Sea.

On November 30, Lieutenant Colonel Martin sent out a party of 40 men under Lieutenant Magee to forage. The party was cut off by Rebel cavalry and Martin had to take the entire regiment to rescue it.[15] Martin suffered no losses in this encounter and was commended for his prompt action.[16]

Scooping Up Yankees

The extent to which the Confederates were successful in scooping up Yankees can be seen in the following casualty figures for the March to the Sea.

	Killed	Wounded	Missing	Total
Entire Army[17]	63	245	295	567
Morgan's Division—XIV Corps[18]	8	16	57	81

The number missing is an indication of how successful the Confederates were in picking off those who strayed, straggled, or foraged. The ratio of missing to total losses for the entire army was 52%; for Morgan's Division it was a whopping 70%!

At Savannah, Hardee had an estimated 8,000-10,000 mongrel mass of artillery, infantry, and militia.[19] Sherman demanded that Hardee surrender on December 17, intimating that he would treat Hardee as Hood treated Union forces at Resaca on October 12; i.e., if assault were necessary no prisoners would be taken.[20] Hardee refused to surrender and Sherman prepared to assault on December 20. Orders were given to make fascines and to carefully examine the line in front.[21] Morgan responded, "I am sorry to say I have no place from which one [an assault] could be made with any reasonable hope of success." Morgan's men found they faced a swamp in the front and a well-built fort on the left.[22] Fortunately for them, Hardee evacuated Savannah on December 20, and the Federals took possession of the city on December 21.[23]

Sherman had reached Savannah and he had set out to "make Georgia howl." Davis' Corps alone reported this destruction:

-48 miles of railroad and four large bridges, destroyed
-12,000 bales of cotton, destroyed
-1,770 draft and saddle animals, 1,500 cattle, and several hundred sheep, captured
-1,340 able-bodied negroes followed the column
-1,000,730 pounds of fodder and 1,474,834 pounds of grain taken
-The corps left Atlanta with seven and one-half days' supply of rations; it reached Savannah with five days' supply—virtually all the rest of the food was foraged en route.[24]

The effects on the countryside were devastating as Sherman and his army burned buildings and laid land to waste. Sherman certainly accomplished his objective.

Highlights

1. Westervelt's Commission: Westervelt writes that he was promoted from first sergeant to second lieutenant after Jonesboro. There is no record that the promotion was ever processed. His official records show him as being jumped to first lieutenant on May 30, 1865, and he was mustered out with that rank on July 13, 1865. It is understood that Westervelt's experience was not atypical for Union officers near the end of the war.

2. Milledgeville: Westervelt notes that some of the officers went into Milledgeville, then capital of Georgia, took possession of the Legislative hall, held a mock session and voted the state back into the Union. It was a rowdy time that attracted thousands of officers and men. What started as a humorous event turned ugly as the statehouse was looted and valuable books were stolen or destroyed. The Left Wing and Kilpatrick were responsible for this atrocity. Sherman noted the event in his memoirs but made light of it.

3. Lawlessness: Westervelt expresses concerns about stealing and the demoralizing effect living off the land and taking possessions from the citizens of Georgia had upon the men. He wasn't alone in his concern; General Davis was also concerned. He issued a circular (order) on November 18, 1864, in which he said, "Men must be taught that, even in the midst of an enemy's country, the dictates of humanity must at least be observed, and that no good can result to the cause of their country from indiscriminate destruction of property or burning of the homes of women and children....The general commanding the Military Division of the Mississippi has forbidden men entering houses on any pretense."[25]

Regretfully, Sherman knew what was happening and made no real attempt to stop it.[26]

THE MARCH TO THE SEA

The next day we left Atlanta and found ourselves fairly started on what proved to be "Sherman's famous march to the sea." Just as we were called in line an order was read to us that had probably been written for the army who had remained at Atlanta since its capture, but we thought it did not fit our case at all, as it told how we had enjoyed a long rest after the arduous summer campaign and had been rested and clothed, and were now starting to win new honors! We thought this decidedly refreshing, as to the rest and clothes, as we had been on the move most of the time since Atlanta was captured, and were now starting again, and not one in twenty had a change even of underclothing, and many of our men were nearly barefoot, as their shoes were worn and broken.

Yet we were not so badly off as would at first appear, as the troops who started ahead of us had been so well supplied they had overloaded themselves, and the usual result followed. The first day out they began to reduce baggage by throwing away what they could not carry. Our men quietly came after and picked up by the roadside shirts, drawers, shoes, socks and everthing requisite for a complete outfit, and in two days' time we had all we wished to carry, without the trouble of a requisition on the quartermaster.

We were now fairly started on Sherman's "March to the Sea." Of course our destination was unknown, but, with an intuitive sense that comes to an old campaigner, we concluded we were starting on a long march, and were to live on the country we were marching through, so we laid our plans accordingly.

After our last engagement at Jonesboro I had been appointed 2d lieutenant, but as my commission failed to arrive I was still 1st sergeant. Our captain was on other duty, leaving me in command of the company, so I selected four good genial fellows to comprise our mess. One of them was sent out as a forager, knowing he was well adapted to that line of duty, and he filled his part of the work so well that our mess were seldom hungry. The remainder of us divided up our cooking utensils and baggage, with a portion of each to carry, while our work was so arranged that each one had a certain part to perform, all of which we were willing to do, and a little more if necessary. So we always ran our mess without any growling or faultfinding, so common in the army. Our noon halt was from forty minutes to an hour, and so systematically was our work performed that in that time we would start a fire, boil coffee, cook meat and potatoes, eat a hearty dinner, wash and pack our mess kit, and often have a few minutes left to wash ourselves, or if any preferred it, enjoy an after dinner smoke, before the bugle sounded to "fall in." At night, when ordered to camp, it was the duty of one who carried a small hatchet to cut tentpoles and put up our small shelter tent; another to make fire and cook supper; the third brought water and made coffee, while the fourth would look up a back load of straw for a bed. By this means our mess often had our tent up, a good bed provided, and were sitting around a steaming supper of coffee, fresh pork, and sweet potatoes, before some had even got their tents up.

On Sunday, Nov. 20, after a long day's march, we camped for the night near the village of Eatonton. We soon had our tents up and everthing comfortable for the night, when orders came for two companies to go on picket. Co. A and our Co. K were selected, and placed in command of the captain of Co. A,

Sherman's Foragers in Georgia

who, in order to give his company an easy tour of duty, remained with them at the reserve, and ordered me to take my company about a half mile in advance, and occupy the outpost. This would give his men a chance to sleep all night, while our company would have to stand guard, and be deprived of sleep, leaving us in poor shape for a long march the day following. But he being captain and I sergeant there was nothing for me to do but obey.

We advanced about a half mile, when, seeing a much better place beyond the village, we advanced to it, where we found a covered bridge over a branch of the Oconee river. This gave us a vantage ground, as the river guarded our flanks, so it was only necessary to post two pickets at the end of the bridge, giving the remainder of the men a chance to sleep. Soon a thunder shower came up, and for two hours the wind blew and the rain seemed to pour down in sheets, but we, with the tight roof of the bridge over our heads, could laugh at the storm, as we were dry and comfortable as in a house, and of course felt very sorry for company A, who, though occupying the reserve, were exposed to the full fury of the blast.

The next morning we leisurely cooked our breakfast, then packed up our tents and blankets all dry and in good order, and at eight o'clock A.M. were called back to the reserve, and we found them in a pitable condition. They had been stationed in a corn-field, and put up their tents congratulating themselves on being on the reserve, with but little to do. But the first blast of the storm had taken down most of the tents, while the rain soon changed the ground to the consistency of a bed of mortar, and in that unenviable condition they had passed the night. Now they were busy wringing the water from their tents and blankets, and with their clothes thoroughly saturated were getting ready to march.

Monday, Nov. 21. — We were quite late in starting, and were then sent to guard our wagon train. This gave us a hard day's march and deprived us of our dinner hour. We did not reach camp until eight P.M., when, with appetites sharpened from a day's fasting, we were in good condition to enjoy our supper.

Tuesday, Nov. 22. — Seeing no signs of a move I managed to secure a horse and went out with a party for a day's foraging. The horse I rode was a captured one, and proved a good mount. He would take any fence or ditch I rode him to, so we took our course right across the country. At noon we had ridden about twenty miles, when we stopped at a plantation for dinner, then loaded an ox cart and two wagons with potatoes and pork, with which we started to return. All went merrily for a few miles, when, on ascending a hill, as we reached the top we met a squadron of rebel cavalry coming up on the opposite side. As our party numbered but six, we saw there was no show of fighting, so concluded it was to be a foot-race, and setting an example to the rest of our party, I wheeled, gave my horse the spur, and started down the hill, leaving our loads of forage for the enemy. Half way to the foot of the hill we turned to the right, leaped the fence, and, with about fifty yelling rebels at our heels, struck for a piece of woods near by. The shots from their carbines flew thick and fast, and how we all escaped was a mystery. Not one of us were hit, not even our horses. We soon reached the wood, and the enemy retired, when we, taking a round-about course, reached camp soon after dark, having ridden over fifty miles since starting in the morning.

Thursday, Nov. 24. — To-day was Thanksgiving in N.Y., and as we saw no signs of moving we commenced cooking Thanksgiving dinner. Just as we had it nearly started orders came to move, and as we could not carry a half-cooked dinner we had to throw it away.

At noon we reached Milledgeville, the capital of the State, and halted just outside the city. The fog was so heavy we could see but little of the place. The state house loomed up in the distance, but we could see nothing distinctly. While we halted here some of our officers went into the city, and taking possession of the legislative hall, organized a mock legislature, and proceeded to vote Georgia back into the Union.

We passed through the suburbs and crossed a covered bridge that spans the Oconee river. From here we traveled on slowly until four P.M., when we went into camp. Soon our forager arrived well loaded, and our Thanksgiving dinner, that was thrown away in the morning, was more than made up at night. Instead of enjoying it at 12 o'clock noon, it was 12 o'clock midnight. Nevertheless, with appetites sharpened from long hours of fasting, we did ample justice to a bill of fare of no mean order.

First, there was boiled turkey and roast sweet potatoes; then came baked corn bread, dressed with sorghum syrup. This, washed down with a quart cup of coffee, made a meal plenty hearty enough to retire immediately after. But nothing seemed to disturb the digestion of a soldier. Dyspepsia was an unknown disease in the army.

The enemy seemed now to have got an idea of what our march meant, and determined, if they could not stop us, to annoy us all they could. They gathered together all the cavalry that could be spared from other places, and placing them under command of Gen. Wade Hampton, hung upon our advance and flanks, ready to pick up any forager who strayed away too far from our line of march. Most of the skirmishing was done by the foragers, who went in advance of our main army. They were composed of a reckless dare-devil sort of rough riders, each one striving to take the advance, and with a dash drive the enemy back, and then be the first to reach a plantation, as the first ones in usually had the best picking, and the foraging was not always for the benefit of the army. Self was not forgotten. If money, watches or jewelry was found it was invariably confiscated. Some of them who never owned even the cheapest kind of a watch, or any jewelry before entering the service, were now sporting expensive gold watches and diamond rings. This had a very demoralizing effect upon the men. Even those who were considered honest before the war soon learned to gather in anything of value that they considered portable. And I believe there are in prisons today, in different parts of the country, men who took their first lessons in theiving while acting as one of Sherman's foragers.

Saturday, Nov. 26. — Revielle at four, and at seven we were on the road. For the first few miles we moved slowly and could hear the foragers skirmishing quite lively. Sometimes the firing would be by volleys almost as heavy as a line of battle. The 20th corps were moving on a road parallel to the one we were on, and a few miles to our right, and we could hear them popping away about as lively as our own advance. Soon the work became too heavy for the foragers, when our regiment were sent forward to help them. Now a running fight commenced that was kept up until about ten A.M., when we reached Sandersville, a small station on the Savannah & Macon R.R. Here the road traveled by the 20th corps and the road our corps (the 14th) were on came together. We found the 150th N.Y. regiment, of Dutchess Co., were on one road while our regiment was in advance on the other,—so there was not only a running fight with the enemy but a foot race between the two regiments, to see which would first enter the village. I guess "honors were easy" between us, as we came into the place neck and neck, and found some good foraging on our arrival. We saw several of our men, as well as the enemy, dead by the roadside, showing that the skirmishing had not been for nothing. A mile from here we camped and could hear Wade Hampton's cavalry skirmishing with our pickets all night.

Sunday, Nov. 28. — On starting we found the enemy's cavalry still hovering about our advance, trying to annoy us all in their power. They destroyed the road bridges to delay us, while we destroyed the railroad tracks to cripple them, but they neglected one important factor which, had they taken in consideration, would have made Sherman's raid almost if not entirely a failure—that is to have destroyed all the forage in advace of us and have driven off all cattle, horses, and mules. As it was, we lived entirely on the country, while our drove of cattle, numbering some three thousand when we started from Atlanta, from which we killed as needed all the way through, numbered more than twice that amount when we arrived in front of Savannah. Worn out mules we left, and took good ones in their places, while our cavalry were never so well mounted. All this was our gain and at the same time impoverished the South, as it left them no animals to work their land.

About noon of the 28th we reached a small branch of the Ohoopee river, and found Wade Hampton's troops had burned the bridge just before our arrival, so we turned aside and rested until near sunset, while our engineers put down a pontoon bridge. These pontoon boats were different from the heavy lumbering concerns that were used in Virginia, requiring five to ten teams to transport them. These were made with light frames covered with canvas. They were easily taken apart and were so light that one team would carry several of them, and yet they possessed sufficient strength and buoyancy to bridge the swiftest running stream. After crossing the stream we passed through the town of Louisville and a few miles from there went into camp.

We remained in camp at Louisville two days, which gave us a chance to close up and get the army in good shape, as the army in front of us were increasing in numbers, rendering it necessary to be always ready for an attack. Here Gen. Sherman showed his superior military genius in deceiving the enemy. He faced the whole army towards Augusta, leading the enemy into the mistake of concentrating their forces at that place, which they commenced to fortify. He then quickly turned towards the seacoast, making Savannah the objection point.

The second day we stopped near Louisville, and the enemy made a dash on our pickets and drove them in. We were hurriedly called in line and moved out to their support at a double quick. On our arrival we looked across some open fields and, about half a mile distant, saw the enemy's line of battle of cavalry over a mile long. We quickly formed our line and advanced. Just before we came *within gunshot of them, they wheeled and rode off at an easy walk, while a mounted band struck up "Dixie." We followed them about a mile, they keeping just their distance from us, when we turned about and returned to camp. An hour after we were sent on picket. Being on the reserve we had a very quiet tour of duty.*

The next morning we found our mess entirely out of meat. While we were discussing the uncertainties of living on an enemy's country, a nice fat calf came running past our lines, and in less than half an hour a good supply of veal cutlets was frying on our fire.

In the afternoon we continued our march towards Savannah. Rainy weather now set in, and the roads soon became very muddy, obliging us to build considerable corduroy road to get our trains over. On the 9th we passed Springfield, and camped at night in front of a rebel battery that was posted across the road, and fired on our advance as they came up, and at night we went to sleep with the comfortable assurance that we were to charge the battery in the morning. But when we got up we found the enemy had very kindly withdrawn during the night, leaving the road clear for us.

We continued our march, and about four P.M. on the 11th we went on picket about two miles from Savannah, just to the right of the turnpike that runs from that city to Augusta. Our camp was formed just in the rear of our picket lines and here we commenced to fortify. The heaviest guns in the city were those just to the left of us, commanding the turnpike, and it soon became evident that we would be obliged to take this battery before we could gain possession of the city. Some of our troops were employed

making faciences,* and when enough were completed they were placed in a convenient position in the woods by the side of the turnpike, as that was the most exposed place to put guns in battery.

Finally, on the night of December 20, a detail was called for, of three men from each company, to dig a trench across the road, throw up breastworks, and put our guns in position to open on the enemy's works in front, while the infantry were to advance and carry them by assault. Our detail moved forward carefully, while sheltered in the woods, until they reached the proper place, when each man taking a facience [sic] in front for shelter, began to dig. As soon as the enemy saw them they opened fire with three thirty-two pounders, which would throw about a peck of grape shot at every discharge. I need not add that our men worked lively until the trench was sufficiently deep, and the bank high enough to shelter them, but with all their exposure our casualities were less than would have been expected.

The firing was kept up steadily until midnight, and I believe the last gun fired from the city was from this battery, as in the morning, when we were forming in line to charge it, it was found that the city was evacuated, and our troops moved forward without opposition and took possession.

Gen. Geary's division was the first to enter, and on this it seems his friends have tried to build for him a heavy reputation, as being the first to enter both Atlanta and Savannah. It always seemed like building on a slight foundation, as an inverted pyramid standing on its apex, to base any man's brilliant military record on the mere fact of

---

* fascines

having been the first to enter and take possession of two cities, whose evacuation had been forced by other troops besides his command. That will do for a brilliant military record during a political campaign, but will not stand the test of time, or the pen of the future historian.

Savannah was now in our possession, and we moved inside the fortifications and camped in a swamp, where we remained until Jan. 20, just one month from the time the city was evacuated. While here we had our usual number of reviews, drills, etc. Once I went to the city to attend church. I was a little late in getting there, and the morning service had commenced when I arrived. The church was comfortably filled, but not crowded, and as I entered, no one offering me a seat, I walked to one of the windows, which was about breast high, and springing up seated myself on the window sill. The audience seemed to divide their attention between the pastor and my
zouave uniform, with probably the largest share directed to me. I tried to pay attention to the sermon, which was a sort of a blue brimstone harangue. One could see his sympathies were strongly with the Southern cause, but there were enough officers of our army scattered through the church to make him guarded in his expressions. I don't think the service was of any spiritual benefit to me, as the glances from many of the citizens and their families were not of brotherly love, and I was just human enough to return their gaze of hatred with one of defiance, and as the last words of the benediction were said I dropped from my perch on the window, and sticking my zouave fez on the back of my head, walked out of the church, while the audience gave way on either side, as though fearing contamination by touching my zouave dress, which was a uniform hated above all others by the chivalry of the South.

THE MARCH TO THE SEA

Notes — Chapter 30

1. Bowman and Irwin, *Sherman and His Campaigns,* p. 250.

2. Lewis, *Sherman—Fighting Prophet*, p. 429.

3. Guernsey and Alden, *Harper's Pictorial History of the Civil War*, pp. 677-681.

4. Ibid., p. 750.

5. Burke Davis, *Sherman's March* (New York: Random House, 1980), p. 24.

6. Ibid.

7. Lewis, *Sherman—Fighting Prophet*, pp. 429-430.

8. *O.R.*, Vol. XLIV, p. 16.

9. Lewis, *Sherman—Fighting Prophet*, p. 435.

10. Davis, *Sherman's March*, p. 27.

11. Bowman and Irwin, *Sherman and His Campaigns*, p. 257.
    O.R., Vol XLIV, p. 783.

12. *O.R.*, Vol. XLIV, p. 190.

13. Ibid., p. 182.

14. Ibid., pp. 185-186.

15. Ibid., pp. 189-190.

16. Ibid., p. 185.

17. Ibid., p. 15.

18. Ibid., p. 182.

19. Ibid., p. 728.

20. Ibid., p 737.

21. Ibid., pp. 747-748.

22. Ibid., p. 769.

23. Ibid., p. 216.

Notes — Chapter 30

24. Ibid., pp. 166-7.

25. Ibid., pp. 489-490.

26. Davis, Sherman's March, p. 43.

Chapter 31

THE CAROLINAS CAMPAIGN

Savannah to Averasboro

Background

Even before Sherman appeared in front of Savannah, Grant was thinking about Sherman's next move. He proposed that Sherman put his infantry aboard transports and sail north to help him deal with Lee.[1]

Sherman had other ideas; he preferred to march through the Carolinas to reach Grant. Sherman wanted to destroy the railroads in the Carolinas, isolate Charleston, South Carolina, so General Foster at Hilton Head could capture the place; go through Columbia, the capital of South Carolina, and Fayetteville, North Carolina, and meet up with the navy at Wilmington, North Carolina.[2] Grant authorized Sherman's march near the end of December 1864.[3]

The organization of the army for the Carolinas was the same as the March to the Sea. Slocum had the Left Wing. Changes in Morgan's Second Division involved leadership moves. Westervelt's Brigade was now under the command of Brigadier General William Vandever in lieu of Colonel Smith; and the 17th New York was now led by Lieutenant Colonel James Lake; Lieutenant Colonel Joel Martin having resigned on January 4, 1865.

The pattern of movement for Sherman's army was essentially the same as that for the March to the Sea. The Left Wing, under Slocum, prepared to cross the Savannah River at Sister's Ferry beginning January 29, 1865. Slocum's assignment was to make a feint towards Augusta, Georgia while the Right Wing, under Howard, made a similar feint towards Charleston, South Carolina. This would divide the Confederate forces between those two places.[4] After that, the Left Wing was to go near Columbia, South Carolina while the Right Wing went into that capital. Railroads were to be destroyed as the army marched.

Both Wings would then proceed to Fayetteville, North Carolina where the old U.S. Arsenal was located and where most of the machinery from the Harpers Ferry Arsenal had been sent by the Confederates. March 12, 13, and 14 were spent destroying the arsenal and other property that Confederates used in pursuing the war.

General Terry had captured Fort Fisher and Wilmington, North Carolina and Schofield had captured New Bern, North Carolina. These successes changed Sherman's objective to that of meeting up with Terry and Schofield at Goldsboro, North Carolina. That city was an important transportation center for Sherman because it had two railroads back to the seaports of Wilmington, North Carolina and Beaufort, North Carolina.[5]

The problems facing Sherman's army in the Carolinas were much the same as the ones in the March to the Sea. In addition to limited resistance, attacks on foragers, and Rebel efforts to take prisoners of those who foraged and strayed, there was the problem of rain.

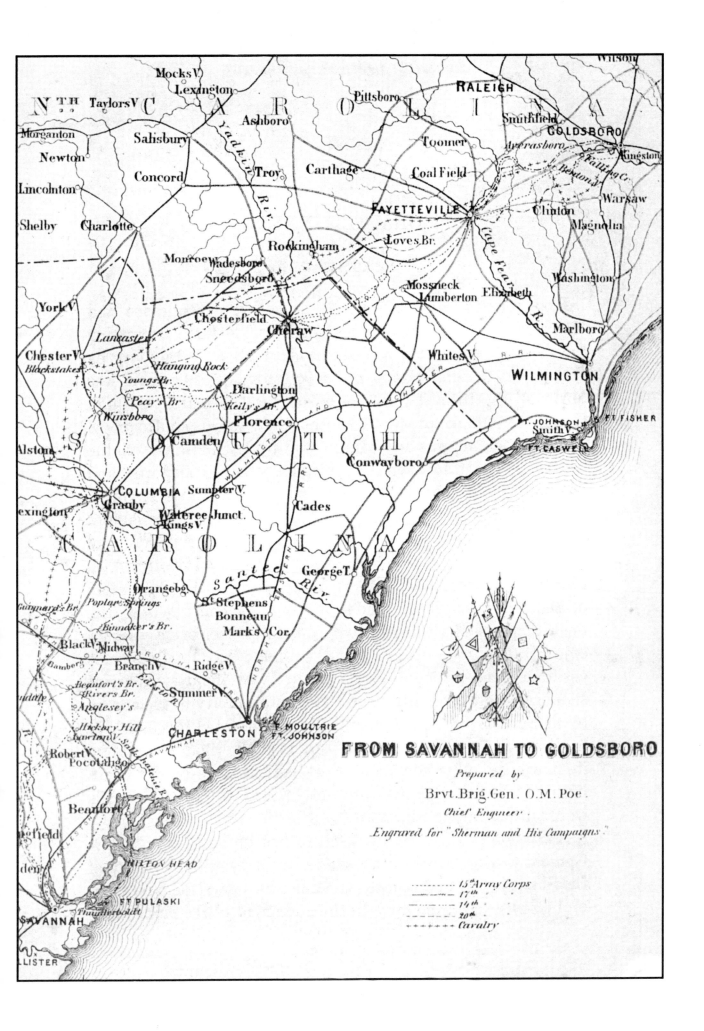

FROM SAVANNAH TO GOLDSBORO

Prepared by

Brvt. Brig. Gen. O. M. Poe.

Chief Engineer.

Engraved for "Sherman and His Campaigns."

··············	15th Army Corps
————	17th
— — —	14th
—·—·—	20th
+++++++	Cavalry

Marching through the Swamps

THE CAROLINAS CAMPAIGN

Rain

The land was deluged with water—rain fell on twenty-eight of the first forty-five days of the campaign[6] (see Picture on page 238). The rain delayed the start of the campaign and the Left Wing lost a week and was forced to move upriver to Sister's Ferry before it could cross the Savannah River. At Sister's Ferry, the river overflowed until it was three miles wide.[7] The weather was bitter cold. Some of Slocum's pickets patrolled their campsites in canoes. One night, a *New York Herald* reporter found the XX Corps commander, General A.S. Williams, perched in a tree, swathed in a blanket, and smoking a cigar.[8]

Confederate General Hardee telegraphed General Joseph E. Johnston, "The Salk is impassable." After the war, Johnston told General Jacob Cox, "But when I learned that Sherman's army was marching through the Salk swamp, making its own corduroy roads at the rate of a dozen miles a day and more, and bringing its artillery and wagons with it, I made up my mind that there had been no such army in existence since the days of Julius Caesar."[9]

Limited Resistance

For the most part, Kilpatrick's cavalry led the way and screened the army. Resistance was primarily Hampton's and Wheeler's cavalry. The first significant resistance encountered by Vandever's Brigade was at the Cape Fear River and is described below; it was the Battle of Averasboro.

Attacks on Foragers

In the March through the Carolinas, foraging was far more difficult than in the March to the Sea. Food was scarcer since it was the end of winter; only stored foods, livestock, and poultry were available. Farms were poorer than in Georgia and foragers had to go farther, usually on horseback, to get food.

General Hazen, commanding the Second Division of the XV Corps said that he had to put five percent of his total force into the saddle to collect the 7,000 pounds of food his troops needed daily.[10] The range of food was more limited than it was in Georgia.[11] Sherman reported that his troops "traversed the country from Savannah to Goldsborough, with an average breadth of 40 miles, consuming all the forage, cattle, hogs, sheep, poultry, cured hams, corn meal, etc." In this same report, he gives another rationale for foraging by saying, "The public enemy [the South] instead of drawing supplies from that region to feed his armies, will be compelled to send provisions from other quarters to feed the inhabitants."[12]

Westervelt tried his hand again at foraging on February 25, and, as he recounts, barely escaped with his life. The Confederates were agressively trying to capture or kill foragers and the situation became very nasty.

Union foragers foraged at a home north of Columbia and raped a teenage girl. Wheeler's men captured and killed the alleged rapists, cutting their throats, and leaving a sign, "these are the seven."

THE CAROLINAS CAMPAIGN

On February 27, eighteen of Kilpatrick's men were killed in the same manner, some with messages attached, "Death to all foragers."[13]

Some of the Union men had gone completely overboard. General Morgan, in his report, said that some of his foragers had become highwaymen; their victims usually old men, women, children, and negroes whom they rob and maltreat. Morgan went on to say, "These men are a disgrace to the name of soldier and the country."[14]

Capturing Foragers and Stragglers

Losses due to those missing during the campaign from Savannah to Goldsboro (minus losses at the Battle of Bentonville) show the following:

	Missing
Morgan's Division	163
Vandever's Brigade	106
17th New York	14

Captain Marshall, who commanded the 17th New York after Averasboro, reported that, during the campaign, "we have lost from our foraging parties, captured 1 commissioned officer, 2 non-commissioned officers; drowned, 1 private."[15]

The comparable numbers for Morgan's Division for the two campaigns are as follows:

	Total Missing
March to the Sea	57
Carolinas Campaign	163

Thus, losses due to missing in the Carolinas Campaign were nearly three times those in the March to the Sea.

The Battle of Averasboro

On March 15, the Left Wing was ordered to follow Kilpatrick to Averasboro and beyond.[16] Hardee, with approximately 7,500 men tried to stop it.[17] This occurred on March 16 at a point where the Goldsboro Road branches off towards Goldsboro through Bentonville.[18] The XX Corps had the lead and found the Confederates behind breastworks. Vandever's Brigade was ordered to the extreme left of the line in an attempt to turn the Confederate right. The brigade's extreme left rested on the Cape Fear River with deep ravines along its front, separating it from the works of the enemy.[19]

Vandever's report states, "I succeeded in pushing across the ravine two companies of the Sixteenth Illinois on my extreme left and three companies of the Seventeenth New York; but they had to remain under cover of the opposite bank being too close to the enemy's works to withstand his fire unprotected. The firing all along my line was heavy and protracted. The matters remained until near dark, when the firing slackened and almost ceased...and so matters remained until the following morning when the enemy was found to have decamped during the night."[20]

At Averasboro, the 17th New York lost Lieutenant Colonel Lake—wounded; Captain Barnett killed. The total loss for the regiment in this battle was:

	Officers	Enlisted Men	Total[21]
Killed	1	8	9
Wounded	2	23	25
	3	31	34

The totals for the XIV Corps were 116 killed and wounded.[22]

Highlights

1. <u>The Burning of Columbia, South Carolina</u>: One of the most memorable events of the March through the Carolinas was the burning of Columbia. It started an immediate controversy that continues and probably will continue forever. Sherman, in his report, blames Confederate General Hampton for setting the fires.[23] Citizens of the city appointed a committee which reported that without question, "Columbia was burned by the soldiers of General Sherman; that the vast majority of incendiaries were sober."[24] Many reasons have been given for the allegations that Union soldiers burned Columbia; one, that it was the birthplace of secession, and two, that it was burned in retaliation for the Rebels burning Chambersburg, Pennsylvania on July 30, 1864.

Westervelt notes that his division did not enter Columbia, so the blame could not be placed on it. Beyond that he is rather blasé about the whole affair.

2. <u>Corduroy Roads and Pontoon Bridges</u>: Every report in the Carolinas Campaign contains references to corduroy roads and pontoon bridges.

Corduroy roads were simply logs put on roads crosswise so that horses, wagons, and men could go across a marsh or wet area. What is remarkable about the use of corduroy roads on the march is the speed with which they were laid. Assume that the logs that had to be cut and laid down were a foot in diameter, that means cutting and laying 5,280 logs per mile. Consider the feat when, as cited earlier, the army corduroyed as many as a dozen miles a day!

At the beginning of the war, pontoons were heavy boats carried on wagons, as at Fredericksburg in December 1862. Later, and in this campaign, pontoons were made by stretching canvas over wood frames. The boats were placed in the water so that planks, carried with the army, could be stretched across the top of the boats to form a roadway. In his report, Sherman refers to the pontoon bridge over the Savannah River as the "Union Causeway."[25] Persons handling the pontoon bridges were called engineers or pontooniers.

3. <u>Lieutenant Colonel Lake and Captain Marshall</u>: Lieutenant Colonel Lake was the 17th New York's commanding officer from Savannah to Averasboro, where he was wounded.

James G. Lake was mustered in as captain, Company G, on Oct. 17, 1863. He served in that capacity until January 4, 1865, when he was appointed lieutenant colonel. While he served in a colonel's slot, he was never promoted to colonel, and was mustered out with the regiment on July 13, 1865.[26]

When Lieutenant Colonel Lake fell at Averasboro, Captain Alexander S. Marshall became the commanding officer of the 17th New York. Marshall had served from 1861 to 1862 as first lieutenant and adjutant in the 7th West Virginia. He joined the 17th New York as first lieutenant and adjutant in July 1863, served as captain, Company B, and finally as major, from March 17, 1865, to the day the regiment was mustered out, July 13, 1865. He was the fourth commanding officer under whom Westervelt served in the 17th New York.[27]

THE CAROLINAS CAMPAIGN

From Savannah to Averasboro

Friday, Jan. 20. — At four reveille sounded and woke us from our morning nap, when we received orders to march. Two hours after we bid good bye to Savannah. On leaving the city we took the turnpike towards Augusta. After a march of eleven miles we camped and remained about a week when we resumed our march. The weather was cold and frosty. In fact for a week we experienced the coldest weather we had felt in Georgia. On the 27th we forded a stream about waist deep and some fifty yards wide, it being covered with ice a good half inch thick. It was, to say the least, decidedly refreshing to plunge into the cold water, and after fording the stream to throw ourselves on our backs, and with our feet in the air let the water run from our shoes; then up and start on a double quick for a few miles to warm ourselves, and march the remainder of the day in our wet clothes. We thought nothing of it then but now, many of us are paying the penalty in rheumatic pains or other complaints.

On the 29th we camped near the Savannah river at a point called Sister's ferry, about forty miles from the city of Savannah. Here we remained until Feb. 5th, while our men built corduroy roads across the swamps on either side of the river and a pontoon bridge across the stream, which was guarded by one of our gunboats to prevent the enemy from running down from Augusta with some of their small steamers, and destroying the bridge.

On the night of the 5th we crossed the river and for the first time found ourselves on the sacred soil of South Carolina. We continued on our march passing through Barnwell on the 11th. Our troops seemed determined to make the power of Sherman's army felt in this part of the South, and burned all the dwellings. Churches and what few school houses we passed were spared. On the 16th we passed through Lexington, and about noon halted within three miles of Columbia. Our division did not enter the city, so the blame of burning that place could not be attached to us. From our halting place we could see the smoke of the burning city, but burning buildings were an every day occurrence, and we took but little notice of it. In the afternoon we moved off to the left of the city and crossed the south branch of the Santee river on a pontoon bridge, and after a day's march of about twenty miles we camped near the north branch of the Santee, and while we enjoyed a good night's sleep our engineers took up the bridge we had crossed and put it down across the north branch of the Santee, which we crossed on the following morning, and continued our march in a northeasterly direction.

Rainy weather now set in, making the roads heavy, and marching very tiresome for the men. When the mules on the wagons trains gave out the men were employed to pull the wagons out of the mud, or up some steep hill where the wet clay was about as slippery as grease. This work was done by attaching a long rope to the side of a wagon, so that from fifty to one hundred men would take hold, and with a cheer we would "whoop her up" as hard as we could run, and woe unto the unlucky man who lost his footing and fell. He was apt to be trampled by all who were behind him, or run over by the wagon, unless he had presence of mind and strength in his hands sufficient to hold fast to the rope and allow himself to be dragged through the mud until the wagon stopped, when on regaining his feet he would look as though he had been buried in the yellow clay, and by some special resurrection had once more come back to earth.

Every day it rained and there was so little sunshine that our clothes and blankets could not dry. At night we went to sleep with clothes wet and got up in the morning with them steaming, and after wringing out the surplus water to lighten the load would start again on our weary march. But with all our discomforts one thing favored us. We were marching through a good section of the country, and forage was plenty. In fact, at times the men became so fastidious that they would not take chickens or turkeys as it required too much labor to cook them, but would take hams as they could be eaten raw as well as cooked.

Sunday, Feb. 19. — At five reveille sounded and in an hour we were on the road. A mile brought us to the Wateree river which was swollen by the recent rains, and the current was running like a millrace. Our engineers had succeeded in throwing a pontoon bridge across. How they had done it was a mystery, but there the bridge was, as a triumph of their skill and perserverance. It was anchored as firmly as they could make it, but the centre of the bridge was carried down stream until it was in the form of a quarter circle, and looked decidedly uninviting to venture over with troops and artillery. Yet we all passed over safely. A few miles brought us to the railroad which runs from Camden to Wateree. Here we halted and worked the remainder of the day tearing up and destroying the railroad track. It seemed like labor lost, as that road had such a worn out appearance that it looked unsafe to run over. However, we tore up the rails and burned the

ties, and when the rails were heated red hot they were twisted in all kinds of geometrical lines.

A few miles from here we camped, and by the time our tent was up our forager arrived well loaded, and soon our supper was spread, consisting of ham, sweet potatoes, cornbread and, as an extra touch, some sorghum molasses was added to our meal, and was heartily enjoyed by all.

Friday, Feb. 24. — About ten A.M. we packed up and started on our march in a furious rain storm. The mud was from six inches to as many feet deep, and of about the consistency of mortar. A mile brought us to the river, a branch of the Peedee, which was greatly swollen with the rain. Our engineers had thrown a pontoon bridge across it at the cost of one of their number lost by drowning. On crossing we came to a steep hill composed of clay, and so slippery that most of us crawled up on our hands and knees. We finally reached the top, where we halted two hours in the rain, then marched on for an hour, when we went into camp. Day's march, five miles. That was about as hard a five miles as I ever marched. The next day, our train having stuck fast in the mud, we did not break camp, but employed the men building corduroy roads and pulling the wagons out of the mud on to higher ground, and as the sun shone warm and clear we dried our tents and blankets and, for the first time in many days, enjoyed the luxury of dry clothing.

On the day following, seeing no prospects of a move, I thought I would try my hand at foraging, so procuring a mule I started forth. After a ride of some ten miles I stopped at a plantation, where my mule was soon loaded with a pair of hams, a bag of sweet potatoes and some meal, when casting my eyes around to see if there was anything more that would be either useful or ornamental to a soldier, I chanced to see a shoemaker's awl, and knowing my shoes were broken and needed repairing I dropped it into my pocket, and leisurely walked out of the house and mounted my mule. Just then I heard a shout of alarm from some of our men who were in the yard on the same honest errand as myself, when looking I saw a company of the enemy's cavalry tearing down the road at a fearful rate. I turned the mule towards our camp and started, but the mule, with the peculiar cussedness of his race, refused to go any faster than a slow trot. I coaxed him with my spurs, clubbed him with my gun, even reduced my load by throwing away—first, the bag of meal, then the potatoes, and at last the two hams were sacrificed to his obstinacy, and yet he would not go. By this time all our men had passed me, and I was left alone, while the enemy were coming up uncomfortably close, when in desperation I pulled the awl from my pocket and commenced stabbing him in the side with it, in hopes he would run into a swamp near by, where I might hide if not run away, when, instead of going ahead, he commenced a rotary motion on his hind legs, but did not advance a yard. The enemy were now so near they called out to me to surrender, which I had not the slightest idea of doing, but as my animal swung around I tried to cover the nearest rebel with my rifle and fired. The result was that as I fired my gun the mule fired me, and the next instant I found myself in a sitting position on the ground with the breath nearly knocked out of my body. Quickly gathering myself I ran for the swamp, and with bullets flying thick about me, was soon under cover of the swamp. About two hours after I trudged into camp, wet, muddy

and tired, and amid the gibes of my company resolved to do no more foraging.

On March 8th we again broke camp, and in a few days crossed into North Carolina, when we came to what is called the "Sand Hills" which is said to be the poorest land on the Atlantic coast, which report is no doubt true. Very little of the ground is cultivated, being mostly covered with a large growth of pine. The gathering of pitch and distilling turpentine seemed to be the principal industry. Every few miles we passed one of the stills where there were large quantities of rosin stored. These were frequently set on fire by our advance, which would oblige us to make a detour to the right or left to get past. At one place where we could not turn out of the road but had to march past, the heat was so intense it singed the hair from our heads and beards and from the sides of the mules in passing, while the smoke almost stifled us.

I asked one of the natives what they raised to live on. He looked at me for a moment with an indescribable twist in his eye as his mouth closed on his Linchburg plug, until his long hooked nose and longer chin almost came together like the handles of a nut cracker, as he replied "Why, stranger, we don't raise nothin', don't have ter. Any man in these diggins kin live on a pine knot and a quart of whiskey a day, that is, if he is a Christian."

For some days forage was very scarce and we began to think we would be obliged to put ourselves on this native diet. One night on reaching camp all we had for supper was about a pint of raw peanuts, so we did not spend much time over our evening meal. In the morning thinking there was no breakfast we did not get up very early. Soon Sergt. Crist called me, with the announcement that "breakfast was ready. I jumped up thinking the foragers had brought in something, but on looking into the pot I found my chum had found somewhere a large pumpkin, and this boiled in water constituted our morning meal. It was, to say the least, thin diet, but we filled ourselves as full as possible and started on our day's march. After traveling some twenty-five miles we camped for the night and found our foragers on hand, one with a live calf, another with a bag of sweet potatoes, while the third contributed a bag of corn meal and a canteen of sorghum molasses, and from dark until midnight we cooked and ate. It seemed as though we never would get filled. At last one after another would give up and roll himself in his blanket for the night, and be soon dreaming the dreams of a well fed soldier.

Thursday, March 16. — Reveille at six, but we saw no signs of a move until nine A.M., when "general" sounded, and soon after we were on the road as wagon guard. After traveling two miles orders came to hurry forward as the troops were engaged, so off we went at a double quick through the woods and mud. Soon we began to hear cannonading and musketry ahead of us, and saw the wounded carried to the rear.

At one P.M. we came to the first line of Rebel works, then in our possession. Here we found some of the enemy's dead, showing that the works had been well defended. We now formed our line of battle and moved off to the left, through the woods and across a deep ravine, and finally took up our position on the extreme left of our line, with our left on the Cape Fear river. Directly in front of us was a line of the enemy's works, and as soon as we were in position they opened fire on us, to which we replied, keeping up a dull scattering fire for about two hours. The woods were quite thick and we could see but little of the enemy.

Finally the fire slackened, when Col. Lake, our commander, thinking the enemy were falling back, ordered Capt. Barnett to take his company forward as skirmishers, and as soon as he found the position of the enemy to send word back, when the remainder of the regiment would advance on a charge. Before the skirmishers had gained the position assigned them the brave Barnett fell, shot through the head, dying almost instantly. In his death our regiment lost one of its finest officers. Brave even to rashness, yet gentle and kind-hearted as a woman. One whose gentlemanly conduct had endeared him to all with whom he was brought in contact. Just as his remains were carried back to our line Col. Lake was struck in his right forearm, when, quietly slipping the sword knot from his wrist, he grasped his sword in his left hand, and was about giving an order "Forward on a charge!" when he fell, severely wounded in the groin, and was carried to the rear.

Before Capt. Marshall could assume command orders came for us to hold the line we then occupied, and not try to advance. So we kept up a dull skirmishing fire until dark, when some other troops came forward and took our place, while we moved back towards the centre and held the rear line for the night. That closed the battle of Averysboro.*

---

* Averasboro

Notes — Chapter 31

1. Guernsey & Alden, *Harper's Pictorial History of the Civil War*, p. 713, Footnote 1.

2. Ibid., Footnote 2.

3. Ibid., p. 714.

4. *O.R.*, Vol. XLVII, Part 1, p. 17.

5. Ibid., p. 27.

6. Lewis, *Sherman— Fighting Prophet*, p. 491.

7. *O.R.*, Vol. XLVII, Part 1, p. 19.

8. Davis, *Sherman's March*, p. 145.

9. Lewis, *Sherman—Fighting Prophet*, p. 490.

10. Ibid., p. 488.

11. Ibid., p. 497.

12. *O.R.*, Vol. XLVII, Part 1, p. 28.

13. Davis, *Sherman's March*, p. 187.

14. *O.R.*, Vol. XLVII. Part 1, p. 487.

15. Ibid., p. 508.

16. Guernsey & Alden, *Harper's Pictorial History of the Civil War*, p. 721.

17. *O.R.*, Vol. XLVII, Part 1, p. 1054.

18. Guernsey & Alden, *Harper's Pictorial History of the Civil War*, p. 721.

19. *O.R.*, Vol. XLVII, Part 1, pp. 495-496.

20. Ibid., p. 496.

21. Ibid., p. 508.

22. Ibid., p. 66.

23. Ibid., p. 21.

Notes — Chapter 31

24. Lewis, *Sherman—Fighting Prophet*, p. 505.

25. *O.R.*, Vol. XLVII, Part 1, p. 17.

26. Phisterer, *New York in the War of the Rebellion, 1861-1865*, p. 1943.

27. Ibid.

Chapter 32

THE BATTLE OF BENTONVILLE

Background

After Averasboro, Hardee fell back and the Left Wing moved towards Bentonville. Sherman remained with Slocum until the morning of March 19, and then he joined the Right Wing which was miles away on the shorter route to Goldsboro.[1]

Before long, the two wings of the army were approximately a half day's march apart; the Confederate commanders, Johnston and Hampton, believed they were a full day's march from each other.[2]

Joseph E. Johnston, relieved at Atlanta, was now back in charge of all Confederate forces from North Carolina to Florida. Lee took this action on February 23, 1865.[3] Johnston's force consisted of Hardee's two divisions with 7,500 men; pieces of Hood's Army of the Tennessee, Hoke's Division from the Army of Northern Virginia, and miscellaneous units from along the Atlantic Coast. His total strength was around 20,000.[4] The units had never fought together before and were a mixture of strong and weak organizations under new leadership. Kilpatrick told Sherman that Johnston announced his strength as 40,000[5] and apparently Sherman accepted that number.

Johnston's only hope of defeating Sherman was to attack the Wings when they were apart, and before they united with Terry's and Schofield's forces at Goldsboro. Thus, he chose to make a stand at Bentonville.[6]

The morning of March 19, the XIV Corps had the lead for the march. Carlin's Division was in front, followed by Morgan's. Sherman had anticipated no attack.[7] Carlin met resistance but thought it was cavalry. His men felt the resistance stiffen and reported back, "They don't drive worth a damn."[8]

Despite this omen, Slocum sent word to Sherman that no help would be necessary to handle the skirmishing. Carlin's Division moved to attack and then Slocum sent word to Sherman asking for help. It was now 11:00 A.M. The Rebels easily repulsed Carlin's attack and then they rolled over his division opening holes in the Union line.

Now the blow fell on Morgan's Division. It had found time to make breastworks and these were put to good use. The result of the battle hinged on the fighting by Morgan's men. Jefferson Davis, corps commmander, told one of his staff, "If Morgan's troops can stand them, all is right; if not, the day is lost. There is no reserve—not a regiment to move—they must fight it out."[9]

The Confederates made a frontal assault and were beaten back. The Union troops rushed over the breastworks and took a large number of prisoners and the colors of the 40th North Carolina.[10]

Brigadier General Vandever picks up the next events in his report:

> About this time, in consequence of movements on our left, the left flank of the brigade became uncovered and the rebels pressed forward with a view to flanking us. Capt. A.S. Marshall, Commanding the Seventeenth New York, quickly wheeled his regiment and in the most gallant manner succeeded in repelling the attack at this point.[11]

THE BATTLE OF BENTONVILLE

Then, an unknown force moved to the rear of Morgan's Division. After a volley, the Federal troops recognized them as the enemy; jumped to the other side of the breastwoks and fought them off. At this point, Cogswell's Brigade from the XX Corps arrived and fell upon the Confederates (D.H. Hill's Brigades) as they attacked Morgan's rear. This was the turning point in the battle.[12]

Later in the day, the Confederates attacked the XX Corps but were beaten back with severe losses.[13] The next day units from the Right Wing came on to the field and finally, all of Sherman's army was united.[14]

Johnston remained at Bentonville until the early hours of March 22, when his army left its trenches and headed towards Smithfield.[15]

Luvaas points out that, "On the Union side, Morgan...emerges as the real hero and for his work he was recommended for promotion to the rank of Major General."[16]

The 17th New York Veteran Volunteers lost 14 at Bentonville; 3 killed, 10 wounded, and 1 missing. Westervelt's report of Bentonville understates the role and activities of the regiment.

Highlights

1. General Morgan: Brigadier General James D. Morgan was the Union hero at Bentonville. He is a virtual unknown in terms of Civil War generals.

Morgan was born in Boston, Massachusetts in 1810. He moved to Illinois, became a merchant, and served in the local militia. He was a captain with the 1st Illinois in Mexico. In the Civil War, he served as lieutenant colonel and colonel in the 10th Illinois.

He was at Island No. 10, at the "siege of" Corinth after Shiloh, and then on garrison duty until the Atlanta Campaign. He commanded a brigade and, at times, a division in the XIV Corps in the Atlanta Campaign. He commanded a division in the March to the Sea and the Carolinas Campaign. Warner says that at the war's end, "he was made a major-general of volunteers—an advancement which he seems to have richly deserved."[17]

2. Confederate Generals at Bentonville: The smallness of the Confederate force, less than 20,000, and the number of high ranking officers at Bentonville, indicate the sad plight of the Rebels at the end of the war. There were:

1 General -	Joseph E. Johnston	
5 Lt. Generals -	Wade Hampton	
	William Hardee	
	Joseph Wheeler	
	Alexander P. Stewart	
	Stephen D. Lee	
10 Maj. Generals -	William Bate	Patton Anderson
	John C. Brown	Edward C. Walthall
	Robert F. Hoke	Daniel H. Hill
	Benjamin Cheatham	Carter Stevenson
	William W. Loring	M.C. Butler

In addition, there were at least 18 brigadier generals at Bentonville. There may have been more, counting cavalry.[18]

3. <u>Union Infantry Regiment Leadership at Bentonville</u>: The senior position in a Union regiment is colonel, and one would normally expect the position would be filled at that rank. Therefore, it would seem unusual to have a captain leading the 17th New York at Bentonville.

Such was not the case. A review of 127 reports submitted by infantry regiments for the Carolinas Campaign shows a remarkable array of rank in regiment positions:

Rank	Number	Percent
Bvt. Brig. General	2	2%
Colonel	13	10%
Lt. Colonel	60	47%
Major	24	19%
Captain	28	22%
	127	100%

Marshall's situation wasn't that unique after all.[19]

4. <u>Westervelt's and Crist's Promotions</u>: At the end of the chapter, under the date of March 22, Westervelt indicates he was promoted to first lieutenant. Despite this, he never received his promotion officially until June 3, 1865, and he never officially served as second lieutenant.

Westervelt was also recommended for an award. Captain Marshall recommended Westervelt and six other enlisted men for "the medal of honor awarded by the War Department to meritorious non-commissioned officers and soldiers." This was done on March 24, 1865.[20] There is no indication in his records that Westervelt received the award.

Westervelt's friend, Sergeant Crist, was also promoted to officer rank based on his valor at Bentonville. The records indicate that Christian B. Crist was appointed second lieutenant but never served in that grade.[21]

5. <u>Rebel Boys at Bentonville</u>: One of the saddest parts of Bentonville was the loss of young boys in the battle. Hardee's only son, 16-year-old Willie, enlisted to participate in the battle and was mortally wounded.[22] Hoke's North Carolinians who attacked Morgan had a group, "The First Regiment of Junior Reserves," none of whom were over 18 years old and were led by a 17-year-old, Major Walter Clark. Their losses were "40 or 50."[23]

The Battle of Bentonville

THE BATTLE OF BENTONVILLE

Friday, March 17. — At daylight we were on the alert when we found the enemy were retreating. We soon sent out a party to bury the dead. About noon we started on our march right across the country.

We soon came to a stream that we had to ford. This was a commencement we kept it up all the afternoon, fording streams at almost every mile. After once wet we did not mind it, but pushed through with a good will, some of them so deep the men had to carry their cartridge boxes on their guns to keep them out of the water.

About eight P.M. we camped, where, around some blazing fires of pitch pine, we dried our clothes and were soon dreaming of an expected fight on the morrow. The next day we continued the pursuit of the enemy. About noon our advance came up with them and skirmished awhile, but when our artillery opened they fell back, and seemed to be forming their lines for an engagement. We now formed in line of battle and advanced about a mile, when we stacked arms, and at sundown went into camp.

Sunday, March 19. — Reveille at six and soon troops began to pass, and soon after the skirmishing commenced. At eight A.M. we fell in, and as we moved off we heard heavy cannonading in front, accompanied by lively musketry. About noon we were hurried to the front, and our brigade was posted on the extreme right, where we threw up some heavy breastworks. Soon after we were ordered to advance, when we left our works and moved forward about one hundred yards, when we quickly engaged the enemy. The woods on our left were on fire, and the smoke was so thick we could see but indistinctly. Soon the troops on our left fell back, and the enemy followed them, gaining possession of the

works we had just built. We saw them moving on our left, but in the thick smoke could not tell the color of their uniforms, and the first notice we had of their position was on receiving a volley from them into the rear of our line. So turning from the enemy in our front we gave those in our rear our undivided attention, by a volley and then by a charge, that was gallantly led by color sergeant C.S. Crist, who here won his commission. This drove them from the works, leaving the ground strewn with their dead and wounded, capturing many prisoners, and the regimental colors of the 49th Virginia.

This turned the tide of battle, and the troops on our left soon regained their old position and established their lines, with our artillery massed across a wide road near the centre of our lines. Here the enemy charged six times, showing a courage we could not help but admire. This was kept up until it was so dark we could only see by the continued flash of the guns, when the enemy withdrew. We continued on the alert all night, as we expected they would make another attempt to break through our lines, and we determined not to be caught napping.

About sunrise the next morning the enemy made a dash on our lines to the left of us, but were quickly driven back, when all became quiet and remained so most of the fore-noon. About noon our brigade advanced and captured the first line of the enemy's works, giving us some very lively fighting, and we got roughly handled while driving them back, losing many of our men and several of our officers before we got firmly established on our new line.

Soon heavy firing began on our right, that proved to be the 15th corps, which had just arrived on the field. The woods were so thick we could not see them, but from the direction of the firing we knew they were driving the enemy back. About dark the firing ceased, and we lay down behind our stack of guns for the night. But after the excitement of the day, and with the expectation of a fight on the morrow, and the responsibility of the command of a company, it was a long time before I slept.

Tuesday, March 21. — At daylight the first blast of the bugle woke me, when I called the men, who packed up lively and got breakfast, as we expected there was some sharp work waiting for us. Soon the firing commenced on the right, when we again advanced our lines, meeting with but little opposition, as the enemy fell back with a few shots—just enough to make it interesting for us. On gaining our position we threw up some breastworks that showed we had come to stay. In the afternoon there was a general engagement all along our lines, but we merely held our own, determined not to retreat, and yet not caring to advance.

At dark rain came on, but being worn out with fighting and excitement of the past three days, I threw myself on the ground and slept soundly through the rain all night.

Wednesday, March 22. — Just before daylight I went to the picket line, when we found that Gen. Johnston, not daring to risk another day's battle, had withdrawn his force during the night. This, the battle of Bentonsville,* was the last general engagement we were in, and, with the exception of some slight skirmishers, we did no more fighting.

After our breakfast, we sent out a burial party, and when their work was completed took up our line of march, and the next day reached Goldsboro. Here we remained nearly three weeks, and while here heard of the evacuation of Richmond, and began to count the time that would intervene before we would take up our line of march for home. I also received my promotion to 1st lieutenant.

---

* Bentonville

Notes — Chapter 32

1. *O.R.*, Vol. XLVII, Part 1, p. 25.

2. Luvaas, *The Battle of Bentonville* (Smithfield, North Carolina: Medlin Printing Co.), p. 2.

3. Ibid., p. 1.

4. Ibid., pp. 1-3.

5. Lewis, *Sherman—Fighting Prophet*, p. 515.

6. Luvaas, *The Battle of Bentonville*, pp. 4-5.

7. Ibid., p. 6.

8. Davis, *Sherman's March*, p. 233.

9. Ibid., p. 236.

10. *O.R.*, Vol. XLVII, Part 1, p. 496.

11. Ibid., pp. 496-497.

12. Luvaas, *The Battle of Bentonville*, pp. 15, 16.

13. Ibid., p. 17.

14. Ibid., p. 19.

15. Ibid., p. 24.

16. Ibid., p. 26.

17. Warner, *Generals in Blue*, pp. 334-335.

18. *O.R.,* Vol. XLVII, pp. 1061-1065.

19. Ibid., pp. 6-13.

20. Ibid., pp. 508-509.

21. Phisterer, *New York in the War of the Rebellion*, p. 1938.

22. Davis, *Sherman's March,* p. 239.

23. Luvaas, *The Battle of Bentonville*, p. 30.

Chapter 33

THE END OF THE WAR — THE GRAND REVIEW

Background

After Bentonville, Sherman assembled his army at Goldsboro, uniting with Schofield and Terry. He refitted and reorganized. The Left Wing under Slocum, now adopted the title,"Army of Georgia." Schofield's X and XXIII Corps became "the Centre," and the Right Wing under Howard continued as "The Army of Tennessee."[1]

Johnston was at Smithfield.[2] Grant and Sherman anticipated that Lee would leave the Richmond/Petersburg area and unite with Johnston somewhere in the Carolinas. To forestall such a move, on April 5, Sherman issued orders for his troops to move north to Warrenton, North Carolina to get between the two Confederate armies.[3]

Thinking he saw an attempt by Lee to leave Petersburg, Grant had attacked Lee on March 30. By April 6, Sherman learned of Grant's action and Lee's retreat. Now his sole objective was Johnston's army.[4] Accordingly, Sherman issued new orders aimed at defeating Johnston and cutting off his retreat or escape.[5]

On April 11, Sherman learned of Lee's surrender.[6] Then, on April 14, Johnston initiated his surrender.[7]

The first surrender agreement was worked out by Johnston and Sherman on April 18, 1865. It was sent to Washington for approval and was rejected. Halleck and Stanton were major players in the rejection. Three of the main reasons for the disapproval were, (1) the hysteria in the North over Lincoln's assassination, (2) the attempt by Stanton to smear Sherman, and (3) the efforts of the Northern Radicals to overturn Lincoln's approach to reconstruction with their much harder version.[8] Grant went to North Carolina and worked behind the scenes to obtain a new surrender agreement which was signed on April 26.

Now it was time for the troops to head home. Orders were issued on April 27, for most of Sherman's army to go to Washington via Richmond. They were to leave Richmond by the middle of May and were "to march slowly and in the best order."[9] Westervelt indicates that his regiment marched from Raleigh, North Carolina to Richmond, Virginia—about 200 miles—in seven days. His estimate of the distance may be high (approximately 160 miles on today's maps), but 28.6 miles a day (or 22.9) is far from a slow march! The rumor was that corps commanders had bets as to whose corps would reach Richmond first. The infantry was sacrificed. Sunstroke affected many of the men; some died from it.[10]

The army rested in Richmond three days, and after seeing the city and having some altercations with the Easterners of the Army of the Potomac (no love was lost between the two armies), moved on to Alexandria.[11] The 17th New York arrived in Alexandria on May 20, 1865.

Grant proposed the Grand Review which was held in Washington on May 24 and 25.[12] The armies started from the Capitol, marched down Pennsylvania Avenue, and passed the reviewing stand at the White House. The Army of the Potomac marched in May 23 and Sherman's on May 24. Comparisons were made. The Army of the Potomac were all "spit and polish." Sherman's army was a mixture of new uniforms and old (like Westervelt's); the Westerners were taller and leaner, and spectators had difficulty in distinguishing between officers and enlisted men.[13]

256

The Grand Review at Washington

Sherman feared that his men would not march well when compared to the Army of the Potomac.[14] As he neared the Treasury Building, he looked back and said, "They have swung into it." Later, he said, "I believe it was the happiest and most satisfactory moment of my life."[15]

On May 30, Sherman bid farewell to his troops. His final admonition was, "You have been good soldiers, so in peace you will make good citizens..."[16]

Highlights

1. The Review in Richmond: After Lee surrendered, Halleck was moved from Washington to Richmond. As Sherman's troops arrived, Halleck ordered the XIV Corps to enter Richmond and pass in review before him. Sherman refused, angry over Halleck's role in rejecting the first surrender of Johnston. Thus, Westervelt was saved from parading in Richmond.[17]

2. Publicity about the Grand Review: Despite Sherman's concerns about the comparison of his army with the Army of the Potomac, the general public saw Slocum leading the march on the second day of Sherman's Veterans.[18] These were the photographs and prints in *Harper's Weekly* the public saw.[19]

3. Westervelt's Last Assignment: From Atlanta to Washington (November 15, 1864-June 8, 1865), Westervelt had been under the command of his first commanding officer, Henry Slocum—first colonel of the 27th New York and finally commander of Sherman's Left Wing, the Army of Georgia.

On June 9, 1865, his regiment was transferred to the XXII Corps until it was mustered out on July 13, 1865. The commanding officer of the XXII Corps was Major General Joseph J. Bartlett, Westervelt's second commanding officer of the 27th New York.

Westervelt would join Slocum and Bartlett in the 1880's in writing the *Regimental History of the 27th New York*.

Full Circle!

Thursday, April 11. — At 2 A.M. the sergeant of the guard woke me, and told me we would move at five, and soon after that hour we were on the march, taking the road towards Smithfield, where Gen. Johnston was said to be waiting to give us battle. In two hours we reached his outpost and commenced a lively skirmish with some artillery, losing several men from the western regiments of our division, but none from our regiment. At noon we took an hour for dinner, and as soon as we started the skirmishing commenced, proving that the enemy were close on our front, and were falling back. Soon, however, they came to a stand, and showed a stronger force than our skirmishers could manage. Our wagons were then parked, and, we formed our line of battle, where we remained all the afternoon, expecting every moment to hear the fight open on our front, when we would be called forward to take a hand ourselves. For some reason, however, the attack was not made, and we rolled up in our blankets and slept soundly all night.

At daylight the next morning we were in line, and while cooking our breakfast the 3d division of our corps was sent on the advance. As soon as they started the skirmishing commenced, assuring us that the enemy were still there. At sunrise we started, and soon passed a line of earthworks where the enemy made a stand the night before. About dark we halted at the town of Smithfield, while our engineers put down a pontoon bridge across the Nuese river. As soon as the bridge was completed our regiment crossed over. We advanced carefully in the darkness, and soon came to the enemy's pickets, who gave us a few shots and fell back. A mile from the shore we went on picket and remained quiet all night.

The next morning the 20th corps crossed over and took the advance. They brought us the news of the surrender of Lee's army, when we concluded the fighting was about over. Still we continued our pursuit of Gen. Johnston's army, and on April 16th we camped on the bank of the Cape Fear river, with the enemy's army on the opposite bank.

Here an armistice was agreed upon, ending in the surrender of Johnston's army, when we took up our line of march for home.

The first march was from Raleigh to Richmond, a distance of about two hundred miles, which we accomplished in seven days. Here we rested three days, when we started for Washington. On our way we passed over some of the ground we fought on in '61 and '62. On the night of May 11 we camped on the battlefield of Bull Run, and from here to Washington we passed over a portion of country that had perhaps felt the effects of the war worse than any part of the South.

When we passed through in '61, and again in '62, there were fine large dwellings, good orchards, and railroads in operation. Now the whole country appeared like a barren waste. The railroad track was torn up, and overgrown with grass and weeds, so that it was difficult at times to locate where the road had been. Every house was destroyed. The fences, orchards and woods had all been used for fuel or wantonly destroyed by the different armies as they passed through. On our way we passed fortifications, around which were many graves, as silent monuments for "the lost cause."

On the afternoon of May 20th we reached Alexandria, and on the 25th took part in the grand review in Washington. That was no doubt the biggest review ever held on this continent, and as I look back to that occasion

I see some things that border strongly on the ridiculous Just before the review I took an inventory of my wardrobe, and found it consisted of just what clothes I had on, and they were well worn. The only shirt I had was of red flannel, and that had done duty ever since leaving Savannah. Whenever it became soiled I took it off and washed it, sometimes in hot water, other times in cold, by some brookside—and while it was drying would button my coat close to my chin, and sit down and watch the shirt lest some one should steal it. That would have been an irreparable loss. Every time it was washed it grew "smaller and beautifully less," until the second button of the bosom came tight under my chin, and the corners of the collar stood up just behind my ears, as though placed there for a rear guard. This, with a coat frayed at the sleeves, and broken at the elbows, with pants and shoes threatening at each moment to disintegrate.

Clad thus I marched at the head of my company past the reviewing stand, where stood the President, Gen. Grant, and many high dignitaries of our own and foreign nations—and without money enough in my pocket to bless myself with a good dinner. Yet the government was indebted to me nearly a year's pay.

We remained camped at Alexandria and Washington until July 13, when we were mustered out of service, and ten days after we received our discharge at Hart's Island, N.Y., having served in the 17th regiment just one year and ten months, or three years and eleven months altogether in the United States' service. Thus ended the Barley Que papers.

Notes — Chapter 33

1. Bowman and Irwin, *Sherman and His Campaigns*, pp. 378-390.

2. Ibid., p. 385.

3. Ibid., pp. 381-387.

4. Ibid., pp. 384-385.

5. Ibid., p. 385.

6. Ibid., p. 386.

7. Ibid., p. 390.

8. Lewis, *Sherman—Fighting Prophet*, pp. 549-555.

9. Bowman and Irwin, *Sherman and His Campaigns*, pp. 438-439.

10. Davis, *Sherman's March*, pp. 280-281.

11. Ibid.

12. Bowman and Irwin, *Sherman and His Campaigns*, p. 441.

13. Lewis, *Sherman—Fighting Prophet*, pp. 575-576.

14. Davis, *Sherman's March*, p. 288.

15. Lewis, *Sherman—Fighting Prophet*, p. 575.

16. Bowman and Irwin, *Sherman and His Campaigns*, p. 446.

17. Davis, *Sherman's March*, p. 284.

18. Ibid., pp. 180-181, centerfold.

19. Guernsey and Alden, *Harper's Pictorial History of the Civil War*, p. 790.

APPENDIX I

Civil War Engagements
in which
William B. Westervelt
took an active part

First enlistment—May 8, 1861, to May 31, 1863

No.	Engagement	Date(s)
1	Bull Run, Virginia	July 21, 1861
2	Pohick Church, Virginia	Oct. 3-4, 1861
3	West Point, Virginia	May 7, 1862
4	Hanover Court House/ Mechanicsville, Virginia	May 22-24, 1862
5	Gaines' Mill, Virginia (First Cold Harbor)	June 27, 1862
6	Crampton's Pass, Maryland (South Mountain)	Sept. 14, 1862
7	Antietam, Maryland	Sept. 17, 1862
8	Fredericksburg, Virginia	Dec. 12-15, 1862
9	Franklin's Crossing, Virginia (Chancellorsville Campaign)	April 29-May 2, 1863
10	Salem Church, Virginia (Chancellorsville Campaign)	May 3-4, 1863
11	Chunky Creek, Mississippi	Feb. 14-15, 1864
12	Decatur, Alabama	May 2, 1864
13	Near Decatur, Alabama	May 26, 1864
14	Hillsboro and Courtland, Alabama	May 27, 1864
15	Near Decatur, Alabama	June 26, 1864
16	Moulton, Alabama	June 28, 1864
17	Atlanta, Georgia	Aug. 8-31, 1864
18	Jonesboro, Georgia	Sept. 1, 1864
19	Sandersville, Georgia	Nov. 26, 1864
20	Savannah, Georgia	Dec. 11-26, 1864
21	Averasboro, North Carolina	March 16, 1865
22	Bentonville, North Carolina	March 19-21, 1865

APPENDIX II

Losses of the 27th New York Infantry
(Union Regiment)

May 1861-May 1863

During its service the regiment lost by death, killed in action, 1 officer, 61 enlisted men; of wounds received in action, 1 officer, 11 enlisted men; of disease and other causes, 2 officers, 72 enlisted men; total, 4 officers, 144 enlisted men; aggregate, 146; of whom 7 enlisted men died in the hands of the enemy; and it took part in the following engagements, etc.:[1]

PLACE	DATE	KILLED O / EM[2]	WOUNDED O / EM	MISSING O / EM	TOTAL
Bull Run, Va.	July 21, 1861	1 / 25	2 / 42	.. / 60	130
Pohick Church, Va.	Oct. 4, 1861	.. / ..	.. / ..	.. / ..	...
Westpoint, Va.	May 7, 1862	.. / 1	.. / ..	.. / ..	1
Mechanicsville, Va.	May 22, 1862	.. / ..	.. / ..	.. / ..	...
Mechanicsville, Va.	June 1, 1862	.. / ..	.. / ..	.. / ..	...
Seven Days' Battle, Va.	June 25-July 2, 1862	.. / 26	10 / 108	.. / 18	162
Crampton's Pass	Sept. 14, 1862	.. / 6	2 / 25	.. / ..	33
Antietam, Md.	Sept. 17, 1862	.. / ..	.. / ..	.. / ..	...
Fredericksburg, Va.	Dec. 11-15, 1862	.. / ..	.. / ..	.. / ..	...
Franklin's Crossing, Va.	April 29-May 2, 1863	.. / ..	.. / ..	.. / ..	...
Marye's Heights and Salem Church, Va.	May 3-4, 1863	.. / 3	1 / 12	.. / 3	19
TOTAL LOSS		1 / 61	15 / 187	.. / 81	345

---

[1] Frederick Phisterer, *New York in the War of the Rebellion, 1861-1865*, Vol. III.

[2] Officers/Enlisted men

APPENDIX III

Losses of the 17th Veteran New York Zouaves

September 1863-June 1865

PLACE	DATE	KILLED O / EM	WOUNDED O / EM	MISSING O / EM	TOTAL
Meridian Campaign	Jan. 18-March 4, 1864	.. / 1	.. / ..	.. / 10	12*
Atlanta Campaign	Aug. 8-Aug. 20, 1864	.. / 1	.. / 8	.. / ..	9
Jonesboro, Ga.	Sept. 1, 1864	2 / 23	.. / 70	.. / ..	95
Savannah, Ga. (March to Sea)	Nov. 16-Dec. 12, 1864	.. / 1	.. / 2	.. / ..	3
Averasboro, N.C.	March 16, 1864	1 / 8	2 / 23	.. / ..	34
Bentonville, N.C.	March 19, 1864	.. / 3	.. / 10	.. / 1	14
March through Carolinas (foraging)	Jan. 20-March 16, 1865	.. / 1**	.. / ..	1 / 12	13
TOTAL[1]		3 / 38	2 / 113	1 / 23	180

* Includes 1 who died
** Drowned

[1] Data from official reports, as cited in chapters, does not show losses due to diseases.

BIBLIOGRAPHY

Abbott, John Stevens Cabot. *The Civil War in America.* Springfield: Gurdon Bill, 1863-1866. 2 volumes.

Bearss, Margie Riddle. *Sherman's Forgotten Campaign—The Meridian Expedition.* Baltimore: Gateway Press, 1987.

Bowman, S.M., and R.B. Irwin. *Sherman and His Campaigns.* New York: Charles B. Richardson, 1865.

Carter, Samuel III. *The Siege of Atlanta.* New York: Ballantine Books, 1973.

Catton, Bruce. *Glory Road.* New York: The Fairfax Press, 1984.

___. *Terrible Swift Sword.* New York: Doubleday and Co., 1963.

Cox, Jacob. *Campaigns of the Civil War, Atlanta.* New York: Scribner and Sons, 1882.

Davis, Burke. *Sherman's March.* New York: Random House, 1980.

Davis, William C. *Battle of Bull Run.* New York: Doubleday and Co., 1977.

Doubleday, Abner. *Campaigns of the Civil War—Chancellorsville and Gettysburg.* New York: Charles Scribner and Sons, 1882.

Dyer, Frederick H. *A Compendium of the War of the Rebellion.* 3 vols. Cedar Rapids, Iowa: 1908; Reprint, Dayton, Ohio: Morningside Bookshop, 1978.

Esposito, Col. Vincent J. *The West Point Atlas of the Civil War.* New York: Frederick A. Frazer, 1962.

Fairchild, Charles Bryant. *History of the 27th Regiment, New York Volunteers.* Binghamton, New York: Carl and Matthews, 1888.

Foote, Shelby. *The Civil War.* 3 vols. New York: Vintage Books, 1986.

Freeman, Douglas Southall. *Lee's Lieutenants.* 3 vols. New York: Charles Scribner's Sons, 1942.

Glathaar, Joseph T. *The March to the Sea and Beyond.* New York: New York University Press, 1986.

Guernsey, Alfred H., and Henry M. Alden. *Harper's Pictorial History of the Civil War.* 3 vols. New York: Harper and Bros., 1866-68.

Headley, J.T. *The Great Rebellion: A History of the Civil War in the United States.* 2 vols. Hartford, Conn: Hurlbut, Williams and Co., vol. 1, 1862; and American Publishing Co., vol. 2, 1866.

Holland, J.G. *The Life of Abraham Lincoln.* Springfield: Gurdon Bill, 1866.

Johnson, Edwin Rossiter. *Campfires and Battlefields.* New York: The Civil War Press, 1967.

Johnson, Robert V., and C.C. Buel, eds. *Battles and Leaders of the Civil War.* 4 vols. New York: The Century Company, 1884-1887.

BIBLIOGRAPHY

Ketchum, R.M., and Bruce Catton. *The American Heritage Picture History of the Civil War.* New York: American Heritage Publishing Co., 1960.

Leslie, Frank. *The American Soldier in the Civil War.* New York: Stanley-Bradley Publishing Co., 1895.

Lewis, Lloyd. *Sherman—Fighting Prophet.* New York: Harcourt, Brace, and Co., 1932.

Long, E.B. *The Civil War Day by Day.* Garden City, New York: Doubleday and Co., 1971.

Lossing, Benson J. *Matthew Brady's Illustrated History of the Civil War.* New York: The Fairfax Press, 1912. Originally published as *A History of the Civil War.*

Luvaas, Jay. *The Battle of Bentonville.* Smithfield, N.C.: Medlin Printing Co., 1956.

Luvaas, Jay, and Harold Nelson, eds. *The U.S. War College Guide to the Battle of Antietam, The Maryland Campaign of 1862.* Carlisle, Pa: South Mountain Press, 1987.

Lytle, Andrew Nelson. *Bedford Forrest and His Critter Company.* New York: Minton, Balch and Co., 1931.

Miller, Francis T. *The Photographic History of the Civil War.* 8 vols. New York: Castle Books, 1911.

Murfin, James V. *The Gleam of Bayonets.* New York: Thomas Yoseloff, 1968.

Newburgh (New York) *News.*

Palfrey, Francis A. *Campaigns of the Civil War, The Antietam and Fredericksburg.* New York: Scribners and Sons, 1882.

Phisterer, Frederick. *New York in the War of the Rebellion 1861-1865.* 3 vols. Albany: J.B. Lyon Company, Publishers, 1912.

Pollard, Edward A. *The Lost Cause.* New York: E.B. Treat and Co., 1866.

Pratt, Fletcher. *Stanton—Lincoln's Secretary of War.* New York: W.W. Norton and Co., 1953.

Schmucker, Samuel M., and L.F. Brockett. *The History of the Civil War in the United States.* Philadelphia: Jones Brothers and Co., 1865.

Sears, Stephen W. *Landscape Turned Red: The Battle of Antietam.* New Haven and New York: Ticknor and Fields, 1983.

Stackpole, Edward J. "Showdown at Sharpsburg—Story of the Battle," *Civil War Times Special,* August 1962.

Thomas, Benjamin. *Abraham Lincoln.* New York: Alfred Knopf, 1952.

United States House of Representatives. *Report No. 65: Fort Pillow Massacre.* Washington, D.C.: Government Printing Office, 1864.

___. *Executive Document 15: Letter of the Secretary of War Transmitting McClellan's Report.* Washington, D.C.: Government Printing Office, 1864.

BIBLIOGRAPHY

United States War Department. *War of the Rebellion. A Compilation of the Official Records of the Union and Confederate Armies.* 128 vols. Washington, D.C.: Government Printing Office, 1881-1902.

Victor, Orville J. *History of the Southern Rebellion.* 4 vols. New York: James D. Torrey Publishers, 1863-1865.

Warner, Ezra J. *Generals in Blue.* Ann Arbor, Mich.: Louisiana State University Press, Cushin-Malloy, Inc., 1964.
___. *Generals in Gray.* Baton Rouge: Louisiana State University Press, 1959.
Webb, Alexander. *Campaigns of the Civil War, The Peninsula.* New York: Charles Scribner's Sons, 1881.
Webster's Ninth New Collegiate Dictionary.
Weigley, Russel F. *History of the United States Army.* New York: The Macmillan Co., 1967.
Wiley, Bell I. *The Common Soldier in the Civil War.* Jamestown, Va.: Eastern Acorn Press, 1987.
Williams, T. Harry. *Lincoln and His Generals.* New York: Alfred A. Knopf, 1952.
Wilson, John Laird. *Pictorial History of the Great Civil War.* n.p.: 1878
Wyeth, John Allan. *That Devil Forrest.* New York: Harper and Brothers, 1959.

INDEX

Note: Ranks of officers shown are those when first mentioned in the book.

INDEX

INDEX

INDEX

Williamsburg, 27, 31, 32, 34, 36, 41, 56
Woodbury's and Alexander's Bridge, 47, 53

Y

Yorktown, 27, 31, 32, 34, 36